The First Book of

Microsoft® Windows 3.0

The First Book of

Microsoft® Windows 3.0

Jack Nimersheim

A Division of Macmillan Computer Publishing
11711 North College, Carmel, Indiana 46032 USA

For De, my oldest and dearest friend. (Somewhere along the way, De was converted into a Mac zealot. Hope springs eternal, however, and there's a good chance Windows 3.0 will compel him back to our side of the PC fence.)

© 1990 by SAMS

FIRST EDITION

SECOND PRINTING — 1991

International Standard Book Number: 0-672-27334-9

Library of Congress Catalog Card Number: 90-62682

Acquisitions Editor: *Linda Sanning*

Production Coordinator: *Steve Noe*

Cover Art: *Held & Dietrich Design*

Production Assistance: *Claudia Bell, Brad Chinn, Denny Hager, Chuck Hutchinson, Bob LaRoche, Joe Ramon, Dennis Sheehan, Mary Beth Wakefield*

Indexer: *Hilary Adams*

Technical Reviewer: *Greg Schultz*

Printed in the United States of America

Contents

vi

Part Two   The Windows Accessories

viii

8 *Calendar, 159*

9 *Paintbrush, 179*

ix

Part Three   Beyond Windows

13   *A Windows Sampler, 259*

14   *The Windows/DOS Connection, 277*

Introduction

Permit me to reveal a little secret: I've never really liked Windows.

I don't know how to say this diplomatically so I'll just come right out and say it: Previous releases of Windows simply didn't cut it! They were unwieldy, unimaginative, undependable, and, despite grandiose claims to the contrary on the part of Microsoft's massive marketing machine, decidedly *ungraphic* in their approach to personal computing. In fact, only a fool would have identified those early versions of Windows as representing even a pale imitation of the convenience and, yes, "user friendliness" that has been available to Macintosh users for several years. And although I may act foolish at times, I like to pride myself in thinking that, underneath it all, I am no fool. Consequently, try as I might, I could not buy into the advantages supposedly associated with turning the majority of my PC operations over to Microsoft Corporation's much ballyhooed graphics operating environment.

This said, however, let me make another critical confession: My attitude changed when I started messing around with Windows 3.0.

Imagine seeing true graphic icons on your DOS display. Imagine being able to load and run any DOS program—or, alternately, Windows application—by simply double-clicking on its corresponding icon. Imagine being able to organize all the programs and data files relating to a given project into a single, logical group and then assigning that group to its own icon. Imagine being able to move a file around within a hard disk's directory structure by simply dragging its icon from one position on your PC monitor to another.

Imagine being able to perform multiple tasks on your PC concurrently, and even switch between them, without interrupting what has gone before. Imagine being able to transfer data between different application programs with a quick drag of an on-screen arrow and a couple of clicks on a mouse button. Imagine all this, and more. Then you'll begin to comprehend the joys of working with Windows 3.0.

Now, imagine knowing what all those admittedly obscure buzzwords and procedural descriptions in the previous paragraph mean—even if you've never used Windows before. That's what this book, *The First Book of Microsoft Windows 3.0*, is all about.

Over the course of the next 14 chapters, we'll examine what Windows 3.0 is, what it does, and what you need to do to take full advantage of this next phase in the on-going evolution of personal computing. That's much ground to cover, to be sure, but we'll manage—and manage in a way that's comfortable and constructive for all readers, regardless of their level of PC expertise.

xii

If you're a relative newcomer to personal computers or Windows, don't worry. I've designed this book to get you up and running, then gradually increase your understanding of how a graphical user interface (or GUI) like Windows can simplify most PC operations. Experienced Windows users, on the other hand, will find practical information in this book about how the new features incorporated into Windows 3.0 overcome many of the frustrations associated with using earlier Windows releases. Everyone, I hope, will find the journey from here to there educational, entertaining, and, who knows, maybe even enjoyable. After all, what fun is learning something new, if an element of fun is not somehow incorporated into that learning process?

So, what's my overriding message about what Windows can help you accomplish on your PC? How's this: Move over Mac zealots, move in DOS users; after several abortive attempts at simplifying our PC lives, Windows has finally arrived!

That sounds good to me.

Jack Nimersheim
Vevay, Indiana
July 1990

Acknowledgments

How do you thank all the people who made completing a project like this one possible? That's the question every writer faces when the time comes to write acknowledgments. I'm always concerned that I'll overlook someone. If, in this case, that someone is you, I apologize. Here, however, are those folks I haven't forgotten.

▶ Linda Sanning at Macmillan Computer Publishing, whose enthusiasm, patience, and diplomacy guided this book from its initial proposal to final production.

▶ All the good people at all the software companies and PR firms who sent me the various programs profiled in Chapter 13. There are simply too many of you to mention individually; so, consider this a "group thanks."

▶ Doug Kilarski and Craig Patchett, the editors of Vulcan's *Computer Monthly* and *PC Laptop*, respectively. These two guys financed my trip to Spring COMDEX, which is where I made initial contact with many of those good people mentioned in the previous acknowledgment.

▶ Finally, and as always, Susan and Jason, my wife and son. Living with any writer is no easy task. Living with this particular writer is no exception to this general rule. They take it all in stride and, in the process, make my life wonderful.

xiii

Trademarks

All terms mentioned in this book that are known to be trademarks or service marks are listed below. In addition, terms suspected of being trademarks or service marks have been appropriately capitalized. SAMS cannot attest to the accuracy of this information. Use of a term in this book should not be regarded as affecting the validity of any trademark or service mark.

IBM® is a registered trademark of International Business Machines Corporation.

1-2-3® is a registered trademark of Lotus Development Corporation.

dBASE® is a registered trademark of Ashton-Tate Corporation.

Part One

The Windows Environment

1

The five chapters comprising Part One describe what you could call, for want of a better term, Windows itself—that is, the graphical user interface that Windows positions between you and your computer's operating system. Individual chapters in Part One contain information on what Windows is and how it allows you to simplify many of your PC operations. You'll also learn how to install Windows and configure it to run properly on your PC. Finally, Part One contains information on the procedures used to initiate specific activities during a Windows session.

2

Chapter 1

Welcome to Windows

In This Chapter

3

- ▶ *An explanation of Windows*
- ▶ *The contents of the basic Windows package*
- ▶ *The new features that have been added to Windows 3.0*
- ▶ *The hardware that you will need to run Windows*

What Is Windows?

Let's start by discussing the most obvious answer to this question. Specifically, Windows is a program designed to run on personal computers that use the MS-DOS operating system—or, to use the terminology commonly applied to such computers, an IBM or IBM-compatible PC. As is true of any computer program, Windows consists of a series of coded instructions. These instructions, in turn, make the computer on which Windows is running perform a special operation, using very precise and predetermined procedures. In this respect, Windows is much like other computer programs that also run on MS-DOS systems (e.g., Lotus 1-2-3 or dBASE, to name but two popular application programs). Beyond this simple comparison, however, Windows is much more than either Lotus 1-2-3 or dBASE. This is true not because of what Windows is—that is, a program designed to run on an MS-DOS personal computer—but because of what Windows includes, how Windows works, and what Windows itself is designed to accomplish.

Have you ever heard of a Chinese puzzle box? This is an intriguing little brain twister that consists of one small box inserted into a slightly larger, second box, which then fits within a third box (only slightly larger still), which then fits within a fourth box, and so on. Windows incorporated a similar structure in that it is, in actuality, several programs sold as a single package. Programs within a program, or a "Chinese puzzle program," if you please.

For example, the basic Windows package includes its own word processor, called Write, that, while certainly not as powerful as a stand-alone word processor like WordPerfect, can be used to compose and edit fairly complex documents. Windows also includes a telecommunications program, a module that it refers to as Terminal. Again, you won't be able to do all the things with Terminal that are possible using a more advanced (and more expensive) program like CrossTalk, for example. Still, Terminal is flexible and may just surprise you with what it can accomplish. Perhaps even more important, Terminal is always available and only a few keystrokes away whenever you're in Windows. The basic Windows package includes other application modules as well, all of which I'll get into more completely in Part Two, "The Windows Accessories."

"Okay," you may be thinking, "so Windows is a bunch of different applications sold in a single box. Big deal! How does that make Windows any different from any other integrated package?" In truth, it doesn't. But now, let me tell you something that differentiates Windows from every other stand-alone PC program or integrated package, let me tell you about the "real" Windows.

Will the "Real" Windows Please Stand Up?

All the attributes I've described up to this point are secondary to Windows' most important feature—they are merely icing on the electronics cake, so to speak. For beneath its bundled application modules, beneath several additional utilities I've not yet mentioned (but will, as this book progresses), beneath everything else that makes Windows special, Windows is, first and foremost, a *graphics-based operating environment.*

And exactly what does this strange buzz-phrase mean? I'm glad you asked. In essence, it means that Windows (the "real" Windows, as opposed to the bundled applications, utilities, and accessories also included in the Windows package) is capable of managing other PC programs—not just those bundled with the basic Windows package itself, but also any additional applications that you use regularly on your IBM or IBM-compatible PC. Windows manages these other programs by presenting visual elements that you, in turn, use to communicate with your PC. This is what truly makes Windows a *graphical* user interface.

Figure 1.1 shows a typical MS-DOS display screen. Not very impressive, is it? In fact, it's downright dreary. To tell the truth, DOS is a boring operating system. Even the most dedicated DOS advocates—a group within which I hold a charter membership—find it difficult to argue that DOS, a utilitarian but admittedly ambiguous operating system, offers much in the way of assistance for the inexperienced PC user. Let's face it, the information contained in Figure 1.1, such as it is, does not indicate what you are expected to do next, if you expect to accomplish something concrete with your PC.

5

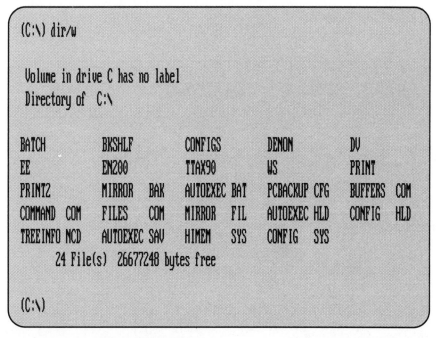

Figure 1.1. Dreary DOS.

▶ **Note:** DOS is one of those generic terms used to describe several variations on the same theme. There's MS-DOS, Microsoft's version of its venerable operating system, and PC DOS, IBM's "official" version of MS-DOS. Windows will run under either of these two operating systems. To avoid clutter, I'll refer to either MS-DOS or use the generic term DOS throughout this book to indicate MS-DOS or its electronic sibling, PC-DOS.

Now, feast your eyes on Figure 1.2. A pretty impressive display, isn't it? It also happens to be a display that's fairly typical of what you'll see when you get Windows 3.0 up and running. To put it bluntly, Windows looks good—especially when compared with the uninspired appearance of Figure 1.1, or what I like to refer to as "naked DOS."

6

Most experts agree that graphics-based environments are the wave of the future for PC operations. People simply want more information about what goes on inside that black box called a personal computer than tired, antiquated, boring DOS, by itself, provides. Windows, on the other hand, puts a whole new face on your PC to provide this higher level of information. As a rule, Windows offers assistance in the form of prompts and dialog boxes

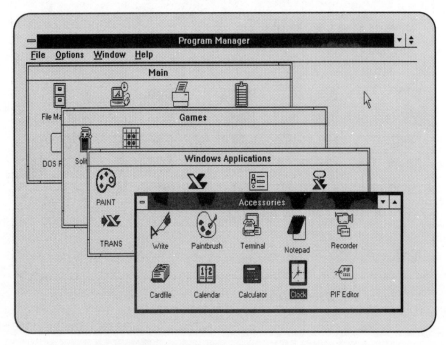

Figure 1.2. Wonderful Windows.

to help you accomplish something with your PC. Consequently, Windows is easy to learn and intuitive to use. In fact, working in Windows can actually be fun. But you'll discover this yourself, as we examine some of the various Windows features throughout the rest of this book. For now, we still have some more fundamental ground to cover, beginning with an explanation of why Windows may be the ideal graphics-based operating environment for people who already own an IBM or compatible PC that uses MS-DOS.

Windows Does DOS

For all its inherent shortcomings, MS-DOS excels at one thing. It supports more, and more varied, types of hardware and software than any other operating system that has appeared since the dawn of the so-called computer age. Either DOS has something of value to offer, or 25 million people have been bamboozled by one of the most successful scams in human history.

It is generally estimated that 25 million personal computers that use MS-DOS have been manufactured and sold since Big Blue introduced the first first-generation IBM-PC way back in 1981. (Because the "P" in PC stands for "personal," I feel justified in assuming a one-to-one relationship between the number of units sold and the number of people sold on DOS.) 25 million! That's quite a few little black boxes that have found their way into the hands of the public over the past decade or so. And those "little black boxes" are only the tip of the proverbial iceberg. Think about the time and money that has been invested in learning how to work with all those DOS computers and how to effectively use the software they were designed to run. It would be a shame if all this time and money ended up being wasted simply because someone decided we needed to put a new face on our PCs.

The good news is, Windows doesn't demand this sacrifice. Because Windows itself runs under DOS, it's capable of peacefully coexisting with the rest of the DOS world. Chances are that the IBM-compatible hardware sitting on the table in front of you will run Windows fine, just as it is. And see all those MS-DOS application programs lining your bookshelf? They also have a few good years left in them. That's because Windows was designed to supplement, rather than supplant, DOS.

7

Windows places itself between you and the admittedly minimalist design of MS-DOS. Consequently, you no longer need to memorize a series of complex commands to get something done. Rather, as I'll demonstrate shortly, Windows allows you to accomplish many tasks by managing and manipulating visual elements on your PC's display screen. Stated simply, Windows makes DOS look good. As a wise person once pointed out, however, looks aren't everything. To be truly useful, Windows must do more than merely spruce up the appearance of DOS with pretty pictures. Don't worry. It does.

More Than Pretty Pictures

8

Did you notice all those stylized illustrations in Figure 1.2? There's that two-drawer file cabinet near the upper left-hand corner located in a partially obscured box marked "Main." One of my favorites is the artist's palette and paintbrush, which can be found in that portion of the screen labeled "Accessories," down in the lower left-hand corner of our representative Windows display. These are but two examples of *icons*, a new element Microsoft introduced to the MS-DOS environment, when it introduced Windows 3.0.

Icons are much more than pretty pictures. As will be demonstrated throughout the remainder of this book, icons are actually graphic tools designed to simplify many operations that, without Windows installed on your PC, would require you to memorize and then know how to properly enter long and often convoluted DOS commands.

As potentially useful as icons are, however, they represent only one of many enhancements Windows brings to DOS. There are other enhancements. Perhaps the most impressive is the manner in which Windows transforms normally cryptic DOS into a truly interactive operating environment, one in which information on the exact steps required to perform a specific operation is always, quite literally, at your fingertips.

Let's Get GUI

The computer industry thrives on acronyms—those cute, little nonwords generally derived from a technical and totally obscure phrase someone, somewhere, came up with to identify his or her latest digital brainstorm. (In fact, MS-DOS itself is an acronym, one that stands for the Microsoft Disk Operating System.) It shouldn't surprise you, therefore, to discover that there's an acronym used to describe what a program like Windows is and what it does. That acronym is GUI—or "gooey," for those of you into phonetics.

GUI stands for *graphical user interface*. Stated simply, a GUI is a graphics-based program that can be used to organize and manage other PC operations. As a rule, working in a GUI like Windows offers the added attraction of simplifying these operations, by converting the procedures required to perform them into a series of interactive steps rather than a list of commands typed in at a system prompt. Let me give you an example of what I mean.

9

Suppose you wanted to relocate a file on one directory on your drive C hard disk to a different directory on a second hard disk, drive D. The series of commands required to perform this operation on a DOS machine without Windows would resemble the following:

```
COPY C:\WS\1\RESNICK.LET D:\LETTERS
DEL C:\WS\1\RESNICK.LET
```

The first command line in this sequence makes a duplicate copy of the specified file on your drive D hard disk, placing it in a directory called LETTERS. Because DOS doesn't support a MOVE command, the DEL command is required to remove the original file from its initial location—that is, the \WS\1 subdirectory of drive C. Admittedly, the procedure I've outlined here is not overly complex. But what if you were just learning how to use your PC? DOS, by itself, provides no assistance in determining the exact steps required to perform even this simple move (or, more correctly, COPY/DEL) operation. With Windows running on your PC, however, the situation is quite different.

Figure 1.3 shows a Windows *pull-down menu*; specifically, the Files menu from File Manager, a Windows utility represented by the two-drawer file cabinet icon shown in Figure 1.2. Pull-down menus are only one way in which Windows simplifies using your PC. Rather than forcing you to type in the precise DOS command required to initiate an activity, you use pull-down menus to tell

Windows what type of operation you want to perform. Windows simplifies many operations even more through its use of *dialog boxes*, interactive display prompts that you use to verify or, where necessary, modify information Windows itself presents about the activity you are performing.

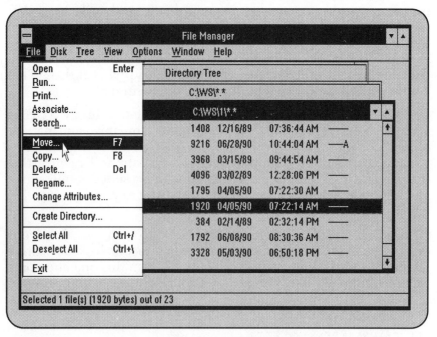

Figure 1.3. Windows provides pull-down menus to simplify operations.

Figure 1.4 contains the dialog box that appears when you select the Move option from the pull-down menu shown in Figure 1.3. (Unlike DOS, Windows does allow you to move a file directly from one location to another, without requiring the two-step procedure outlined earlier.) Notice that Windows itself is already aware of most of the information it needs to complete the requested Move operation. For example, Windows already knows what file you want to move and where that file is currently located. (You'll learn how Windows determined this information in a later chapter; for now, take my word for it.) All you need to do to complete the Move operation, therefore, is supply Windows with the information specifically requested by the dialog box shown in Figure 1.4—that is, the location you want this file moved to. Thanks to this interactive

10

design, where selecting one option causes Windows to request any subsequent information it needs to perform the specified operation, Windows may be the ideal operating environment for neophyte PC users.

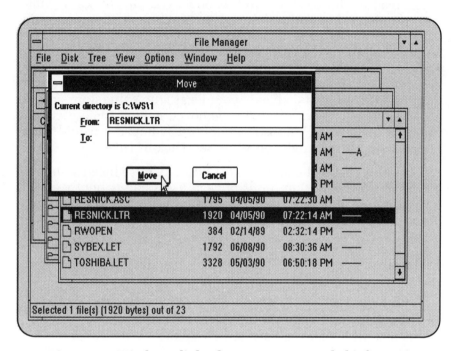

Figure 1.4. Windows dialog boxes request needed information.

11

Experienced users, too, can profit from incorporating Windows into their daily PC operations. As the Move option outlined in the previous example demonstrates, Windows supports some procedures that can't be performed directly in DOS. For this introductory tour of the Windows environment, I purposely selected a relatively simple example. The deeper we delve into Windows 3.0, the more you power users out there will realize how truly flexible and powerful the new and improved Windows GUI can be.

In other words, we've barely scratched the surface when it comes to demonstrating what Windows 3.0 can do. Please have patience. After all, we're only halfway through Chapter 1. Besides, before I get down to the details of how to install and use Windows 3.0, we need to cover some general ground.

New Features of Windows 3.0

If you read the introduction to this book, you already know that I have not always been an avid supporter of Windows. In my opinion, Windows releases prior to Windows 3.0 simply did not live up to Microsoft's promise of a true graphics-based operating environment for MS-DOS personal computers. Add to this the fact that those early versions were slower than molasses and demanded more hardware than you'd find on the shelves of your local True Value store, and it's easy to understand why Windows enjoyed neither the critical nor financial acceptance Microsoft undoubtedly hoped it would when the company first introduced Windows back in 1984.

All this changed when Microsoft finally introduced Windows 3.0. Here was the GUI millions of DOS users had patiently—well, let's be honest, quite impatiently—been waiting for, lo those many years.

12

With Windows 3.0, Microsoft finally succeeded in creating a true graphical interface that offers such advanced features as:

▶ A completely revamped Setup program, designed to simplify the steps required to install Windows on your PC.

▶ A vastly improved user interface that includes true graphical icons, which can be used to initiate most Windows operations.

▶ The ability to modify your system configuration without having to reinstall Windows completely, as was required in previous versions.

▶ The ability to organize program and data files into logical groups, regardless of their physical location on your system disk drives.

▶ The ability to perform file-related operations—copying files, moving files, deleting files, and the like—using on-screen icons.

▶ True multitasking of both Windows and standard DOS applications, when Windows is installed on a system with as little as 2 megabytes of RAM.

▶ A single Windows version that uses improved memory management techniques to run in one of three operating modes: Real mode, Standard mode, and Enhanced 386 mode. (As I will explain later, the mode which will be best for your situation depends on the type of system you own.)

▶ Compatibility with a number of popular networks.

▶ A built-in macro recorder that allows you to record keyboard and mouse sequences, which can later be used to automate virtually any Windows operation.

▶ Printer support for Hewlett-Packard, PostScript, or compatible laser printers.

This list contains only the major enhancements that have been added to Windows 3.0—Windows dressing, if you'll forgive me an obvious pun. Veteran Windows users will find enough of the flavor of previous releases in the new version that switching over to Windows 3.0 presents no problem. (Don't panic if you're confused by some of the "technobabble." Everything will be explained as we move along.)

As I stated earlier, Windows is more than just a visually attractive enhancement for standard DOS. The basic Windows package also includes a number of useful application programs and utilities, designed to let you immediately begin working in the Windows graphical environment. These include:

13

Write	The Windows text editor.
Paintbrush	A graphics program based on the popular PC Paintbrush program from Z Soft.
Terminal	A telecommunications program that allows you to communicate with other personal computers, electronic bulletin boards, and commercial information services from within Windows.
Calendar	A monthly calendar and daily electronic appointment book you can use to organize your time more efficiently.
Cardfile	A flat-file database for organizing and managing information on your PC.

We'll examine each of these, and many others, as we learn more about the Windows environment and the applications it is designed to run. Before getting into the specific steps involved in using this impressive graphics-based operating environment, however, it might be a good idea to take a look at the equipment you'll need, if you want to use Windows effectively on your PC.

What You'll Need to Run Windows

I alluded earlier to the diversity that exists in the MS-DOS community. This is not mere hyperbole. If you need to get something done, chances are that someone, somewhere, produces a piece of hardware or software that is capable of doing it. And more often than not, this piece of equipment was designed to run on an MS-DOS computer. As is often the case, however, this convenience carries with it an accompanying curse: As more (and more varied) products enter the DOS marketplace, you need to be especially careful to purchase only those PC tools that will work properly on your PC.

14

Previous releases of Windows took an unorthodox approach to this dilemma in that different versions were recommended for use on different types of systems. With Windows 3.0, all of this changed. (You must be getting tired of such statements by now, but, as they say, facts are facts. Windows 3.0 represents such a major improvement over its electronic ancestors that I feel obligated to hammer this point home whenever the opportunity presents itself—at least in the early stages of our discussions. To be honest, I was the last person I ever expected to sing the praises of Microsoft Windows based on its previously anemic attempts at producing a true GUI, but here I am writing a book about Windows. Who can figure it?) About the only prerequisite for running Windows 3.0 is that, due to Windows emphasis on icons and other visual elements, your PC must include a graphics display.

Beyond this single caveat, the type of system on which you choose to run Windows is precisely that, your choice. I don't mean to imply, however, that all PCs are created equal. They aren't. Consequently, the specific hardware installed in a given system will influence how well it handles Windows.

We'll look at some specific examples of how certain hardware components influence the Windows operating environment in a moment. First, let's list the basic equipment you'll need to run Windows 3.0.

The minimum hardware requirements for Windows 3.0 include:

- ▶ An IBM or IBM-compatible personal computer.
- ▶ 640K of random access memory (RAM).
- ▶ The MS-DOS operating system, version 3.1 or higher.
- ▶ A hard disk with 6 to 8 megabytes of free space.

▶ One 3 1/2- or 5 1/4-inch floppy disk drive (needed to install Windows on a hard disk from its distribution diskettes).

▶ A graphics monitor.

In order to get the most out of Windows, however, you'll probably want to install it on a system that exceeds these minimum requirements. In some cases, you may choose to equip your system with a more powerful variation of one of the components listed above, as would be the case if you installed a VGA (Video Graphics Array) rather than a CGA (Color Graphics Adapter) monitor on your system. Another way to enhance Windows' performance is to add a few "extras" to this basic system, additional hardware components that make Windows easier to use or to increase its capabilities. Let's look at some of these variations on the basic Windows theme and examine the different ways in which they can improve how well Windows performs on your PC.

PCs, a Potpourri of Power and Price

15

Personal computers come in all shapes and sizes. An 8088-based PC/XT system like the original IBM PC is now considered to be almost an anachronism—the Model-T of modern PC technology. Newer, faster, and more advanced systems have been introduced at a breakneck pace since the PC/XT's initial introduction way back in 1981. Today's so-called "third-generation" systems (that is, personal computers based on Intel's 80386 microprocessor) are capable of running over 35 times faster than the original PC/XT.

Of course, the type of PC on which you run Windows is totally your decision—a decision that will probably be based on how much power you need and, even more important, how much money you can afford to spend. The critical point to realize here is that, although Windows will run on any DOS-based personal computer, its performance is influenced by the kind of system you own. (In all honesty, Windows' performance on an 8088/86-based PC/XT is sluggish, at best.)

Display Options

As pointed out in the previous list of Windows' "bare-bones" system requirements, it will run on any monitor capable of generating graphics. Unfortunately, the PC marketplace is overflowing with graphic alternatives, which makes picking the right display for your

Windows operations anything but a simple task. Over on the color side, you can choose from the CGA, EGA (Enhanced Graphics Adapter), or VGA "standards." For people who don't feel the need for color, a Hercules-compatible video card and monitor should suffice. In fact, a Hercules-compatible display may represent the most logical choice for a number of reasons.

First, aside from the "golly gee" factor of being able to generate pretty tints and hues, a color monitor does not contribute that much to your overall PC productivity. Second, the resolution of a Hercules display—and, therefore, its image quality—is actually higher than either the CGA or EGA standard. Finally, a Hercules-compatible display card and accompanying monitor can be picked up for under $100. Unless color is mandatory for your Windows operations, I strongly recommend you go the Hercules route.

Of Mice and Menus

16

If you allow yourself one luxury item when gathering together the hardware for your Windows system, make it a mouse. While it is possible to run Windows exclusively from your computer's keyboard, doing so is comparable to reaching for the hand brake each time you want to stop a car. Sure, this technique will work and may even be required in an emergency situation, but who wants to go through all that hassle when a better and more convenient alternative is readily available?

A GUI like Windows is ideally suited for the kinds of "point and click" operations at which a mouse excels. Selecting menu items and initiating operations from the Windows display are greatly simplified when a mouse is available. Furthermore, if you plan to work extensively with graphics applications like Windows' Paintbrush accessory or other, similar programs, a mouse crosses over the line from being a luxury item to becoming a real necessity. A mouse's ability to emulate paper and pencil simplifies using such programs.

Windows can use virtually any PC buss mouse designed to be compatible with MS-DOS systems—both buss model mice and those that connect through the serial ports COM1 through COM4. The type of mouse you own is one of the items you specify during Windows installation, as explained in the next chapter, "Getting Started."

Printer Power

You will also need a printer if you wish to generate a permanent record of any work you perform in the Windows environment. The quality of those printouts will be determined by what type of printer you choose.

Given Windows' reliance on graphics, one of two types of printers seems a logical choice for a Windows-based PC: a dot-matrix or a laser printer. Because Windows includes a driver capable of supporting over 150 popular printers in these two categories, the actual brand of printer you buy is up to you.

Modem Madness

A modem puts your PC in touch with the rest of the world. One of the built-in Windows accessories, Terminal, requires a modem to run properly. You will also need a modem if you plan to install any other communication packages into your Windows environment.

Modems come in two basic types: internal and external models. An internal modem plugs directly into one of the expansion slots located inside your PC's system unit. External modems communicate with your PC through a standard serial port. Keep in mind, however, that should your system include a serial mouse, you will need two serial ports, if you also want to use a modem from within Windows.

A second consideration when selecting a modem for your system is the maximum data transfer rate that a modem supports. Commonly referred to as a modem's *baud rate*, this specification determines the speed with which your system will be able to exchange data with another, remote PC. Common transfer rates for PC communications include 1200, 2400, 4800, and 9600 baud, with the first two being the most widely used. Windows supports modem communications anywhere within this range.

Additional Hardware

Personal computers are extremely flexible. Given their modular nature, you can customize a DOS-based PC to include a wide variety of hardware options—called *peripherals*, in the PC vernacular. The items outlined previously represent merely the most common hardware components that can be found on many PC systems. They are by no means the only ones you can attach to a personal computer. While none

17

of the following additional peripherals will be addressed in this book, you should know that they exist and are compatible with Windows.

Other peripherals you may want to incorporate into your total Windows environment include:

▶ Alternate "mouse input" devices (for example, a joystick or a trackball).

▶ An A/B switch, which will allow you to use a single serial port for multiple purposes.

▶ A printer buffer.

▶ A network board.

Starting with version 3.0, Windows, which was previously network ignorant, can recognize several popular PC networks, including any networks that adhere to the Novell and 3Com standards.

18

During installation, Windows itself assumes responsibility for determining much of what it needs to know about the hardware comprising the system on which it is being installed. In other cases, the person installing Windows will need to provide this information. One good place to go from here, therefore, would seem to be installing Windows on your PC. And that's what we'll do in the next chapter.

What You Have Learned

▶ Windows is a collection of programs designed to be used with IBM and IBM-compatible personal computers. Beyond this, however, Windows is also the graphical user interface under which all these programs run.

▶ Windows includes a number of applications you use to perform specific tasks on your PC. Write, for example, is the Windows application used for word processing. Other Windows applications include Paintbrush, Calendar, Terminal, and Cardfile.

▶ Windows will run on any personal computer that uses the MS-DOS or PC DOS operating system, version 3.1 or later, so long as that computer is equipped with a graphics display and a hard disk. Windows is also compatible with a variety of additional hardware peripherals that can be installed on an IBM or IBM-compatible personal computer.

Chapter 2

Getting Started

In This Chapter 19

▶ *How to start the Windows Setup program*

▶ *How to access the Windows on-line help feature*

▶ *How to modify the system configuration Setup uses to install Windows*

Installing Windows

Now that you have a basic idea of what Windows is, it's time to begin transferring the various programs included on the Windows distribution diskettes to your hard disk. During installation, you will be asked to provide or, in some cases, verify certain information about how Windows should be configured to run properly on your system.

Installing Windows isn't as difficult as you may think. Microsoft provides a special installation program, Setup, that walks you through each of the steps required to get Windows up and running on your PC. Part of Setup's job is to configure Windows to take full advantage of the hardware and software installed on your PC. Setup also converts several Windows files that have been compressed for distribution back into usable programs. Consequently, Windows will not run properly if you simply copy the files contained on its distribution diskettes to your hard disk, as can be done with some other PC applications. You must run the Setup program to install Windows.

Specific information requested by Setup during Windows installation includes:

▶ The disk drive and directory on which you want Windows installed.

▶ The type of computer you have.

▶ The kind of monitor it uses.

▶ Whether you own a mouse and, if so, what kind of mouse it is.

▶ The type of keyboard connected to your PC.

▶ The language Windows should use in its screen messages and displays.

▶ Whether your PC is connected to a network and, if so, what kind of network protocol it uses.

20

▶ Whether you own a printer and, if so, what kind of printer it is and how that printer is connected to your PC.

▶ What application programs on your hard disk you want installed as icons within your Windows environment.

You will find the Setup program on Disk 1 of the Windows distribution disks. During installation, Setup will also need to access files stored on several other disks shipped with Windows. Make certain that you have all of the Windows distribution disks (or copies of these disks, as explained in the next section) available before beginning the installation procedures outlined in this chapter.

Protecting Your Programs

Most programs today, including Windows, are shipped on several distribution disks. These are the disks included in the original packaging for a given program. Although floppy disks (both the 5 1/4- and 3 1/2-inch varieties) are extremely durable, no one has yet invented the perfect diskette—one that is invulnerable to accidental damage or unable to be erased inadvertently. For this reason, it's always a good idea to make copies of a program's distribution disks before installing that program. This way, you always have your original disks to fall back on, should something go awry (as George

Bernard Shaw tells us "oft times" will for mice and men) somewhere down the road.

The easiest way to protect your Windows software against accidental damage is to create an exact copy of each distribution diskette, using the DOS DISKCOPY command. After duplicating your distribution disks, place the originals in a safe place and install Windows from this second set of disks.

> **Note:** Your DOS manual includes complete instructions on how to perform a DISKCOPY operation.

Starting Setup

21

You can run Setup from any floppy disk drive. The drive you use will be determined by the type of disks included in your Windows package. On my system, for example, I had to run Setup from drive B, my 3 1/2-inch disk drive, because Windows was shipped to me on 3 1/2-inch diskettes. If you are installing Windows from drive A, remember to substitute that drive letter whenever drive B is specified in the following exercise.

√ To Install Windows on Your PC

▶ Boot your computer so the DOS prompt (usually C:\>) appears.

▶ Place Disk 1 in the drive you want to use to install Windows.

▶ Type the name of the drive from which you will install Windows (A: or B:) and press Enter.

▶ Type **SETUP** and press Enter. This starts the Windows Setup program, which uses a series of interactive message and prompt screens to walk you through Windows installation. Supplying the information requested by these screens will install Windows to take full advantage of your hardware configuration.

▶ Windows Setup will advise you when installation is complete. At that point, press Ctrl+Alt+Del to reboot your system, incorporating any changes Setup made to your CONFIG.SYS or AUTOEXEC.BAT files, so that it is configured properly to run Windows.

√ **To Begin Setup**

▶ Place the Windows Disk 1 into the appropriate disk drive for your system.

▶ Type **B:** and press Enter.

▶ Type **SETUP** and press Enter.

> ▶ **Tip:** Remember, you may need to specify a different drive letter here, corresponding to the floppy disk drive on which you are running Setup.

After a few seconds, Setup displays its opening message, shown in Figure 2.1. In addition to welcoming you to Windows (Setup's a congenial little program, isn't it?), the opening message screen in Figure 2.1 contains information about what Setup does and how it works. Notice, also, that the bottom line of this screen lists the options available to you at this point in your Windows' installation.

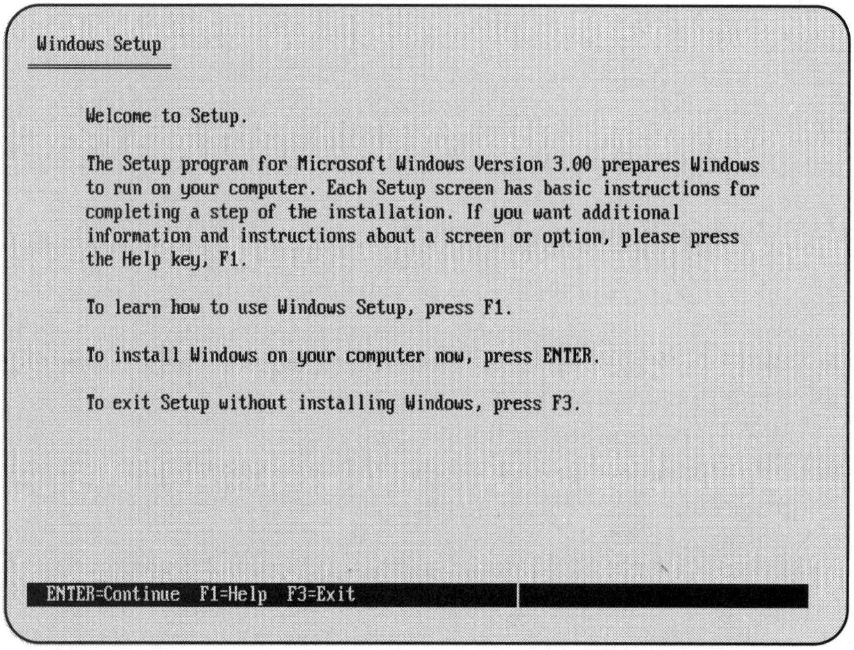

22

```
Windows Setup

    Welcome to Setup.

    The Setup program for Microsoft Windows Version 3.00 prepares Windows
    to run on your computer. Each Setup screen has basic instructions for
    completing a step of the installation. If you want additional
    information and instructions about a screen or option, please press
    the Help key, F1.

    To learn how to use Windows Setup, press F1.

    To install Windows on your computer now, press ENTER.

    To exit Setup without installing Windows, press F3.




ENTER=Continue  F1=Help  F3=Exit
```

Figure 2.1. Use the Setup program to install Windows.

Before telling Setup to continue installing Windows, let's take a short detour to examine an extremely useful Windows feature, its on-line Help system.

Getting Help

As intuitive as Windows is, there may be times when you could use a little more information about the steps required to perform a specific operation. Thanks to Windows' on-line Help system, such information is always a mere keystroke away. On the bottom line of the screen in Figure 2.1, for example, one of the listed options is Help, which you access by pressing the F1 function key. Let's do this now just to see what happens.

√ **To Access the On-Line Help System**   **23**

▶   Press the F1 function key.

Pressing the F1 function key displays the first screen of a multiscreen Setup Help message, as shown in Figure 2.2.

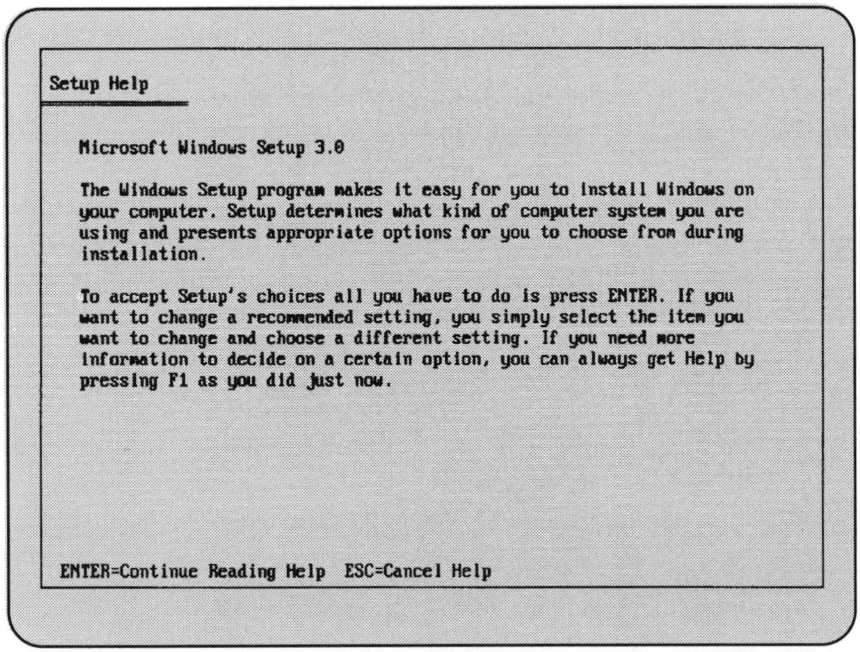

```
┌─────────────────────────────────────────────────────────────┐
│  Setup Help                                                   │
│  ─────────────                                                │
│                                                               │
│     Microsoft Windows Setup 3.0                               │
│                                                               │
│     The Windows Setup program makes it easy for you to install Windows on │
│     your computer. Setup determines what kind of computer system you are │
│     using and presents appropriate options for you to choose from during │
│     installation.                                             │
│                                                               │
│     To accept Setup's choices all you have to do is press ENTER. If you │
│     want to change a recommended setting, you simply select the item you │
│     want to change and choose a different setting. If you need more │
│     information to decide on a certain option, you can always get Help by │
│     pressing F1 as you did just now.                          │
│                                                               │
│                                                               │
│  ENTER=Continue Reading Help  ESC=Cancel Help                 │
└─────────────────────────────────────────────────────────────┘
```

Figure 2.2. On-line Help is available at virtually any time during a Windows session.

Notice that the bottom line of Figure 2.2 contains additional options available in Setup Help. Pressing Enter, for instance, will show the second screen of the current Help message. This is another example of how, whenever possible, Windows itself provides information about its use.

Go ahead and press Enter to view subsequent Setup Help messages. I'll wait here until you're ready to exit Help and continue installing Windows.

√ To Exit Setup Help

▶ Press Esc.

> ▶ **Note:** The next chapter, "Navigating Windows," contains additional information on using Windows' on-line Help feature.

Pressing Esc returns you to the opening Setup screen shown in Figure 2.1. From here, you can inform Setup that you're now ready to install Windows on your computer. Again, notice that the option line at the bottom of your display includes instructions on how to tell Setup you're ready to begin installing Windows on your computer.

√ To Continue Installing Windows on Your PC

▶ Press Enter.

This displays the prompt screen shown in Figure 2.3. Throughout Setup you will be prompted for information regarding your system configuration by several screens similar to this one. Answering these questions correctly ensures the proper installation of Windows.

The Setup program consists of two parts:

1. DOS-related operations.
2. Windows-related operations.

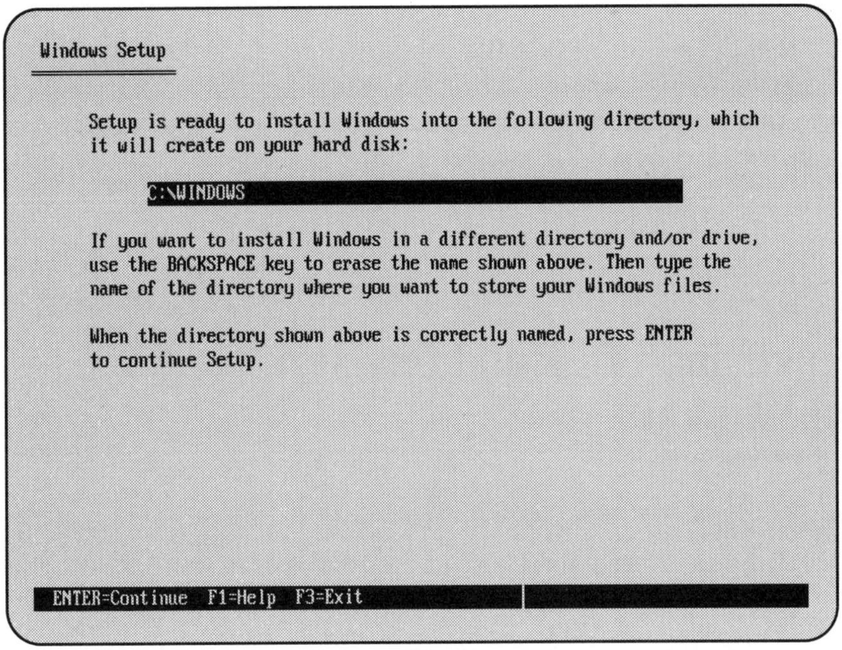

```
 Windows Setup
 ═══════════

        Setup is ready to install Windows into the following directory, which
        it will create on your hard disk:

            C:\WINDOWS

        If you want to install Windows in a different directory and/or drive,
        use the BACKSPACE key to erase the name shown above. Then type the
        name of the directory where you want to store your Windows files.

        When the directory shown above is correctly named, press ENTER
        to continue Setup.




 ENTER=Continue  F1=Help  F3=Exit
```

25

Figure 2.3. Setup asks you to specify the directory where Windows should be installed on your system.

▶ **Note:** Previous Windows users will be thrilled with this new Setup program, which Microsoft introduced in Windows 3.0. By using Windows itself to install Windows—if you'll forgive the redundancy in that statement—Setup greatly simplifies the process of getting Windows up and running. Also, since the Windows portion of Setup is an independent program that can be run from within a Windows session, you no longer need to rerun Setup completely and reinstall the entire Windows package if you modify your hardware configuration at some later date. More on this in Chapter 4.

The actual installation of Windows begins in the DOS portion of Setup, from which several important operations are performed:

▶ Setup first asks you to specify a directory into which it should copy those files required to install Windows on your system.

▶ Setup then analyzes your hardware and asks you to verify that the results of this analysis, on which it bases your Windows configuration, are correct.

▶ After verifying your system configuration, Setup copies several essential files to the specified directory, so that it will be able to start Windows and complete the installation process.

Specifying a Disk and Directory for Windows

You can tell Setup to copy the Windows files to any directory on your hard disk—or, for that matter, to any hard disk installed on your PC. During installation, Setup takes all the necessary steps to ensure that Windows can find these files later, when needed. The default location Setup uses for Windows' installation is a directory called "WINDOWS" on drive C, as shown in Figure 2.3.

To accept this default directory, you would simply press Enter. As I said earlier, however, the choice of where to install Windows is entirely up to you. To illustrate how easy it is to change a default value in Setup, let's specify a directory other than C:\WINDOWS for this installation.

√ To Specify a Different Windows Directory

▶ Press Backspace four times to position the cursor after the "N" in C:\WINDOWS.

▶ Type **3** and press Enter.

This tells Setup you want to install Windows in a directory on drive C called WIN3. Don't worry if this directory does not already exist. Setup will create it before moving on to the next stage of the Windows installation.

Modifying Setup's Analysis of Your System Components

After it records the specified Windows directory (and creates this directory, if necessary), Setup displays a screen similar to the one shown in Figure 2.4. This screen represents Setup's "best guess" as to the type of hardware and software installed on your PC—information it needs to configure Windows to run properly on your system.

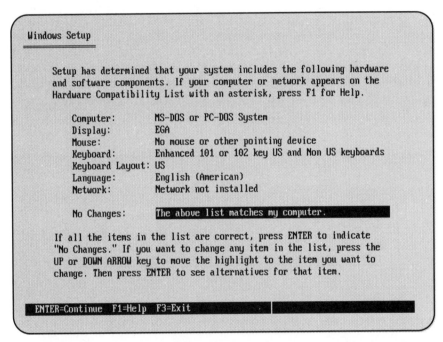

```
Windows Setup

   Setup has determined that your system includes the following hardware
   and software components. If your computer or network appears on the
   Hardware Compatibility List with an asterisk, press F1 for Help.

        Computer:          MS-DOS or PC-DOS System
        Display:           EGA
        Mouse:             No mouse or other pointing device
        Keyboard:          Enhanced 101 or 102 key US and Non US keyboards
        Keyboard Layout:   US
        Language:          English (American)
        Network:           Network not installed

        No Changes:        The above list matches my computer.

   If all the items in the list are correct, press ENTER to indicate
   "No Changes." If you want to change any item in the list, press the
   UP or DOWN ARROW key to move the highlight to the item you want to
   change. Then press ENTER to see alternatives for that item.


   ENTER=Continue  F1=Help  F3=Exit
```

Figure 2.4. Setup automatically analyzes the hardware and software installed on your PC.

▶ **Note:** The individual items displayed on your screen will probably differ from those shown here, which represent the hardware and software Setup discovered on my system.

If the system configuration Setup displays is correct, you can press Enter to specify "No Changes" and have Setup continue

27

installing Windows. But what if Setup did not correctly analyze your system components? That's no problem. As a quick glance at the instructions on in Figure 2.4 reveals, Setup allows you to modify the results of its system analysis easily, should you need to do so.

√ To Modify Setup's System Analysis

▶ Use the arrow keys to highlight the field containing the information you need to change.

▶ Press Enter.

For example, because I did not load a mouse driver into memory prior to installing Windows, Figure 2.4 indicates that Setup discovered "No mouse or other pointing device" on my system. If I want Windows configured to recognize a mouse, therefore, I would need to change this field. Highlighting the Mouse field and pressing Enter displays the screen shown in Figure 2.5, which I could then use to tell Setup what kind of mouse is normally installed on my PC.

28

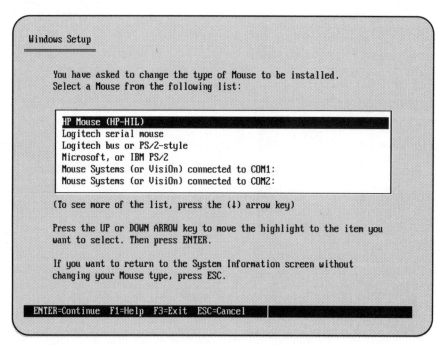

```
Windows Setup

      You have asked to change the type of Mouse to be installed.
      Select a Mouse from the following list:

      ┌─────────────────────────────────────────────────────┐
      │ HP Mouse (HP-HIL)                                     │
      │ Logitech serial mouse                                 │
      │ Logitech bus or PS/2-style                            │
      │ Microsoft, or IBM PS/2                                │
      │ Mouse Systems (or VisiOn) connected to COM1:          │
      │ Mouse Systems (or VisiOn) connected to COM2:          │
      └─────────────────────────────────────────────────────┘

      (To see more of the list, press the (↓) arrow key)

      Press the UP or DOWN ARROW key to move the highlight to the item you
      want to select. Then press ENTER.

      If you want to return to the System Information screen without
      changing your Mouse type, press ESC.

   ENTER=Continue  F1=Help  F3=Exit  ESC=Cancel
```

Figure 2.5. You can modify the results of Setup's system analysis.

> ▶ **Tip:** Pay special attention to the value Setup lists in the Display field of its system analysis. Given Windows' reliance on a graphics-based interface, you want to make sure that it is configured to take full advantage of your monitor.

When all the system components listed on Setup's analysis screen are correct, pressing Enter continues your Windows installation.

√ To Continue Installing Windows on Your System

▶ Press Enter.

At this point, Setup begins copying files from the Windows distribution diskettes to the WIN3 directory you specified earlier. During the initial stage of installation, Setup will need to access files from a distribution diskette other than Disk 1. When this happens, Setup will pause, display information on which diskette it needs, and then instruct you to press Enter to continue installation.

29

At some point in this process, your monitor will go blank for a few seconds. When Setup resumes, you'll see the screen shown in Figure 2.6. Congratulations! Setup has advanced to the Windows portion of its installation procedures, and you are now looking at your first Windows graphics-based display.

At this point, Setup has switched over to the Windows portion of its installation procedures, as mentioned earlier. From here on out, you will actually be using Windows to finish installing Windows on your PC. (Pretty nifty, huh?)

Whereas I would not normally end a chapter midtask, using the Windows interface is what this book is really all about. Strange as it may seem, therefore, I'm going to conclude this chapter here—halfway through Setup. Don't worry. You'll finish installing Windows in the next chapter, where we'll begin looking at the actual procedures used to communicate with your PC, using the Windows graphics-based interface.

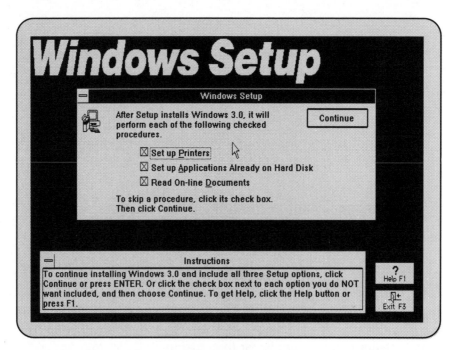

Figure 2.6. Welcome to the Windows GUI.

30

What You Have Learned

▶ Windows includes a special program, Setup, that simplifies the process of installing Windows on your PC.

▶ Setup automatically analyzes the hardware and software installed on your PC and then uses this information to determine the most appropriate configuration for Windows. You can, however, override individual settings that Setup selects, as needed, to ensure that Windows will run properly on your system.

▶ Windows includes an on-line Help feature, which you access with the F1 function key. Help messages contain specific information about a wide range of Windows procedures.

Chapter 3

Navigating Windows

In This Chapter

31

▶ *How to use a mouse with Windows*

▶ *How to finish installing Windows on your system*

▶ *How to rearrange elements of your Windows display*

Let's pick up right where we left off, in the middle of installing Windows. As you'll recall, we ended the previous chapter when Setup completed the DOS portion of Windows installation and switched you over to the Windows GUI, displaying the screen shown in Figure 3.1.

Now that we're actually in Windows, it's time to start taking advantage of the graphics-based interface it provides. We'll begin by examining how Windows uses a mouse to simplify the remaining steps in the Setup installation procedures.

Using a Mouse

As mentioned in Chapter 1, a GUI, like Windows, is ideally suited for mouse operations. Because any procedure you can perform is clearly shown on the Windows display, it's a simple matter to identify a

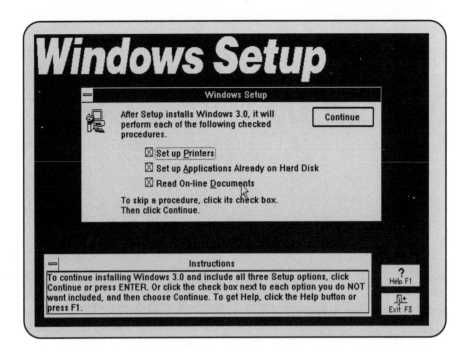

Figure 3.1. Setup switches over to the Windows GUI to complete its installation procedures.

given operation using the two-step "point and click" paradigm common to mouse operations:

1. Use the mouse to point at the procedure you want to initiate.
2. Click the left mouse button to get things underway.

That's really all there is to it. Before showing some examples of what I mean, however, let's determine whether Setup configured Windows so that you can use a mouse.

Notice the small arrow located in the center of Figure 3.1. This is the Windows mouse pointer. If this mouse pointer appears anywhere on your Windows display, then Windows recognizes that an electronic rodent is attached to your PC and is configured to allow mouse operations. If you have a mouse and do not see this pointer, it's possible that Setup did not automatically sense its presence. Don't worry. You can eliminate this problem in one of two ways:

1. Press the F3 function key to interrupt Windows installation at this point and rerun Setup, making sure you specify the appropriate mouse during the DOS portion of that program.
2. Continue on for now and run Setup again, once Windows installation is completed.

32

> ► **Note:** No mouse pointer will appear on your Windows
> display if you did not specify a mouse (or, alternately, if you
> did specify "No pointing device") during the DOS portion of the
> Setup program. While it's technically possible to run Windows
> exclusively from the keyboard, keep in mind that doing so is
> extremely awkward and inefficient. I'm going to assume, there-
> fore, that you have incorporated a mouse in your environment.
> Consequently, I'll mention only keyboard commands when I
> feel doing so is absolutely necessary or, as is sometimes the
> case, when an available keyboard command is more conve-
> nient to use than the corresponding mouse procedure.

Use a mouse for a variety of operations, when working in
Windows, including:

► Selecting menu and dialog box options.

► Choosing and executing on-screen commands.

► Modifying the placement and appearance of elements in
your Windows display.

► Selecting text and objects for additional processing.

Don't worry if the meaning of these various activities isn't clear
to you right now. You'll be performing and practicing each of them,
as we move along. For now, I just want to outline, in a general way,
some of the activities for which you will use a mouse, while working
in the Windows environment. This said, let's perform one of these
activities.

Moving the Mouse Pointer

Are you ready to play with a mouse? (Sounds gruesome, doesn't it?)
Okay, let's begin by using another method to access the Windows
on-line Help feature.

√ **To Access On-Line Help with Your Mouse**

► Move the mouse down and to your right, until the tip of the
mouse pointer is positioned over the button marked Help F1.

► Click the button located on the left-hand side of your mouse.

33

Your display should now resemble Figure 3.2, which shows an outline containing a partial listing of the various topics available under Setup Help. If it does, congratulations! You just learned how to use a mouse! Wasn't that easy? Point and click. That's all there is to it. Now, are you beginning to understand why the PC community is excited about Windows' new and improved GUI?

34

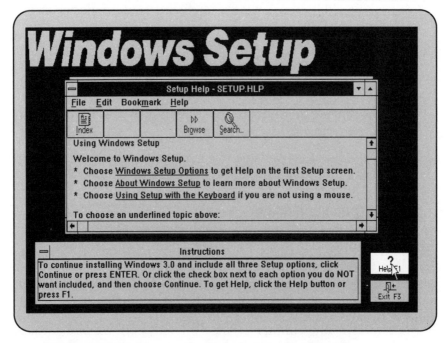

Figure 3.2. Clicking on the Help button displays the Setup Help index.

While we're at this Setup Help screen, let's look at some additional attributes of using a mouse to navigate Windows.

The Chameleon Cursor

It really is a misnomer to refer to a mouse pointer. Certainly, right now, that's what it is. The following exercise, however, points out how problems can arise with this little bit of PC jargon.

√ **To Move the Mouse Pointer**

▶ Move the mouse up and to the left, until the mouse pointer is positioned over the word "Keyboard" in the "Using Setup with the Keyboard" entry in the Setup Help outline.

Suddenly, you may find yourself saying, "What mouse pointer?" Now it's a mouse hand. (A mouse hand? That concept rates right up there with chicken lips.) As this exercise points out, the Windows mouse pointer can and will change shape, depending upon what you're doing at the time. Want to see some more?

√ **To See Some of the Other Available Mouse "Pointers"**

▶ Move the mouse to the left, until the mouse pointer reaches the vertical line marking the left side of the Setup Help display window. (Now it's a double-headed, horizontal arrow.)

▶ Move the mouse down, until the mouse pointer reaches the horizontal line marking the bottom border of the Setup Help display window. (The pointer is still double-headed, but now it's vertical.)

35

As these few examples illustrate, the mouse pointer is an adaptable little creature, indeed. Given this fact, I'll refer to it as the mouse cursor from now on.

Completing Your Windows Installation

There's much more to learn about navigating Windows. And learn it, we will. But we've dawdled enough in the middle of our installation procedures. (Remember, you don't even have Windows totally installed on your system yet.) It's time to move on. So, let's use a keyboard shortcut to exit Setup Help and get the whole Windows package on your hard disk.

√ **To Exit Help and Continue Setup**

▶ Press Alt+F (hold down the Alt key and, while keeping it down, tap the F key).

▶ Press **X**.

This returns you to the Setup screen shown in Figure 3.1. From here, we can tell Setup to finish installing Windows. But first, let's tell Setup we want to skip reading its on-line documents.

√ **To Skip Reading Setup's On-Line Documents**

▶ Move the mouse until the mouse cursor points to the box next to the `Read On-Line Documents` option.

▶ Click the left mouse button to de-select the option.

Now, we can continue our Windows installation.

√ **To Continue Installing Windows on Your System**

▶ Move the mouse until the mouse cursor points to the box marked Continue, in the top-right corner of the Windows Setup display window.

▶ Click the left mouse button.

36

Setup returns to transferring files from the Windows distribution diskettes to your hard disk. Once again, Setup will walk you through all the required procedures. Setup even sounds a distinctive beep and displays an on-screen message, to inform you when you need to place a new distribution diskette in your floppy disk drive and which disk it needs. Follow these instructions, and you'll soon have all the Windows installed on your hard disk. This process will take awhile, because Windows consists of many files.

> ▶ Note: Exactly what disks you'll use, and the order in which you'll use them, is determined by the various hardware and software components installed on your PC. To try to cover all the possible permutations of the Setup procedures would be impossible. The best advice I can give you is read. Read. READ! Specifically, read any instructions Setup displays and then follow those instructions carefully. If you do this, you should have no trouble transferring the remaining Windows files onto your hard disk.

Modifying Your CONFIG.SYS and AUTOEXEC.BAT Files

When Setup has transferred all the necessary files from the Windows distribution diskettes to your hard disk, it displays the message shown in Figure 3.3, requesting whether and how it should modify two critical DOS files on your hard disk: CONFIG.SYS and AUTOEXEC.BAT. I'm going to assume that, if you understand this message, you'll know which option is best for you. If not, let Setup make any changes that are required in these two files.

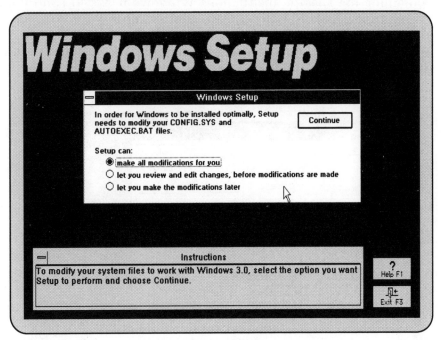

Figure 3.3. Setup allows you to specify whether your CONFIG.SYS and AUTOEXEC.BAT files should be modified for Windows.

37

√ **To Have Setup Automatically Modify CONFIG.SYS and AUTOEXEC.BAT**

▶ Press Enter.

Note: If these files did not previously exist, Setup creates them. If your system already had a CONFIG.SYS and AUTOEXEC.BAT file, Setup makes the required modifications but saves the earlier versions under the names CONFIG.OLD and AUTOEXEC.OLD, respectively. See how considerate Windows is?

Specifying a Printer

Next, Setup asks you to install a *print driver* for your Windows environment, as shown in Figure 3.4. Basically, a print driver is a file containing the specific instructions Windows needs to control a given printer. Installing the correct print driver in your Windows environment is important because any programs you run under Windows that are "Windows-aware" will use the specified print driver for all their print operations.

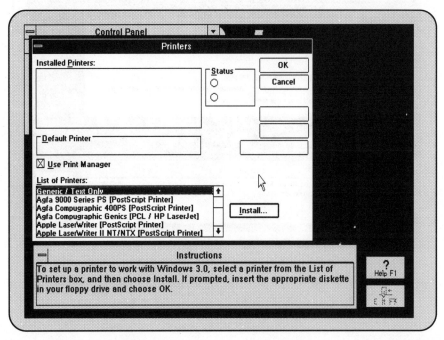

Figure 3.4. Setup requests that you identify what type of printer you will be using with Windows.

Though important, all is not lost if you do not select the correct driver for your printer. As I mentioned in Chapter 1, Windows 3.0 allows you to modify your system setup without completely reinstalling Windows, a process we'll look at more closely in Chapter 4, "Customizing Windows." For now, make your best guess and then follow the screen instruction to complete this phase of the Setup procedures.

Setting Up Applications

As its final step in Windows installation, Setup offers to scan your hard disks and automatically install into your Windows environment any applications programs it recognizes, as shown in Figure 3.5. Once again, unless you understand this option, it's best to let Setup automatically handle everything for you. If it misses some of your favorites (it's not infallible) you can return later to pick them up.

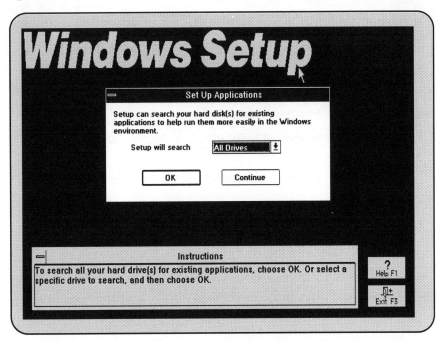

Figure 3.5. Setup can automatically install applications in your Windows environment.

✓ To Have Setup Automatically Install Programs into Your Windows Environment

▶ Press Enter.

After scanning the files on your hard disks, Setup displays a screen similar to that shown in Figure 3.6, giving you one more opportunity to specify which programs it should install in your Windows environment. Different screen, same principle: If you don't understand what this is all about, go ahead and let Setup take care of things.

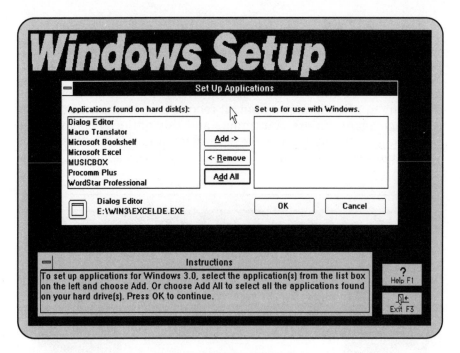

Figure 3.6. Setup lists any application programs it finds.

✓ **To Add Automatically All Applications Setup Finds to Your Windows Environment**

▶ Press Enter to select Add All.

▶ Move the mouse until the mouse cursor points to the box marked Continue.

▶ Click the left mouse button.

Ending Setup and Starting Windows

We're just about finished with your Windows installation. At last! All that remains is to decide what should happen when you exit Setup. As illustrated in Figure 3.7, you have three options:

▶ Have Setup completely reboot your system, so that any changes made to your CONFIG.SYS and AUTOEXEC.BAT files take effect.

▶ Automatically start Windows, without resetting your system to any new parameters established during Setup.

▶ Return to DOS and take no further steps.

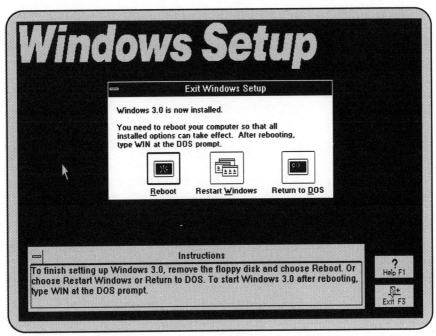

Figure 3.7. The final step in Setup is to specify what should happen when Setup ends.

And yes, I'm going to say this one more time: If you don't understand exactly what all this means, select the default option—rebooting your system—and let Setup itself decide the best alternative.

√ To End Setup and Reboot Your System

▶ Press Enter.

Guess what? Windows is now completely installed on your system. There's still much to do, as we get down to the nitty-gritty of learning how to work within the Windows environment.

Window Parts

You should now be at the DOS system prompt and, I would hope, fairly eager to load Windows. Before doing so, however, let's look at a generic Windows screen and identify the various Windows elements you'll be working with for the remainder of this chapter.

41

Before doing this, however, I must explain the difference between Windows and a window. When I mention *Windows* (with a capital W), I mean the Windows program itself or, in a more universal way, the total Windows GUI environment. A *window* (with a lowercase w) is a discrete portion of the complete Windows screen—generally the outlined display box in which a given application, program, or utility is running. Big Windows vs. little windows; that's not such a bad way of thinking about it.

Figure 3.8 shows a typical Windows screen—a relatively boring one, I will admit, but a Windows screen, nonetheless. Several elements have been pointed out on this screen; you will need to be familiar with these elements as you begin navigating Windows.

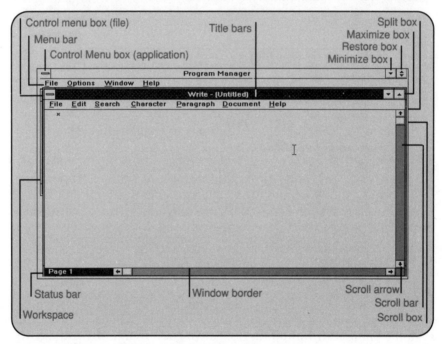

Figure 3.8. Elements of the Windows display.

Specifically, these items are:

Control menu box (application)	Click on this box to display the pull-down Control menu for an application window. The Control menu includes command options for sizing, moving, "shrinking," enlarging, and restoring an application window.

Menu bar	It displays the main Menu options available in a window. Clicking on a Menu item displays a pull-down menu associated with the item that, in turn, lists additional command options. The specific options listed on the Main menu bar depend on the application running in a window.
Control menu box (file)	Click on this box to display the pull-down Control menu for the file on which you are working. The Control menu includes command options for sizing, moving, "shrinking", enlarging, and restoring the active window.
Workspace	This is the area in which your windows are displayed. You can, of course, have multiple windows open in the workspace at any given time.
Status bar	Use the status bar to display information and messages relating to a window's current status or a selected command. Each window open in the workspace will have its own status bar. Most Windows applications allow you to turn off the status, if you so desire.
Window border	Each window has its own border. If your system includes a mouse, you can use a window's border to modify the size of that window.
Title bars	Each window in your workspace contains a title bar, which shows the name of the program, accessory, or utility running in that window. If your system includes a mouse, you can use a window's title bar to change the location of that window.

43

Minimize box	Clicking on this box shrinks a window to icon size. If a window cannot be represented as an icon, that window will not contain a minimize box.
Maximize box	Clicking on this box enlarges a window to its largest possible size, usually to where it occupies the entire screen.
Restore box	Clicking on this box restores a window to the size it was before you performed a Minimize or Maximize operation on that window.
Split box	Dragging your mouse on this box splits a window horizontally. Certain Windows applications also have a vertically split box that, if available, is located to the left of the horizontal scroll bar.
Scroll box	Windows uses this box to indicate your position in a file, relative to its beginning and end. As you drag this box up and down the scroll bar, Windows automatically scrolls you through a file's contents.
Scroll bar	Clicking on this bar moves you through a file too long or wide to be displayed completely in a single window. Most Windows applications allow you to turn off the scroll bar, if you so desire.
Scroll arrow	Clicking on a scroll arrow moves you through a file in small increments, in the direction the arrow "points."

44

Take a few moments to familiarize yourself with these various Window parts and how each is used within the Windows environment. I'll refer to them frequently in the remainder of this chapter—indeed, throughout the rest of this book.

Starting Windows

As part of its installation procedures, Setup appended the Windows directory—WIN3, if you followed the steps in the previous chapter—to a PATH statement in your AUTOEXEC.BAT file. Consequently, DOS will be able to locate the program used to run Windows, WIN.COM, without requiring that you first change to the Windows directory. So, let's begin a Windows session.

√ **To Start Windows**

▶ Type **WIN** and press Enter.

After displaying a brief copyright message, Windows advances to the opening screen shown in Figure 3.9.

45

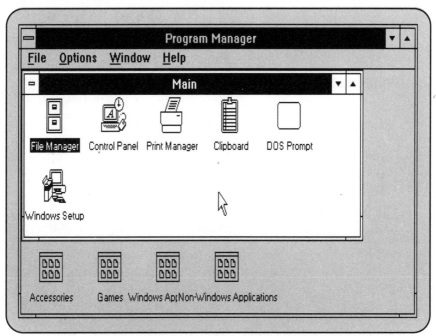

Figure 3.9. The first time you start Windows, it displays a document window marked Main, which contains a group of system applications Setup created during installation.

Windows always starts with a screen resembling Figure 3.9, the first time it is run. Later you will learn how to customize this opening display to correspond more closely with your normal work habits.

The window displayed in the workspace of Figure 3.9 contains several Windows system applications that Setup automatically created and organized into a program group called Main during installation. These include:

File Manager   Performs file-related operations during a Windows session.

Control Panel   Changes how your system is configured during a Windows session.

Print Manager   Manages printing during a Windows session.

Clipboard   Transfers data between windows and applications during a Windows session.

DOS Prompt   Allows you to temporarily exit the Windows GUI and enter commands directly from the DOS prompt during a Windows session.

Windows Setup   Accesses Setup and modifies elements of your Windows environment during a Windows session.

Other icons across the bottom of the workspace represent additional program groups created when you installed Windows. These include:

The Accessories Group   Contains the various applications mentioned in Chapter 1 that Microsoft includes in the basic Windows package (Write, Paintbrush, Terminal, Cardfile, and the like).

The Games Group   Contains two games also included with Windows, Reversi and Solitaire, that offer an ideal diversion from the more important work you'll soon be accomplishing with Windows. (After all, as the old adage states, all work and no play makes Jack a dull boy.)

46

The Windows Applications Group	Contains any Windows-based applications Setup found on your hard disk during installation
The Non-Windows Applications Group	Contains any standard DOS (or non-Windows) applications Setup recognized and incorporated into your Windows environment during installation.

You'll learn how to access each of these groups and work with many of the applications they contain as we dig more deeply into Windows throughout the rest of this book. Our main goal in the remainder of this chapter, however, is to become comfortable navigating the Windows GUI, something we'll accomplish using the various elements contained in the opening Windows display.

Working With Icons

After discussing icons several times, it's finally time to start learning the manner in which icons are used within a Windows session. Put simply, icons provide a quick and convenient method for managing different elements of your overall Windows environment.

For example, rather than forcing you to type in an exact file name and then press Enter to run a program, as is required in standard DOS, Windows allows you to accomplish the same thing by simply clicking on that program's icon. Previously convoluted operations like copying files to a new location are also simplified by Windows' use of on-screen icons. To pull a pathetic pun out of my bottomless bag of literary tricks: "If you can do it in DOS, 'icon' do it more easily in Windows."

Icons can be used to represent a variety of items on your Windows display, including:

▶ Individual program and data files stored on your disks.

▶ Multiple files that have been organized into logical groups.

▶ Special procedures and operations.

Rather than simply telling you about icons, why don't I show you what I mean? Notice that the words "File Manager," the text description associated with the two-drawer file cabinet icon in

Figure 3.9, are displayed in *inverse video*—that is, white letters on a black (or, possibly, blue) background. This identifies File Manager as the active icon. Let's change this.

√ **To Select a New Icon**

▶ Move your mouse until the mouse cursor points to the stylized computer icon, located just to the right of File Manager.

▶ Click the left mouse button.

Notice that this causes the words "Control Panel" to be displayed in inverse video, indicating that it is now the active icon. But what exactly does this mean? This question is answered within our next topic of discussion: the Windows menus.

48

Using Menus

Once an icon is active, you can use the different options accessed through the Windows pull-down menus to quickly perform a variety of operations on the file or group of files that icon represents. Let's look at what I mean by this.

√ **To Access the Files Menu**

▶ Move your mouse until the mouse cursor points to the File option of the Program Manager menu bar.

▶ Click the left mouse button.

Your screen should now resemble Figure 3.10, which shows a pull-down menu containing those File options available in Program Manager.

The availability of pull-down menus in Windows simplifies many PC operations by making them interactive—that is, Windows itself provides information about what you hope to accomplish and you, in turn, fill in the blanks to accomplish it.

Let's see what happens, for example, when you select the Copy option from the File menu.

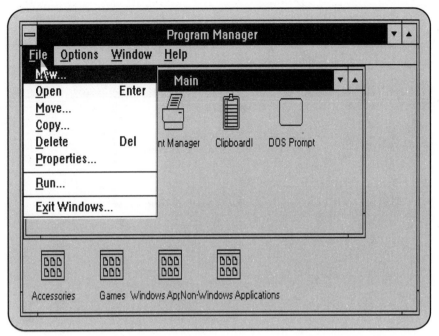

Figure 3.10. The File menu lists file-related operations that you can perform on the active icon.

✓ To Select the Copy Option

▶ Move your mouse until the mouse cursor points to the Copy option of the Files menu.

▶ Click the left mouse button.

This displays the dialog box shown in Figure 3.11.

Notice that Control Panel has already been entered into the field marked Copy Program Item. In other words, Windows assumes that, because Control Panel is the active icon, it is the program you want to copy. All you need to do to complete the Copy operation is specify where you want to copy Control Panel. You'll learn how to accomplish this in Chapter 5, "Managing a Windows Session." For now, let's return to the opening Windows screen, so we can continue our current discussion—that is, the various procedures used to work effectively within the Windows GUI.

49

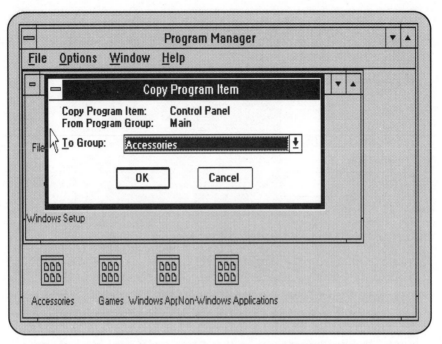

Figure 3.11. Windows automatically identifies the active icon as the item on which you want to perform the current Copy operation.

Canceling a Windows Operation

At this point, your display should still contain the Copy dialog box shown in Figure 3.10. Rather than completing this operation, however, let's assume that you decided to leave the Control Panel right where it was, within the Main program group. Most Windows dialog boxes include a Cancel button that, logically enough, allows you to cancel the current operation and return to where you were before it was initiated.

✓ To Cancel the Copy Operation

▶ Move your mouse until the mouse cursor points to the button marked Cancel.

▶ Click the left mouse button.

Canceling the Copy operation returns you to the opening Windows display shown in Figure 3.9—except that, as you may have noticed, Control Panel remains the active icon.

50

▶ **Note:** It's time to start cutting down on the complexity of the commands included in our exercises. By now you should have a pretty good idea of the steps involved in selecting an icon, menu option, or, as in the previous exercise, a Windows display button. For this reason, I'm going to start referring to this two-step procedure with a single word, *Choose*—the same terminology used in the Windows documentation. From now on, therefore, whenever an exercise contains instructions to Choose an item, it means you should position the mouse cursor over that item and then click the left mouse button. That's easy enough, isn't it?

Opening a Window   51

Icons also provide an easy way to open an *application window*—that is, a window within Windows, containing a program or program group. To accomplish this, you use a special method called "double-clicking" on an icon.

✓ **To Open a Window Containing the Windows Accessories**

▶ Move the mouse until the mouse cursor points to the icon on the bottom of your display marked Accessories.

▶ Click the left mouse button twice, in rapid succession.

Double-clicking on an icon automatically expands that icon to a display window, as illustrated in Figure 3.12. In this figure, a second window has been added to the opening Windows display. This second window contains the icons associated with the so-called Accessories Setup automatically installed in your Windows environment.

▶ **Note:** From now on I'll describe this procedure using the same terminology you'll find in the Windows documentation—*double-clicking*. Whenever an exercise contains instructions to double-click on an item, position your mouse cursor over that item and then quickly press and release the left mouse button twice.

Figure 3.12. Double-clicking on an icon automatically expands that icon to its own display window.

Now that we have two open windows, let's look at some additional features of the Windows GUI.

Working With Multiple Windows

Notice that the title bar containing the name of the window you just opened, Accessories, is now highlighted. This identifies Accessories as the active window. Conversely, the Main window, which was previously active, is now inactive, as indicated by the fact that its title bar is no longer highlighted. Each time you open a new window, Windows automatically places that window in the foreground of your display and makes it active.

You can change the color scheme used to identify the various elements of your Windows display, such as the colors used to indicate active and inactive windows. We'll see how this is done in Chapter 4, "Customizing Windows."

One of Windows' most impressive capabilities is how easily it allows you to manage, manipulate, and move around—or navigate, as I refer to these procedures in the title of this chapter—even the most complex workspace. Let's quickly look at a few examples of how this is accomplished.

Switching Active Windows

Suppose, for example, that you need to access an icon located on the Main window. The quickest way to accomplish this is to once again make that window active.

√ To Make the Main Window Active

▶ Move your mouse until the mouse cursor is pointing to any visible portion of the Main window.

▶ Click the left mouse button.

53

This returns the Main window to the foreground of your display and makes it active. You could now select an item on this window by simply clicking on its icon.

Moving a Window

You can also change the location of a window on your display. This would be desirable, for example, if you wanted to be able to see more of an inactive window, which is almost totally obscured in the default arrangement Windows uses when multiple windows have been opened.

√ To Change the Position of the Accessories Window

▶ Move your mouse until the mouse cursor is pointing to any visible portion of the Accessories window.

▶ Click the left mouse button. (This makes Accessories the active window.)

▶ Move your mouse until the mouse cursor is pointing to the title bar of the Accessories window.

▶ Press and hold down the left mouse button.

▶ Move your mouse slowly down and to the right until the shaded outline that separates from the Applications window is resting against the right-hand side and bottom border of the Windows workspace.

▶ Release the left mouse button.

> ▶ **Note:** Once again, let's standardize our terminology. The Windows documentation refers to this procedure as *dragging* a display element. Sounds good to me. Whenever an exercise in this book contains instructions to Drag an item, therefore, it means you should position your mouse cursor over that item, press and hold down the left mouse button, move the mouse to a new location, and then release the left mouse button.

When you've completed these steps, your screen should resemble Figure 3.13, in which the Accessories window has been moved to a new location on the Windows workspace. Admittedly, this new arrangement is slightly less cluttered than before. Still, the actual Windows workspace seems pretty crowded. It probably won't surprise you to find out that there is a way to enlarge it.

54

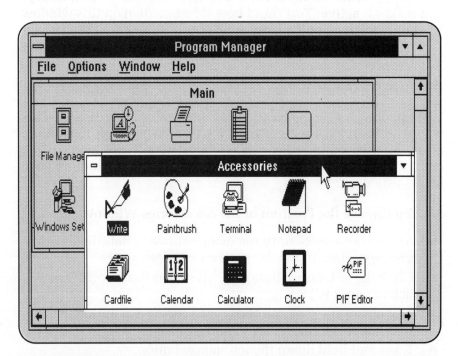

Figure 3.13. Move a window by dragging the mouse cursor on that window's title bar.

Resizing Elements of the Windows Display

It may help to think of your Windows display as resembling a typical desktop. As you've already seen, it's easy to adjust individual windows within this display—in much the same way that, throughout the course of an average workday, you rearrange reports, folders, notepads, and the like, occupying your desk or workspace. If you're like me, however, there have probably been times when you wish your desk could be enlarged temporarily, just to make room for all the different projects you're working on at the time. Whereas it's impractical to think about doing this with a traditional work area, adjusting the size of the various elements comprising your Windows display is child's play. We'll begin by expanding the total Windows work area, so that it occupies your entire display.

Maximizing the Windows Workspace

55

Notice the two boxes located to the far right of the Program Manager title bar. These two boxes, called the Minimize box and Maximize box, allow you to shrink and expand elements of your Windows display quickly. (Refer to Figure 3.8, if necessary, to determine the location and appearance of the Minimize and Maximize boxes.)

✓ **To Expand the Windows Workspace to a Full-Screen Display**

▶ Position your mouse cursor over the Maximize box located in the Program Manager title bar.

▶ Click the left mouse button.

Your screen should now resemble Figure 3.14, in which Windows has been enlarged to fill the entire display. This gives you much more room to work with when arranging the various elements of your Windows workspace. Now that we have all this additional space, let's take advantage of it.

Expanding a Window Manually

Of course, there will be times when you'd like to enlarge a single window, without having that window take over your entire display. This might be the case, for example, if you're working primarily in an application loaded into one window, but need to leave a small portion of a second window visible in order to reference specific material it contains.

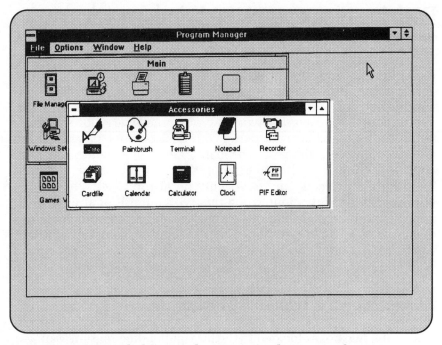

Figure 3.14. Clicking on the Maximize box expands your Windows display.

In such a situation, it wouldn't make sense to use the Maximize box. Rather, you'd want to increase the size of your primary application window only slightly. Windows allows you to do this.

✓ To Increase the Size of the Accessories Window

▶ Position the mouse cursor on the lower right-hand corner of the Applications window. (This should cause the mouse cursor to change to a diagonal, double-headed arrow. If not, keep adjusting the cursor location until this new shape appears.)

▶ Press and hold down the left mouse button.

▶ Drag the mouse slightly down and to the right.

▶ Release the left mouse button.

Your display should now resemble Figure 3.15, which shows the Accessories window slightly enlarged from its previous size. Depending on the border you drag, a window can be expanded horizontally, vertically, or, as we did in the previous exercise, diagonally.

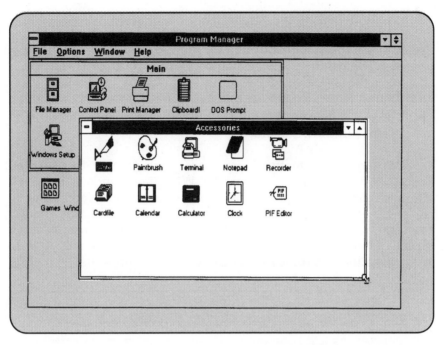

Figure 3.15. By dragging the mouse cursor on a window's border, you can dynamically alter the size of that window.

▶ **Tip:** This same technique can be used to reduce a window's size. For example, positioning the mouse cursor on a window's right-hand border and then dragging the mouse to your left would move the right border in, thus reducing the horizontal dimensions of that window.

Cascading vs. Tiled Windows

Until now, we've been working exclusively with Windows default layout of setting up *cascading windows*—that is, a display arrangement where multiple windows are positioned to overlap one another, with each subsequent window you open automatically located slightly below and to the left of the previous one. Windows supports a second display option, called tiling.

✓ **To Switch Your Windows Display to a Tiled Arrangement**

▶ Choose the Window option on the Program Manager menu bar. (Remember, this means to position your mouse cursor over the specified option and then click the left mouse button.)

▶ Choose Tile from Window options that appear in the subsequent pull-down menu.

Windows automatically redraws your display to use tiled windows, as shown in Figure 3.16. With *tiled windows* in effect, multiple windows are positioned next to one another, rather than in an overlapping configuration, as was the case with the default Cascade arrangement. Personally, I prefer the Cascade arrangement, so let's change back to that. In the process, we'll also be able to examine another Windows feature: keyboard shortcuts.

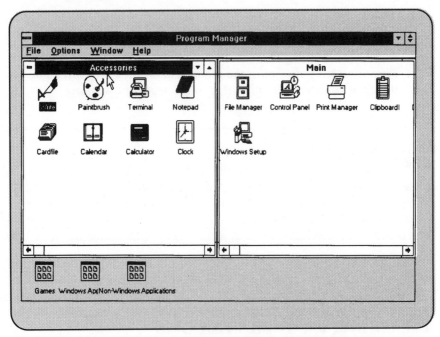

Figure 3.16. Windows displays tiled windows.

Using Keyboard Shortcuts

As I mentioned in Chapter 1, the availability of a mouse greatly simplifies most Windows operations. As is true of any general rule, however, this one does have some notable exceptions. In several cases, Windows provides alternate keyboard commands that you may find more convenient to use than the corresponding mouse sequences. When available, Windows lists these keyboard "shortcuts" on its various option menus. Let's see how this works, by taking another look at the Window options menu used in the previous exercise.

√ **To View the Window Menu**

► Choose the Window option on the Program Manager menu bar.

Notice that the key sequence Shift+F5 appears next to the Cascade option. This is one example of a Windows keyboard shortcut.

√ **To Return Your Display to Cascading Windows**

► Close the menu by clicking the left mouse button while the pointer is outside the menu area. (Key shortcuts don't work with the menu open.)
► Press Shift+F5.

This switches your display back to a cascading windows arrangement, as shown in Figure 3.17.

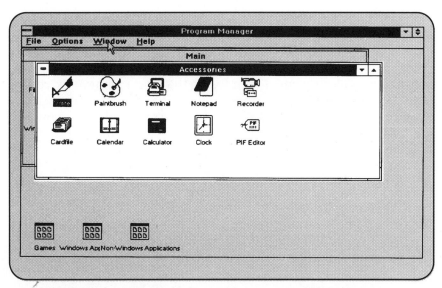

Figure 3.17. Keyboard shortcuts are available for many Windows operations.

> ▶ **Note:** Windows uses the plus sign (+) to indicate a multiple-key command sequence. In this case, for example, Shift+F5 indicates that you should hold down the Shift key while pressing the F5 function key. For the sake of consistency, I'll use this same notation to indicate multiple-key command sequences throughout this book.

In this chapter, we've looked at some of the basic procedures used to navigate and, in some cases, modify the appearance of your Windows workspace. To be honest, we've only scratched the surface. You'll learn many more techniques associated with working in the Windows environment throughout the rest of this book as we examine additional components of the total Windows package. My main goal here was to introduce you to Windows and then have you experiment just enough to feel comfortable with that program's GUI—to stick your head into Windows and then look around a bit. (If I've succeeded, all the exercises that follow should come together like a proverbial piece of cake.) Now that I've gotten you into Windows, though, it's probably a good idea if I show you how to get out—that is, the steps required to end a Windows session.

Exiting Windows

Exiting Windows is a two-step process. To begin with, any programs you have been running in the current Windows session should be closed. This guards against your losing the most recent work you've done. Once these applications are closed, it's safe to exit the Windows GUI and return to DOS. Of course, we didn't open any applications in this, our first Windows session. Ending it, therefore, will be easy.

√ To Exit Windows

▶ Position your mouse cursor over the Control menu box located in the upper-left corner of the Program Manager title bar. (Refer to Figure 3.8, if necessary, to determine the location and appearance of the Control menu box.)

▶ Click the left mouse button.

This displays the Control menu shown in Figure 3.18, which contains several options for managing either the current window or your total Windows environment. When available, selecting the Close option ends the current Windows session.

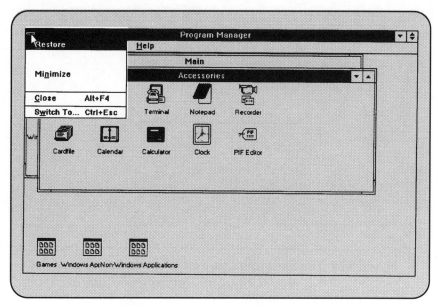

Figure 3.18. Select the Close option of the Control menu to end a Windows session.

61

✓ **To End the Current Windows Session**

▶ Choose Close.

Each time you quit Windows, it displays the prompt box shown in Figure 3.19, asking you to verify that you want to end the current session. This prompt box provides you with an opportunity to save any changes you made in the Program Manager during the current session. If you elect to Save Changes, the next time you open Windows your workspace will be configured the same way it is now.

> ▶ **Note:** This prompt also provides a safeguard, in that it allows you to verify in your own mind that you have indeed closed any applications used during the current session.

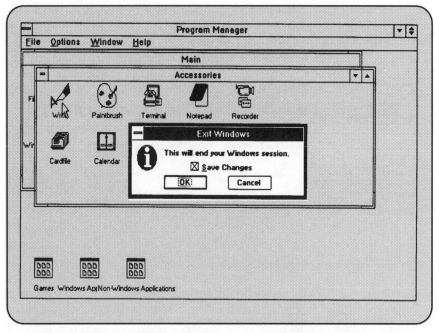

Figure 3.19. The Save Changes option allows you to save the current settings of your Program Manager workspace.

√ **To Exit Windows and Save the Current Workspace**

► Choose OK.

> ► **Note:** If there is no reason to preserve the current workspace, clicking on Save Changes would remove the X from the accompanying check box. You could then choose OK to exit Windows. The next time you started Windows, your workspace would appear exactly as it did at the beginning of the current session.

You should now be back at the DOS prompt. Don't worry, we'll return to Windows in the next chapter.

What You Have Learned

▶ Installing Windows within Windows follows a procedure different from that found in previous releases. In the current release, any future system configuration modifications you make after the initial installation will not require a complete reinstallation of the Windows GUI.

▶ A typical Windows display contains a number of elements designed to simplify the process of working within a graphics-based environment. These include menu bars, pull-down option boxes, dialog boxes, scroll bars, and the like. Positioning the mouse cursor on these visual elements and performing the appropriate action makes working in the Windows environment an interactive process.

▶ Windows allows you to save your current workspace settings so that they will automatically be put into effect the next time you open a Windows session.

63

64

Chapter 4

Customizing Windows

In This Chapter

▶ *The differences between Windows' three operating modes*
▶ *How to specify command parameters when starting Windows*
▶ *How to start applications from within Windows*
▶ *How to use Control Panel and Setup to modify your*
  Windows environment

I know you're probably eager to climb back into Windows. (Don't worry, we soon will.) However, before we actually begin working in a couple of Windows applications, I want to make certain that Windows is set up on your PC to run as efficiently as possible. This requires a short detour to examine the evolution of DOS-based personal computers—a topic that, in turn, leads directly to a discussion of one of the most impressive features of Windows 3.0: its advanced memory management capabilities.

A Short History of PCs

I'm not going to get too technical here. I promise. My primary goal is to dwell on the subject only long enough to ensure that your Windows environment is configured to take full advantage of the memory installed on your PC. This said, let's forge ahead.

We'll begin by looking at the three general categories of personal computers on which Windows will run. Specifically, these include:

▶ Systems built around the Intel 8088 or 8086 microprocessor.

▶ Systems built around the Intel 80286 microprocessor.

▶ Systems built around the Intel 80386 or i486 microprocessor.

It may look like we've swayed off-course here. Trust me, we haven't. As I'll explain shortly, the type of system you own directly influences the degree to which you'll be able to take advantage of Windows' advanced memory management features. Stay with me. Everything will be made clear as we move along.

Somewhere inside every PC sits a *microprocessor*, a special silicon chip designed to coordinate all other operations your PC performs. It is the heart and soul of that magical machine on which you rely so heavily. But all microprocessors are not created equal. As PC technology has evolved, so too have the microprocessors upon which that technology depends. Each subsequent step up this ladder of electronic evolution has been accompanied by comparable improvements in the features and capabilities those microprocessors support. This is especially true in the area of memory management.

Early IBM and compatible personal computers—the so-called PC/XT models based on Intel's 8088 or 8086 microprocessor—were extremely limited in the amount of memory they were designed to support. Practically speaking, the largest amount of memory these first-generation PCs were capable of managing was 1 megabyte, or 1024 individual memory addresses.

If you'd like a useful analogy, picture a memory address as resembling a mail slot in an old-fashioned post office. Like the person distributing mail in our imaginary post office, your PC's microprocessor is responsible for constantly moving items in and out of these individual slots—making sure that the appropriate item (instruction or information) is placed in the correct "slot" and then knowing how to locate that item when it's needed. The original PC/XTs, therefore, could be compared to a post office with only enough space to accommodate 1024 slots. Admittedly, the manner in which your PC manages memory is much more complex; for our purposes here, however, this simple analogy will suffice.

As if this 1-megabyte limit weren't restrictive enough, someone decided that over one-third of a PC's total memory, or 384K, should be reserved for controlling specific activities within that PC— coordinating its display, regulating the system clock, managing disk access, and the like. This left only 640K of random access memory, or RAM, available in which DOS could actually load and run any programs you planned to use, a figure condescendingly referred to as the *DOS 640K barrier.*

Life in PC land improved drastically with the introduction of a second generation of personal computers, dubbed AT systems, which were based on Intel's 80286 microprocessor. In essence, using an AT system resembles working in a post office with 16,384 mail slots, given that the 80286 chip is potentially capable of managing 16 megabytes (or 16 x 1024 bytes) of RAM. There was only one problem: DOS, by itself, still couldn't access these additional memory addresses—a dilemma not unlike building all those extra mail slots and then neglecting to have keys made to open them. Though potentially more powerful than the PC/XT models they improved upon, at least in terms of the memory they could manage, 80286-based AT systems were still crippled by DOS. A frustrating situation for anyone who owned an AT? You bet. But the situation soon got better—or worse, depending on your perspective.

Unlike human evolution, which transpires over periods measured in millennia, improvements in computer technology come fast and furious. Even as it announced the 80286 chip, Intel was already putting the finishing touches on its third-generation microprocessor, the 80386. Remember those 16,384 metaphorical mail slots incorporated into our previous postal annex? Well, how impressed would you be with a structure designed to hold *over 4 million* of them? Symbolically speaking, that's the 80386, which is theoretically capable of managing 4 gigabytes (4 x 1024 x 1024, or 4,194,304 bytes) of RAM! Now we're talking real PC power.

67

> ▶ **Note:** And the recently released fourth-generation i486 chip is even more impressive. At some point, though, the numbers become so large their differences become inconsequential. Consequently, I'll limit our discussion to the three primary PC platforms, grouping the new i483 chip in with its immediate PC predecessor, the 80386.

Despite the availability of all this potential power, the advantages inherent in owning a PC more advanced than the original PC/XT remained largely unrealized. Anyone using standard DOS, even on a 386 system, was still destined to run smack up against the same impasse that existed before: that confounded 640K DOS barrier.

So, did all this technological evolution merely represent an electronic exercise in futility? Hardly. Though fairly rigid, DOS's

RAM restrictions are not impregnable. Methods do exist that will allow you to climb over the 640K DOS barrier, even though you will not be able to raze it completely. If that isn't the perfect cue to introduce the advanced memory management capabilities built into Windows 3.0, I don't know what is. See, I told you we'd get back to Windows, didn't I?

The Three Faces of Windows 3.0

As mentioned in Chapter 1, Windows 3.0 is designed to operate in three different modes:

▶ Real mode.
▶ Standard mode.
▶ Enhanced 386 mode.

The existence of multiple alternatives in both PC platforms and Windows operating modes is no mere coincidence. One, the different configurations in which Windows can run, is a direct result of the other, the various types of DOS-compatible personal computers currently on the market. This isn't surprising, actually. You see, Microsoft planned it that way, with the memory management techniques used by each of Windows operating modes designed to take full advantage of a specific generation of PC hardware.

Real Mode

When operating in Real mode, Windows uses memory management techniques most appropriate to first-generation DOS systems—that is, personal computers built around an 8088 or 8086 microprocessor. In Real mode, all active programs running in a Windows session must reside in that 640K area of memory commonly referred to as conventional RAM, the same 640K of memory comprising the infamous DOS barrier. The memory management techniques Windows 3.0 employs when operating in Real mode are virtually identical to those previously used in Windows/286—the less powerful version of Windows sold by Microsoft back before a single program, Windows 3.0, was designed to be all things to all systems.

Running Windows in Real mode is mandatory if your system is a PC/XT model built around an 8088 or 8086 chip—or, alternately, the NEC V20 and V30 "work-alike" microprocessors used in many PC/XT clones. You will also need to run Windows in Real mode if you have an AT or 386 system with less than 1 megabyte of extended memory. As a rule, if your system includes an 80286 or 386 CPU and does have the required amount of extended memory, the more logical choice is to configure Windows to run in either Standard or Enhanced 386 mode.

> ▶ **Tip:** One exception to this general rule is when you are using Windows programs that have not yet been upgraded to take full advantage of the advanced memory management capabilities built into Windows 3.0. It's possible you may experience difficulties when trying to load older versions of some programs into the newer Windows environment. The only way of resolving this conflict is to force Windows to operate in Real mode, using one of the command switches I'll describe a little later in this chapter, should you have to run an older, problematic Windows application under Windows 3.0.

69

Standard Mode

One step up from Real mode is Windows' new Standard mode. When operating in Standard mode, Windows 3.0 can access so called high-RAM, memory located between 640K and the 1-megabyte memory address that DOS normally ignores. Standard mode also endows Windows with the ability to make *extended memory*—that is, RAM existing above the 1-megabyte memory address—available to those applications designed to take advantage of this feature. Consequently, programs that required the electronic equivalent of a crowbar to fit into previous releases of Windows, and then left precious little free memory for data storage once they were running, work just fine under Windows 3.0.

The basic message lurking behind all this "technobabble" is a simple one: When operating in Standard mode, Windows no longer finds itself on a direct collision course with the dreaded 640K DOS barrier. If you have an AT system, therefore—or, as I'll explain shortly, a 386 or 486 system with less than 2 megabytes of RAM— you'll probably want to configure Windows 3.0 to run in Standard mode. However, don't forget the exception to this rule. If the kinds of software conflicts outlined in the previous section occur, you'll be forced to "get Real," and restrict Windows to running in Real mode.

Enhanced 386 Mode

If your system is an 80386- or i486-based personal computer that includes more than 2 megabytes of RAM, you will be able to run Windows 3.0 in its third, and most advanced, mode: Enhanced 386 mode. Enhanced 386 mode supports all of the impressive features supported by Windows running in Standard mode, as well as providing a pair of additional capabilities only available in systems built around these two state-of-the-art microprocessors.

First, Enhanced mode allows a standard DOS application to run in its own window of a multiwindow display, rather than automatically assigning such applications the entire screen, as happens when Windows is running in Real or Standard mode. Second, and perhaps even more impressive, Enhanced mode allows Windows to convert available storage space on a hard-disk into *virtual memory*—a sort of artificial RAM created when disk space is temporarily used to store applications running in a Windows session—and then use this virtual memory to augment the actual RAM installed on your system. Consequently, the amount of "memory" available to Windows running in Enhanced 386 mode is ultimately determined by the amount of storage space available on your hard disk.

70

Using Command Switches

As I pointed out in Chapter 2, Windows tries, whenever possible, to make a best guess as to how it should configure itself to run most efficiently on your PC. This includes selecting an initial operating mode, based on the hardware components Windows determines are installed on your system each time it is run. As a rule, there should be no reason to modify Windows's default configuration. If you ever do find it necessary to run Windows in a mode other than its default—as would be the case, for example, if Windows normally configures itself in Standard mode and you discover that some of your older programs require Real mode to run properly—there is an easy way to accomplish this.

When starting Windows, you can append one of three special switches to the WIN command, thus forcing Windows to run in a mode other than its default. These include:

/R is used to force Windows to run in Real mode.

/S is used to force Windows to run in Standard mode.

/3 is used to force Windows to run in Enhanced 386 mode.

Entering the following command at the DOS system prompt, for example, would load Windows and instruct it to run in Real mode:

```
WIN /R
```

If you are running Windows in Real mode, you have access to three additional command switches that allow you to control the way Windows uses any expanded memory (EMS) installed on your system. Be aware, however, that the functions of these EMS switches cross over into some fairly technical territory. They should be used, therefore, only if you are familiar with how EMS works and what each switch accomplishes.

The three optional EMS command switches available when running Windows in Real mode include:

71

/E is used to specify how much conventional memory must be available for Windows to use large-frame EMS mode, where the EMS page frame is configured to 64K.

/L is used to move the EMS bank line up or down by 1K increments, if Windows is using a 64K (large-frame) page frame.

/N is used to prevent Windows from using any expanded memory when running in Real mode.

As interesting as the technical aspects of personal computing may be, you are undoubtedly more interested in learning more about using Windows. Let's start another Windows session now from which we'll use the Control Panel and Setup accessories to complete customizing Windows to match your preferences.

√ To Restart Windows

▶   Type **WIN** and press Enter.

> ▶ **Tip:** Entering the WIN command with the appropriate command switch forces Windows to run in a specified operating mode.

This reopens Windows and displays the screen shown in Figure 4.1. Because we used the Save Changes option at the end of Chapter 3, Windows displays the same workspace that was in effect when you ended the previous session. Now that Windows is up and running again, let's look at how you can use its Control Panel to further customize your Windows environment.

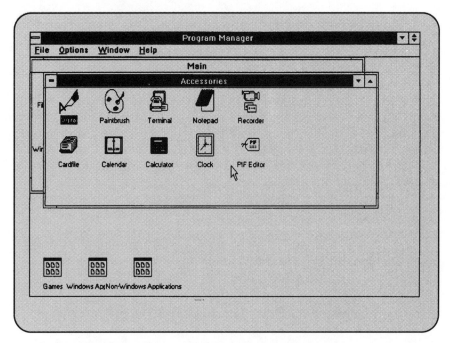

Figure 4.1. Selecting Save Changes causes Windows to redisplay the previous workspace the next time it is started.

The Windows Control Panel

Control Panel provides a quick and easy way for you to modify several hardware and software settings associated with your system. The ability to access Control Panel from within a Windows session, combined with the fact that Windows immediately implements any modifications specified through its Control Panel, means that your Windows environment can be dynamically altered, as needed.

Starting Control Panel

You access Control Panel from within the Main program group.

√ To Start Control Panel

▶ Move the mouse cursor to any visible portion of the window containing the Main program group.

▶ Click the left mouse button.

▶ Double-click on the Control Panel icon.

> ▶ **Tip:** Remember to position your mouse cursor over the specified icon, then rapidly tap and release the left mouse button twice.

73

This opens a window from which you can access the various Control Panel options. Each option is represented by its own icon, as illustrated in Figure 4.2.

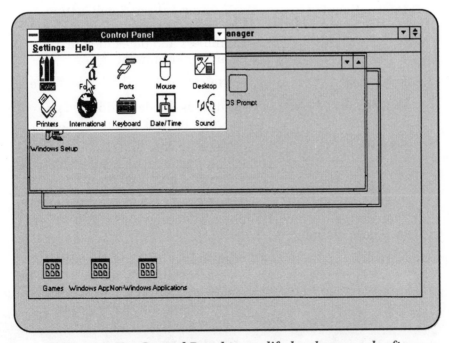

Figure 4.2. Use Control Panel to modify hardware and software settings associated with your Windows environment.

The Control Panel Options

Options available in the Control Panel window include:

Color	Changes the colors used to display specific elements of the Windows GUI.
Fonts	Adds or removes fonts for your printer and display.
Ports	Specifies communication parameters for any serial ports installed on your system.
Mouse	Modifies how your mouse performs within the Windows environment.
Desktop	Modifies the appearance and other aspects of the Windows display.
Printers	Installs and configures printers for your Windows environment.
International	Specifies international setting, such as the format used to display numbers and dates in your Windows environment.
Keyboard	Adjusts the keyboard repeat rate.
Date/Time	Modifies the date and time recorded in your system clock.
Sound	Specifies whether Windows should generate a beep when it detects a potential error.

74

Two additional options may appear in the Control Panel window, depending on how Windows is configured to run on your system. These include:

Network	Controls how Windows runs when installed on a network. (The Network option is only available if the system running Windows is installed on a network.)
386 Enhanced	Specifies how your system resources should be allocated among foreground and back-

ground applications when
Windows is being used to run
multiple programs in Enhanced
386 mode. (This icon only appears
if Windows itself is operating in
Enhanced 386 mode.)

To see how the Control Panel works, we'll modify a Desktop
setting, the one that controls icon spacing on your Windows display.

Modifying Icon Spacing

You may have noticed in Figure 4.2 that Windows' default setting for
icon spacing can cause the descriptions associated with icons to
overlap. The Windows Applications description, for example, is
partially obscured by the text, Non-Windows Applications. You can
correct this problem by increasing the spacing Windows uses to
separate any icons it displays.

75

√ To Access Control Panel's Desktop Options

► Double-click on the Desktop icon.

This displays the Desktop dialog box shown in Figure 4.3. You
can use the various fields located in this dialog box to modify various
aspects of your Windows display.

√ To Increase Windows' Default Icon Spacing

► Place the mouse cursor to the right of the number in the box
following Icon Spacing.
► Click the left mouse button. This places an input cursor in
the Icon Spacing prompt.
► Press Backspace until the Icon Spacing is blank.
► Type **120** and press Enter.

► **Note:** One of the most useful keyboard shortcuts Windows
provides is the ability to select an active button by simply
pressing Enter. Because the OK button was active in the
Desktop dialog box—that is, surrounded by a wide "shadow"—
pressing Enter in the previous step was analogous to positioning the mouse cursor over OK and then pressing the left mouse
button.

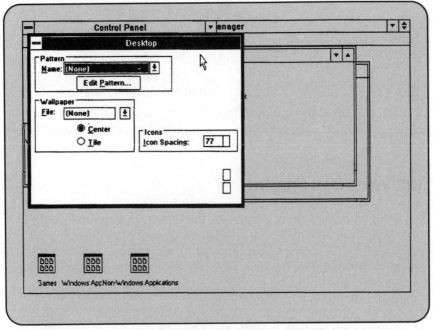

Figure 4.3. Use the dialog box to modify the appearance and other aspects of the Windows display.

This closes the Desktop dialog box and returns you to the Control Panel window. All that remains now is to have Windows implement the new icon spacing, using the Arrange Icons command.

✓ To Implement the New Icon Spacing

▶ Choose the Minimize box to close the Control Panel window.

▶ Choose Window from the Program Manager menu bar.

▶ Choose Arrange Icons.

Windows redraws the active window, using the new icon spacing setting of 120 pixels, as illustrated in Figure 4.4.

✓ To Rearrange Icons in the Remaining Windows

▶ Position the mouse cursor on any visible portion of the Accessories window.

▶ Click the left mouse button.

▶ Choose Window from the Program Manager menu bar.

▶ Choose Arrange Icons.

▶ Choose the Non-Windows Applications icon.

▶ Choose Window from the Program Manager menu bar.

▶ Choose Arrange Icons.

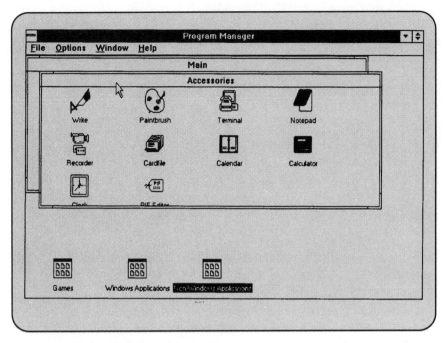

Figure 4.4. The Arrange Icons command redraws the active window using the current icon spacing.

This last step repositions all unopened icons on the Windows workspace, using the new icon spacing. When you've completed this exercise, your display should resemble Figure 4.5, in which all of the screen icons have been rearranged using the new spacing of 120 pixels.

You'll learn more about working with the new Windows Program Manager in Chapter 5, "Managing a Windows Session." For now, let's return to the Main window and look at how the Setup program in Windows 3.0 can be used to modify elements of your system configuration without forcing you to completely reinstall Windows, as was required with earlier versions.

Using Setup to Modify Your System Configuration

As already mentioned, previous Windows releases forced you to run Setup from the DOS prompt. Consequently, if you upgraded your

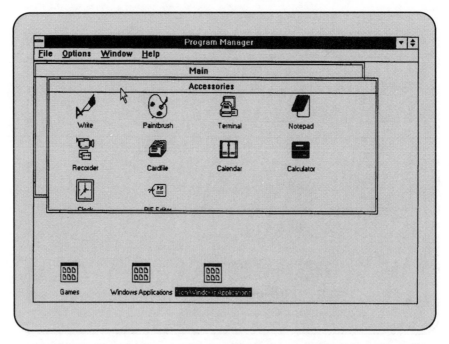

Figure 4.5. Windows redraws all of your windows incorporating the new icon spacing.

printer, for example, you had to reinstall Windows completely before it would recognize this new purchase—a major inconvenience, as almost any Windows veteran will attest to. Another feature new to Windows 3.0 is that it now allows you to access the Windows-based portion of Setup from within a Windows session.

Using the Window Menu to Switch Active Windows

During installation, Windows automatically placed Setup in the Main program group. Before running Setup, therefore, you will need to return that group window to active status. As you've already seen, one way to accomplish this is by clicking the mouse cursor on any visible portion of the desired group window—in this case, the Main program group. But what if you have set up a complex workspace (as, indeed, you can) where one or more group windows are totally obscured? Does Windows provide an alternate method for accessing such windows? You bet.

√ To Switch Windows from the Window Menu

▶ Choose Window from the Program Manager menu bar.

This displays the pull-down menu, as shown in Figure 4.6. The options numbered 1–5 on this menu identify the five program groups in your Windows environment.

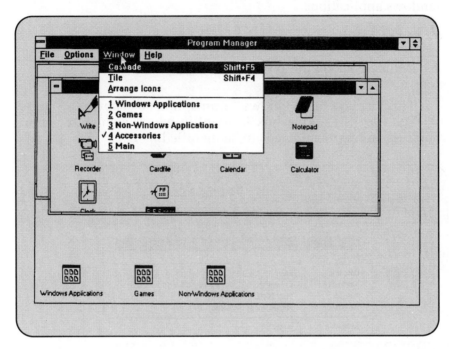

Figure 4.6. Individual program groups in your Windows environment are listed on the Window pull-down menu.

Each time you create a new program group, something you'll learn how to do in the next section, another numbered option is added to the Window menu.

The check mark next to the number 4 in Figure 4.6 indicates that the corresponding option, Accessories, is the currently active window. As you've probably guessed by now, you can change active windows simply by selecting the desired group from this menu.

√ To Make the Main Program Group Active

▶ Choose option 5, Main.

This moves the window associated with the Main program group to the foreground of your display and makes this the active window.

79

Starting Setup

At this point, you can start Setup just as you would any other Windows applications.

√ **To Start Setup**

▶ Double-click on the Windows Setup option.

This displays the Windows Setup option box shown in Figure 4.7. You use this option box to identify which element of your Windows environment needs to be modified.

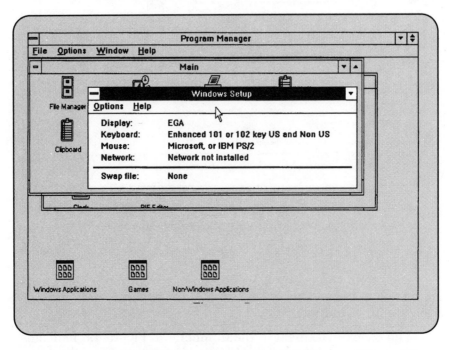

Figure 4.7. The Windows Setup program allows you to modify system components of your Windows environment.

Setup is slightly different from other Windows applications in that you must use its pull-down Options menus to select the item you want to modify. To see how this works, let's assume you've added a network to the system on which Windows is installed. In this situation, you would use the following steps to configure Windows to be compatible with that network.

⊘ **Caution:** Unless you really do need to configure Windows for a network, make sure you follow the steps in the following exercise *exactly*. It's only being presented here as an example of the procedures used to modify a Setup option, when necessary.

✓ **To Configure Windows for Network Compatibility**

▶ Choose Options from the Windows Setup menu bar.

▶ Choose Change System Settings from the resulting pull-down menu.

This calls up the dialog box shown in Figure 4.8. Notice the down arrow to the right of each option displayed in this box. Clicking on one of these arrows displays a listing of available settings for the corresponding item that are compatible with Windows 3.0.

81

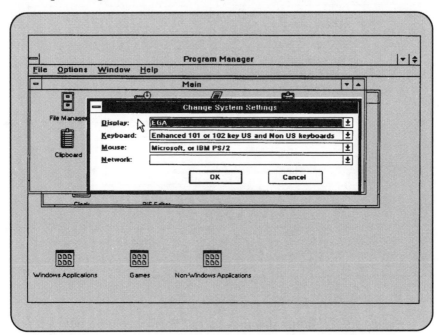

Figure 4.8. The Change System Settings dialog box displays those items you can reconfigure using the Windows Setup utility.

▶ **Note:** Compatibility is critical when modifying Setup options because Windows must have access to a device driver capable of supporting the specified item. In those cases where Windows itself does not support a specific device, check to see if the manufacturer provides its own device driver so its product will run with Windows.

√ To See the Networks Windows Supports

▶ Choose the down arrow to the right of the Network option.

To identify the network installed on your system, simply choose that network from the resulting list of Windows-compatible network drivers, shown in Figure 4.9.

82

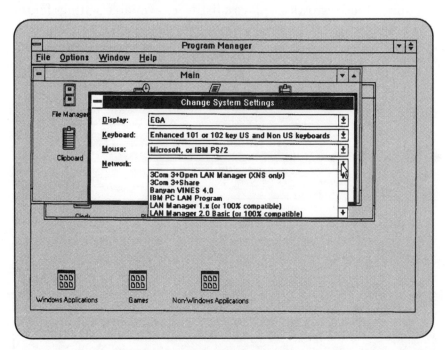

Figure 4.9. Windows displays lists of hardware with which it is compatible in each Setup category.

Now that you've seen how Setup works, let's back out of the current exercise without actually installing a network driver.

✓ **To Exit Setup Without Modifying Your System Configuration**

▶ Choose the Control menu box of the Change System Settings window.

▶ Choose Close. This returns you to the Windows Setup option box.

▶ Choose the Control menu box of the Windows Setup window.

▶ Choose Close.

This closes the Setup window and returns you to the Program Manager, with the Main group still the active window. And speaking of the Program Manager, that's one of the new features of Windows 3.0 we'll be looking at in Chapter 5, "Managing a Windows Session."

What You Have Learned   83

▶ Windows 3.0 can run in three different operating modes—Real mode, Standard mode, and Enhanced 386 mode—each of which is designed to provide maximum support for different types of personal computers. Which mode you should run Windows in depends on the specific hardware comprising your PC system.

▶ It's possible to override Windows' default operating mode by including the appropriate command switch with the WIN command used to start a Windows session. Other command switches allow you to specify how Windows should use any expanded memory installed on your system when running in Real mode.

▶ The Control Panel and Setup utilities allow you to modify your Windows environment. As a general rule, use Control Panel to change settings internal to Windows itself—display colors, fonts, your desktop layout, icon placement, and the like. Setup, on the other hand, provides a way to tell Windows when new or different hardware has been added to your system configuration. You access Control Panel and Setup just as you would any other Windows application.

84

Chapter 5

Managing a Windows Session

In This Chapter

▶ *How the Windows Program Manager works*

▶ *How to use the Windows File Manager*

▶ *How to create and maintain program groups*

Until now we've discussed the more general aspects of the Windows GUI. For example, you now know how to install, customize, and, on a very cursory level, interact with Windows. From here on out, I plan to get a little more specific—to open Windows a little wider and look around—as we discuss the procedures you'll use regularly when running actual applications within the Windows environment. We'll begin by looking at Program Manager and File Manager, two new features of Windows 3.0 that allow you to organize and manage the programs and data files comprising your total PC environment.

The Windows Program Manager

Microsoft designed its new Windows Program Manager to accomplish something that simply can't be done with standard DOS. Specifically, Program Manager lets you organize your disk files logically—that is, based on how those files will be used—rather than strictly reflecting their physical location on your hard disk. That's not self-explanatory, is it? Maybe I'd better use an example.

The DOS Directory Structure

Using the standard DOS directory structure is similar to organizing paper documents with a traditional filing cabinet. On a given hard disk, for example, you may elect to store files associated with your word processing program in one directory, analogous to a single manila folder in a file cabinet, and then create a second directory to hold the documents it generates. Similarly, you could set up a third directory for your spreadsheet program, a fourth directory to store your spreadsheet files, and so on, creating one directory for each of your application programs and a second dedicated to its corresponding data files. While certainly better than no organization at all, DOS's strict reliance on how files are physically stored on a disk leaves much to be desired, especially when you consider the manner in which most people work.

86

When was the last time you put together a project that relied on a single application program? Perhaps a better question would be, have you ever worked on a project that could be completed using a single program? Odds are the answer to this question is no. More likely, the work emanating from your PC contained elements from several sources.

An annual report, for example, may include text files created with a word processor, some tables generated with a spreadsheet program, perhaps a graphic file or two designed to visually emphasize a point, and so on. The problem is, DOS's reliance on directories and subdirectories provides little help in organizing such tasks— forcing you, as it does, to scramble hither and yon through the physical layout of your hard disk when the time comes to gather all the various elements of a given project. Surely, there must be a more logical approach. There is. And the Windows Program Manager provides it.

A More Logical Approach

Unlike DOS, which organizes your files based strictly on their physical location, the Windows Program Manager allows you to gather multiple files into a single program group, regardless of where those files are stored within a disk's directory structure. Sticking with our previous example for a moment, you could use the Windows Program Manager to create a program group called "Annual Report." This group, in turn, would contain an icon representing your word processor, one for a spreadsheet program, a third for a graphics program, as well as individual icons associated with each of the data files created by these various applications, files that ultimately will be combined to produce your final report. Whenever it was time to work on this project, therefore, all you'd have to do is open this program group, and you'd have immediate access to all the application and data files you need.

Program Manager provides the additional convenience of allowing you to include the same application or data file in more than one program group. The same word processing program file assigned to the Annual Report group, for example, could also be included in a program group you've created to manage and organize your personal correspondence. Again, this differs from the standard DOS disk structure, where the only way to have a file exist in more than one directory is to create multiple copies of that file, a waste of valuable storage space.

87

Beyond providing a logical alternative for organizing program and data files, Program Manager includes several additional features designed to simplify managing your PC activities. Rather than merely describing the various capabilities built into the Windows Program Manager, however, why don't we return to our previous Windows session and see just what you can accomplish with this impressive new organizational tool?

Using the Program Manager

You may not realize it, but you're already somewhat familiar with the Windows Program Manager. The Program Manager starts automatically each time you begin a Windows session. Consequently, we've been working in it almost exclusively throughout the previous two chapters. Furthermore, at least three program groups—and possibly more, depending on what types of programs Setup discovered when you installed Windows on your hard disk—already exist in your Windows environment. Rather than letting Setup have all the fun, however, let's create our own program group, one designed to hold the programs and data files you'll be working with in Part Two.

Creating a Program Group

You create a program group using the New command, one of the options listed in the Program Manager File menu.

√ To Create a Program Group

► Choose File.
► Choose New.

This displays the New Program Object dialog box shown in Figure 5.1. Like most Windows operations, creating a new program group is an interactive procedure—that is, Windows requests the details it needs, and you provide the appropriate information

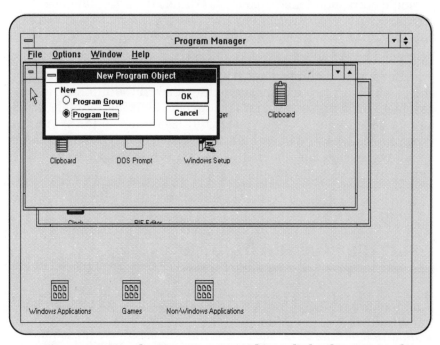

Figure 5.1. Use the New Program Object dialog box to supply initial information about your new group.

The first thing Windows needs to know is whether you want to create an entirely new program group or simply add a new program to a previously existing one.

√ To Tell Windows That You Are Creating a New Group

▶ Click on Program Group.

▶ Choose OK.

This displays the Program Group Properties dialog box, shown in Figure 5.2, which you use to assign a group name to your new program group. Whatever name you enter in the Description field appears in the title bar whenever this group is active. At other times, a group's name is displayed beneath its icon.

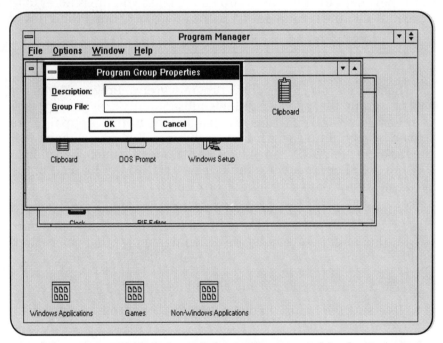

89

Figure 5.2. Windows uses information entered in the Description field as the new program group's name.

▶ **Tip:** Group names are not limited by the eight-character DOS file-naming conventions. Consequently, it's possible to specify a group name that adequately describes a group's function. Keeping group names short prevents them from overlapping one another and conserves space on your Windows display.

√ **To Assign a Name to the New Program Group**

▶ Type **Book Exercises**.
▶ Press Enter to specify OK.

> ▶ **Note:** This is one of those instances where executing a command from the keyboard is more convenient than using its mouse counterpart. Because you were already using the keyboard to enter the group name, I had you press Enter to specify OK, the default button in the Program Group Properties dialog box.

90

Each time you create a new program group, Program Manager sets up a group file, which Windows subsequently uses to keep track of any program and data files assigned to that group. Group files are named by combining a derivative of the specified group name with the file extension GRP. Unless you want a specific name assigned to a group file, therefore, you should leave the Group File field in the Program Group Properties dialog box blank.

After setting up the required files, Program Manager automatically displays a blank window for the new group, as shown in Figure 5.3. At this point, you can begin assigning items—that is, program and data file icons—to your newly created Book Exercises group.

There are three ways you can add items to a group:

1. By using the mouse to move or copy icons from one program group to another.
2. By manually identifying the program item you want added to a group.
3. By using the Windows File Manager to create new program item icons for a program group.

In the following sections we'll look at the first method outlined above. The other two techniques will be covered later in this chapter when we examine the Windows File Manager.

Moving Icons Between Program Groups

The easiest way to add a new item to a program group is to move or copy that item from an already existing group. This method is

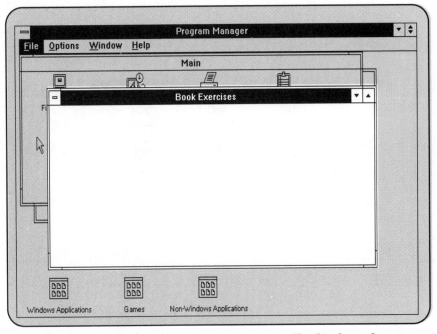

Figure 5.3. Program Manager automatically displays the new program group as the active window.

especially convenient when you need to include an application program in multiple groups. You will probably want to assign your word processing program, for example, to every group in which it will be used to create document files. That's exactly what we're going to do with the Windows Write program.

√ To Assign Windows Write in the Book Exercises Group

▶ Choose Window from the Program Manager menu bar.

▶ Choose Accessories.

This makes the Accessories group the active window and brings it to the foreground of your Windows display, as shown in Figure 5.4.

> ▶ **Tip:** You could have displayed the Accessories group by clicking the mouse cursor on any visible portion of its window. Given that almost all of the Accessories window was obscured, however, I opted to use the menu bar Window command.

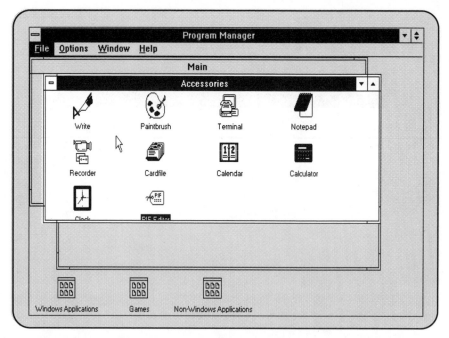

Figure 5.4. The first step in transferring an icon between program groups is to make the group containing that icon the active window.

At this point, you have two options for transferring an icon from the Accessories group to your new Book Exercises group:

1. Dragging an icon exclusively with the mouse moves it from Accessories into the new group—that is, the program associated with that icon will no longer exist in the Accessories group when the move operation is completed.
2. Depressing the Ctrl key while you drag an icon replicates that icon in the new group—that is, the program associated with that icon will be assigned to both groups when moved in this manner.

We'll employ the second method so that you can access the Windows Write program from both the Book Exercises and Accessories groups.

✓ **To Include a Program in a Newly Created Group**

▶ Position the mouse cursor over the Write icon.
▶ Press and hold down the Ctrl key.

▶ Press and hold down the left mouse button.

▶ Drag the mouse until the stylized image of the pen associated with Write is located within the Book Exercises window, the bottom portion of which is still visible beneath the Accessories window.

▶ Release Ctrl and the left mouse button.

Your display should now resemble Figure 5.5, which shows a duplicate copy of the Write icon located in the Book Exercises window. You can now access Write directly by double-clicking on either of the two Write icons that now exist in your Windows environment.

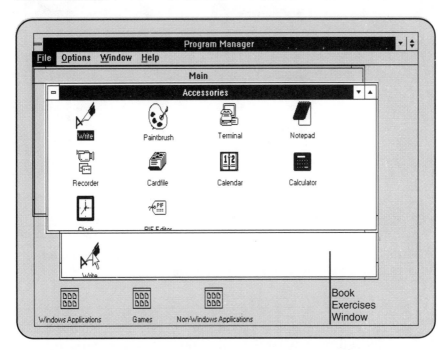

93

Figure 5.5. Dragging the Write icon with the Ctrl key depressed places a copy of that icon in the Book Exercises window.

Keep in mind, however, that a single copy of Windows Write still resides on your hard disk. This is one of the major advantages associated with using the Windows Program Manager to complement standard DOS, which would require that you actually copy a program file in a different directory, if you wanted that program directly associated with other files in a program group—a misnomer in itself, since DOS doesn't support the creation of program groups.

Before moving on, let's copy a few other Windows accessories into the Book Exercises program group, so they'll be available for use in Part Two. Using the same procedures outlined in the previous exercise, replicate the Paintbrush and Cardfile icons in the Book Exercises program group. When you're finished, your screen should resemble Figure 5.6.

94

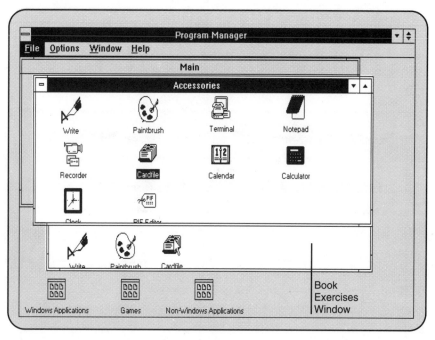

Figure 5.6. We'll use the Windows accessories now assigned to the Book Exercises group in Part Two.

▶ **Note:** Your display may differ slightly from Figure 5.6, depending on where you positioned the Paint and Cardfile icons while copying them from the Accessories window. What's important here is to make certain that you transfer all three of the specified icons into the Book Exercises program group. As I mentioned earlier, we'll use them in Part Two, "The Windows Accessories."

Now that the necessary icons exist in your Book Exercises program group, let's arrange them a little more conveniently for subsequent use.

√ To Rearrange Icons in the Newly Created Group

▶ Click the mouse cursor on any visible portion of the Book Exercises program group to make it the active window.

▶ Choose the Window option of the Program Manager menu bar.

▶ Choose Cascade.

> ▶ **Note:** If your icons weren't repositioned, make sure that a checkmark appears next to the Auto Arrange option of the Options menu, indicating that this feature, which we activated in Chapter 4, remains in effect. If not, activating Auto Arrange and repeating the previous exercise should redraw your screen to match Figure 5.7.

Selecting Cascade redraws your Windows display, automatically rearranging the icons in the Book Exercises program group to resemble Figure 5.7.

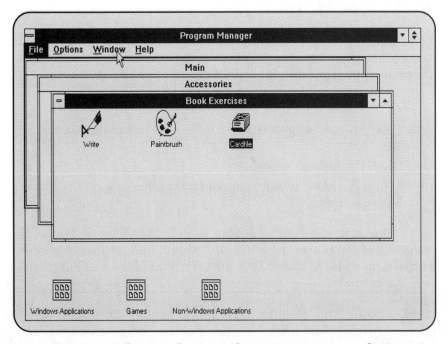

Figure 5.7. Selecting the Cascade option rearranges the icons in all windows to match current display settings.

Now that we have the beginnings of a program group dedicated to future exercises, let's move over to the Windows File Manager to complete this work.

Using the File Manager

File Manager, another feature new to Windows 3.0, resembles the Windows Program Manager in that it simplifies working with various elements of your PC environment. Whereas you use Program Manager to manage programs and groups of programs, File Manager, as its name implies, is designed to help you organize your files and disk directories. File Manager works much like other, traditional DOS shells such as XTree or the Norton Commander. One major benefit File Manager possesses over its standard DOS counterparts is that, being a Windows application, File Manager takes full advantage of the Windows GUI. As we did with the Program Manager, let's see what File Manager allows you to do.

Starting File Manager

During installation, Setup automatically included File Manager in your Main program group. Before actually starting File Manager, therefore, you'll need to make that group the active window.

√ To Switch to the Main Window and Start File Manager

▶ Position your mouse cursor on the title bar of the Main window.

▶ Click the left mouse button.

▶ When the Main window appears, double-click on the File Manager icon.

After a few seconds, during which Windows analyzes the contents of the currently active disk drive, you will see a window containing a File Manager Directory Tree, as shown in Figure 5.8.

▶ **Note:** The specific items listed in your Directory Tree display will differ from those shown here, which reflect the disk drives and directories on my system.

96

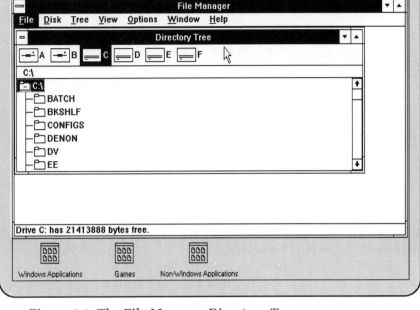

Figure 5.8. The File Manager Directory Tree.

The File Manager Display

Before getting into the different ways in which File Manager can be used, let's analyze the File Manager display. Notice, first of all, that File Manager resembles the Program Manager in that it contains several display windows. First, there is a primary display window, identified in its title bar as File Manager. Additional windows are used to display information you request regarding the individual disk drives installed on your system. In Figure 5.8, for example, a Directory Tree window contains information about the various disk drives installed on my system.

In addition to the standard title and menu bars contained in all windows, the Directory Tree window in Figure 5.8 includes the following display elements:

▶ Individual *disk drive icons* identify all disk drives installed on your system, with different icons used to represent floppy disks, hard disks, network drives, RAM disks, and CD-ROM devices. Figure 5.8, for example, lists six drives, A–F, of which A and B are floppy disks. (No network drives, RAM disks, or CD-ROM devices are represented in this figure.)

▶ File Manager identifies the active drive by highlighting its icon. For example, Figure 5.8 indicates that drive C is currently active.

▶ Immediately below the drive icons is the status line File Manager uses to display the volume label assigned to the active drive (if any) and the complete directory path of the currently active directory. Figure 5.8 identifies the root directory of drive C, which is not assigned a volume label on my system, as the current path.

▶ Windows uses the workspace in a File Manager window to display a visual representation, called a *directory tree*, of those directories that exist on the currently active drive. Initially, File Manager lists only the individual first-level directories, in alphabetical order, below the root directory (\). (As you'll see a little later, you can request that the File Manager display also include any *subdirectories* on your disks—that is, directories attached to the first-level directories shown in the initial File Manager display.)

98

▶ Within this workspace, File Manager highlights the currently active directory or subdirectory.

▶ If more directories exist than will fit in the workspace, File Manager automatically includes scroll bars down the right-hand side of the display window, as shown in Figure 5.8.

▶ A second status bar immediately below the workspace lists the amount of free storage space currently available on the active drive. Figure 5.8, for example, indicates that my hard disk, drive C, still contains over 21 megabytes of free space.

Now that we've listed the various elements contained in the File Manager display, let's see how they are used.

Maximizing a Directory Tree

If you've followed along in previous chapters, you should have no trouble navigating the File Manager display. The basic procedures for accessing the various File Manager features are virtually identical to those you've been using throughout this book. Changing to a different disk drive, for example, is a simple matter of clicking on that drive's icon. Before doing this, however, let's expand the workspace in our current File Manager display.

✓ To Expand the File Manager Workspace

▶ Click on the Maximize box (the up arrow) located to the
extreme right of the Directory Tree title bar.

This changes your Windows display to the configuration shown
in Figure 5.9. Notice that the title bar of this new display, a hybrid
of File Manager and the Directory Tree, contains both the File
Manager and Directory Tree labels. Additionally, the menu bar
previously associated with File Manager remains active.

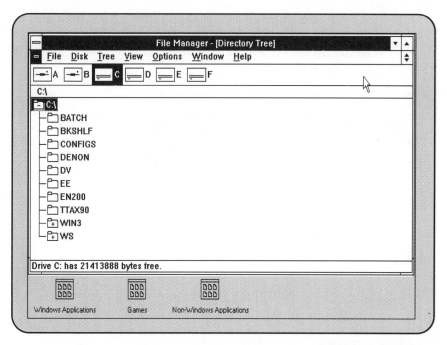

99

*Figure 5.9. Maximizing the Directory Tree workspace creates a
hybrid window that combines elements of both the File Manager and Directory Tree display.*

Expanding Directory Listings

The plus sign (+) in the WIN3 directory icon in Figure 5.9 indicates
that additional subdirectories exist below this first-level directory.
I mentioned earlier that File Manager allows you to request that your
Directory Tree display also include any subdirectories on the currently active drive. Let's do this now for the WIN3 directory.

> ▶ **Note:** If you do not see an icon marked WIN3 on your screen, press Ctrl+[drive], where [drive] is the drive letter of the disk on which you installed Windows. This will make the drive containing your Windows files the active drive.

√ To Display Any Subdirectories Attached to a Directory

▶ Choose the WIN3 icon.

Your screen should now resemble Figure 5.10, which shows two subdirectories, SYSTEM and TEMP, attached to the WIN3 directory. Setup automatically created these subdirectories during Windows installation.

100

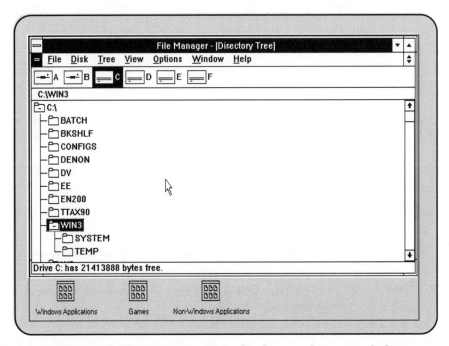

Figure 5.10. The Directory Tree display can be expanded to include any subdirectories attached to a first-level directory.

Notice, also, that the WIN3 icon now contains a minus sign (–). File Manager uses this technique to indicate any directories that have been expanded to include their subdirectory listings. As you may have guessed already, clicking on this minus sign would "collapse" the subdirectory listings back into their parent directory, WIN3.

Opening a Directory Window

Until now, we've been using File Manager to list and analyze only the directories that exist on your disks. But directories hold individual files, and it is these files you'll use most often while working in the Windows environment. So, how can you request that File Manager display the individual files stored on your disks? I'm glad you asked.

√ **To Open a Directory Window**

▶ Double-click on the WIN3 icon.

Your screen should now resemble Figure 5.11, in which a new window has been opened listing the individual files stored in the WIN3 directory.

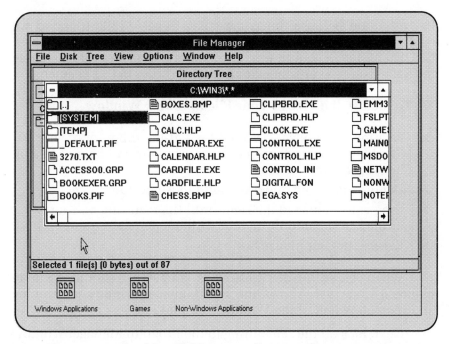

Figure 5.11. Double-clicking on a directory icon opens a new window listing that directory's individual files.

> ▶ **Note:** Are you beginning to see how the "Chinese puzzle box" analogy I discussed in Chapter 1 applies equally to all levels of your Windows operations? Here, for example, as you access additional features of File Manager, the individual windows associated with those features are incorporated into your total Windows environment, very much like smaller boxes being inserted into larger ones to create a Chinese puzzle box. These Windows GUI procedures are pretty nifty.

Working With Multiple Windows

102

Pay attention because things are going to get a little tricky as we continue modifying the Windows workspace. The end result of all these GUI gymnastics, however, will be to simplify the process of fine tuning the Book Exercises program group created earlier in this chapter.

√ **To Modify the Size of Your File Manager Window**

▶ Position the mouse cursor on the left-hand border of your File Manager window. (The mouse cursor will change to a horizontal double-arrow.)

▶ Depress and hold down the left mouse button.

▶ Drag your mouse to the right until the resulting outline is located in the middle of your display.

▶ Release the left mouse button.

When you've finished these steps, your screen should resemble Figure 5.12, which shows the File Manager window occupying approximately half of the Windows display.

Next, let's do the same thing to the Program Manager window but position it on the opposite side of your display.

√ **To Modify the Size of Your Program Manager Window**

▶ Position the mouse cursor on any visible portion of the Program Manager window.

▶ Press your left mouse button to make this the active window.

▶ Choose Window from the Program Manager menu bar.

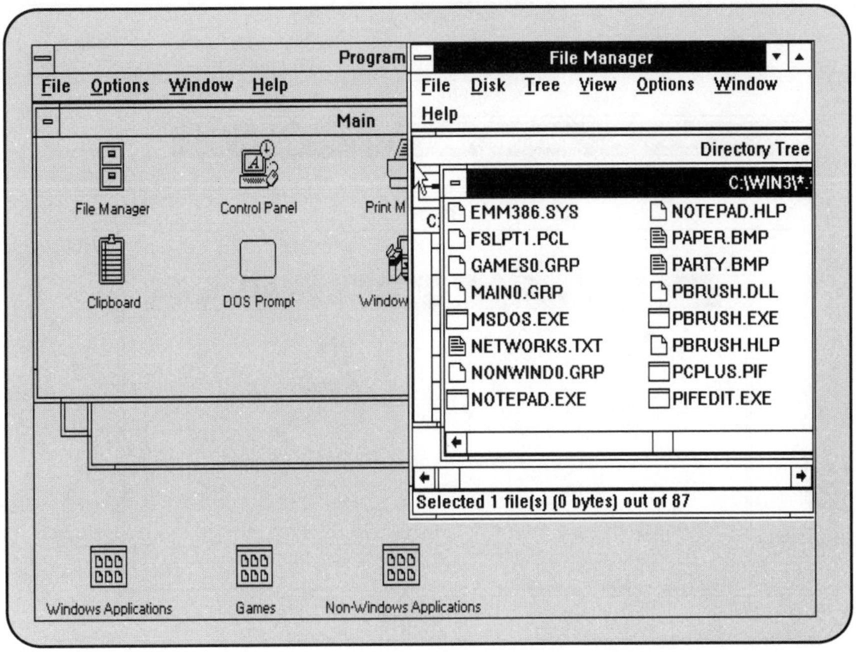

Figure 5.12. Drag your mouse on a window's border to modify the size of that window.

▶ Choose Book Exercises to make this the active window.

▶ Position the mouse cursor over the Maximize box in the upper-right corner of the Program Manager screen, which now shows two small arrows pointing up and down.

▶ Click the left mouse button.

Your screen should now resemble Figure 5.13, which shows a resized Program Manager workspace in which Book Exercises is the active window.

Next, I'm going to let you work with the Program Manager window on your own. Using the techniques you've already learned, modify your display until it resembles Figure 5.14, which shows the Program Manager and File Manager running side-by-side in the File Manager workspace.

Now that we've set up the appropriate Windows workspace— but, keep in mind, one that still only hints at the true flexibility of the Windows GUI—let's use the tools you've established to finish creating the Book Exercises program group that we'll be working in throughout the rest of this book.

103

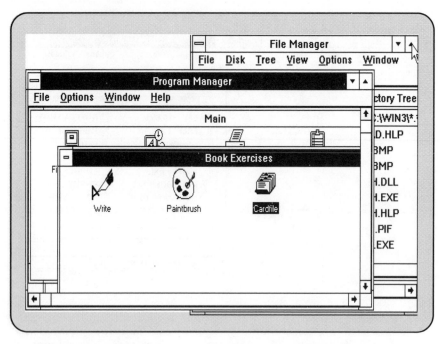

Figure 5.13. Similar steps allow you to resize the Program Manager workspace.

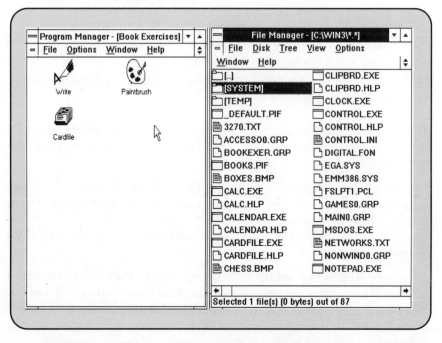

Figure 5.14. When you've finished, Program Manager and File Manager should be sharing your Windows display.

104

> ▶ **Tip:** Remember that dragging the mouse on a window's title bar changes the positioning of that window within your total workspace. Altering a window's size, on the other hand, is accomplished by dragging the mouse cursor on the border corresponding to the direction in which you want its size increased or decreased. Dragging the mouse at the corner of a window expands that window both horizontally and vertically. Once you've established the appropriate positioning for Program Manager and File Manager, clicking on the Maximize box for both Book Exercises and the C:\WIN3 directory listing will expand these two display elements to occupy the full size of their respective windows. Get all this right—a process that really is easier than it sounds—and the display on your monitor will resemble Figure 5.14.

Creating a Directory

105

The first thing we'll do is set up a special directory to hold the various data files you'll be creating in Part Two. Doing so will make it easier to organize these files later.

√ To Create a New Directory

▶ Position the mouse cursor on any visible portion of the Files Manager window.

▶ Click the left mouse button to make this the active window.

▶ Choose File from the File Manager menu bar.

▶ Choose Create Directory.

Windows displays a Create Directory dialog box, as illustrated in Figure 5.15. Use this dialog box to enter WINBOOK, the new name of the directory you want to create.

√ To Name the New Directory

▶ Type **WINBOOK** and press Enter.

File Manager creates the new directory and adds its name to the directory window for WIN3, placing it in alphabetical order immediately after the TEMP directory.

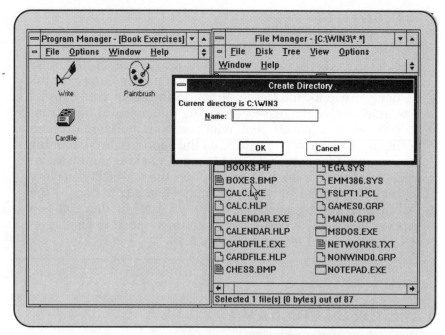

Figure 5.15. Use the Create Directory dialog box to specify a name for your new directory.

Using File Manager to Add an Item to the Program Manager

Next, let's add a file listed in the File Manager directory window to a program group. Specifically, we'll include the Windows Calculator in our Book Exercises group.

> ▶ **Note:** This differs from earlier exercises, where we copied items from the Accessories group to Book Exercises, in that it provides an easy way to incorporate files into one program group that are not already associated with another group. (Yes, I realize Calculator is also in the Accessories group; I needed something to demonstrate this technique.) You could, for example, use the following method to include your own word processor in a program group set up to organize your personal correspondence.

✓ To Add a File from File Manager to the Newly Created Program Group

▶ Position the mouse cursor on filename CALC.EXE in the File Manager directory window.

▶ Depress and hold down the left mouse button.

▶ Drag your mouse to the left until the resulting icon shadow is located within the Book Exercises window.

▶ Release the left mouse button.

When you've finished these steps, your screen should resemble Figure 5.16, which shows a Calculator icon added to the Book Exercises program group.

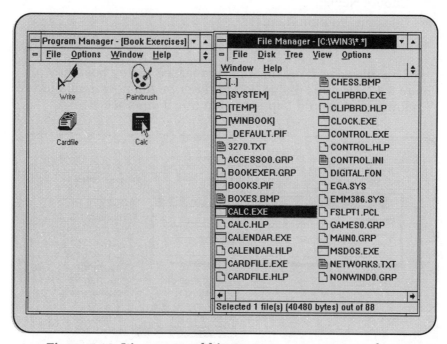

Figure 5.16. It's easy to add items to a program group from a File Manager directory window.

Automatically Loading a Data File with an Icon

The last step we'll perform in this chapter is to create a special icon in the Book Exercises program group that will not only load the Windows Write program but also automatically open a special document file each time that icon is selected. You accomplish this using the New option, which is located in the Program Manager File menu.

✓ To Add a Program Item to the Newly Created Program Group

- ▶ Choose File from the Book Exercises menu bar.
- ▶ Choose New.
- ▶ Click on Program Item.
- ▶ Choose OK.

108

This displays Program Item Properties dialog box shown in Figure 5.17. Use this dialog box to describe the new item and tell Windows what should happen when this item is selected.

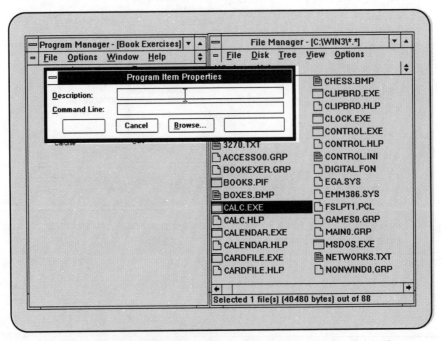

Figure 5.17. Selecting New from the File menu displays the Program Item Properties dialog box.

✓ To Set Up an Icon That Automatically Loads the Program and a Data File

▶ Type **Sample Document** in the Description box.

▶ Press Tab to advance the cursor to the Command Line box.

▶ Type **WRITE C:\WIN3\WINBOOK\SAMPLE.DOC**.

▶ Press Enter or click on the OK button.

When you've completed these steps, your screen will resemble Figure 5.18, which shows that the new item has been added to the Book Exercises program group. Notice that Windows automatically assigned a stylized pen icon to this new item, identifying it as a Windows Write application.

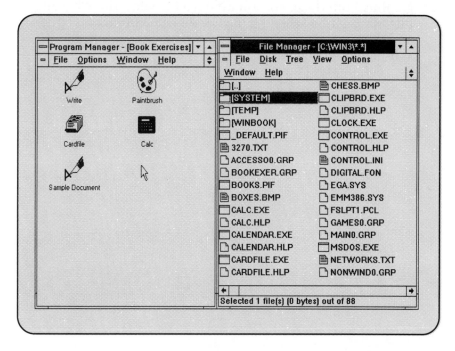

109

Figure 5.18. Program Manager adds the new item to the current program group.

We've examined a number of Windows procedures in this chapter. Specifically, we used the Windows Program Manager and File Manager to create and refine a program group designed to help you organize the various exercises contained in Part Two, "The Windows Accessories."

What You Have Learned

▶ The Windows Program Manager organizes your files into program groups. Program Manager lets you manage your PC activities more logically than relying strictly on the DOS directory structure, since it allows files to be organized according to how they are used rather than by their physical location on a disk. Program Manager allows the same file to be assigned to multiple groups, thus making more efficient use of your valuable storage space.

▶ File Manager simplifies file-related operations by allowing them to be performed interactively from a Windows-like graphical interface. For example, you create a directory in File Manager by selecting the Create Directory menu option and then entering a name for your new directory in the subsequent dialog box.

110

Part Two

The Windows Accessories

111

Now that you've installed and, to some degee, customized Windows for your PC, it's time to look at the individual accessories Microsoft includes in the Windows package. Basically, these accessories include a number of miniprograms designed to let you begin using the Windows GUI quickly and productively. The seven chapters comprising Part Two contain a series of exercises designed to illustrate how the Windows accessories work and the types of work each allows you to accomplish. Chapter 12, "Putting It All Together," the final chapter in Part Two, demonstrates how the Windows Clipboard can be used to combined data elements from multiple accessories into a single file.

112

Chapter 6

Windows Write

In This Chapter

▶ *How to use the Windows Write accessory*
▶ *How to access the various editing features of Write*
▶ *How to format a document with Write*

How Write Lets You Process Words

If statistics can be believed, people love to process words with their PCs. One recent study, for example, revealed that 78% of those surveyed identified word processing as being the primary task for which they use their PC. Perhaps more than any other activity, word processing has assured the success of the personal computer. And why not? Processing words on a PC turns an otherwise tedious chore, writing, into the creative activity it should be.

Writers like myself—indeed, anyone who spends a large portion of the work day chained to a keyboard—understands the advantages of word processing over traditional writing methods. In the "old days" (pre-PC, that is) it was not unusual for me to retype entire documents after proofing and editing my work, simply to include those corrections or revisions I felt needed to be made. Consequently, and with depressing regularity, getting from my first draft to finished copy proved a slow and tiresome process—one that often made me wonder whether the prize (a finished story, article, or book) was worth the price (the days of effort required to complete even a short assignment).

The power of the PC, combined with the panache of word processing, has changed all this. Suddenly, writing is fun, or, at least, as much fun as any job can be. Since adding word processing to my literary arsenal, my assignments are completed more quickly, and, I believe, the finished products are more polished. That's because I no longer view revising my work, a process that generally occurs during the post-draft editing phase, with the same apprehension I once did. And that, in turn, makes it much easier for me (or anyone else for that matter) to make my living as a professional writer.

But enough of the personal perspective. You're probably more interested in the professional advantages inherent in how a word processor works. To be more precise, you're probably interested in how Write, the word processor included in the basic Windows package, can place the power of word processing at your fingertips.

What Is Write?

Put simply, Write is one of the accessories included with every copy of Windows. At its most basic level, Write converts your personal computer into an electronic typewriter. Words you enter at the keyboard when working with Write appear on your display monitor, just as they would on paper if you were using a manual typewriter. But composing text with an electronic word processor like Write allows you to do much more than merely send words to the screen.

Used properly, Write can greatly simplify the writing process by putting a number of advanced editing and formatting capabilities at your fingertips:

▶ Margins of a Write document can be justified or not justified, depending on whether you want that document to look factual (both margins justified), formal (all margins centered), friendly (ragged right margin), or fanciful (try justifying the right margin only to accomplish this).

▶ Assigning different margin settings for different portions of a Write document is a simple point-and-click mouse operation.

▶ Words, phrases, even entire paragraphs can be emphasized using the underline, boldface, and italics features supported by Write.

▶ Should you need to make a point more strongly, Write can even print portions of a document using different type sizes and styles—from that tiny-print footnote that readers love to hate to large, dramatic headline-style type fonts. (Try doing this with a traditional typewriter.)

▶ Write lets you automatically generate headers and footers for every page in your finished document.

▶ Write includes a variety of electronic editing tools that allow you to copy, move, and delete entire passages within your document with only a few, simple menu-driven commands.

▶ Write also supports advanced find-and-replace operations. Suppose, for example, that you write a long article about Ms. Brown and, just before that article is completed, Ms. Brown marries Mr. Smith. If you're writing with Write, updating your document to reflect this new marital status is a simple matter of automatically finding all occurrences of "Ms. Brown" and replacing them with "Mrs. Smith." Now we're talking simple revisions!

▶ You can even incorporate graphic images created with other Windows applications (such as Windows own Paintbrush accessory, which we'll discuss in Chapter 9) into your Write documents.

115

Perhaps most important, Write's reliance on the Windows GUI makes learning how to perform these various operations about as simple as learning how to press a mouse button. As you can see, Write does more than merely emulate a traditional typewriter. Rather, Write transforms your personal computer into a personal typesetting system and does so without forcing you to become a computer scientist in the process.

But there I go again, extolling the virtues of a Windows product when I should be showing you how to use it. Let's get Write down to it, so to speak, and start writing.

Starting Write

Before we actually start Write, let's modify our Windows workspace to one more conducive to working in a single application. We'll begin by closing File Manager, which we left running at the end of Chapter 5.

√ To Close the File Manager Window

▶ Choose File from the File Manager menu bar.
▶ Choose Exit.
▶ Choose OK.

116

> ▶ **Note:** Like Program Manager, File Manager also includes a Save Settings feature. When the Save Settings feature is activated, any settings specified with the View or Options menus will remain in effect the next time you open File Manager.

Next, let's return our Program Manager window, which currently occupies only the left half of your screen, to a full-screen display.

√ To Expand the Program Manager to a Full-Screen Display

▶ Choose the Maximize box.

We're now ready to use Write to compose a sample document. The document you create here also will be used in future chapters, as we examine how the various Windows accessories work together to enhance all your PC operations.

√ To Start Write

▶ Double-click on the Write icon.

This loads the Windows Write accessory and displays its initial editing screen, which is shown in Figure 6.1. Notice that this screen is almost empty, resembling a blank piece of paper. That analogy, as you will soon see, is certainly apropos.

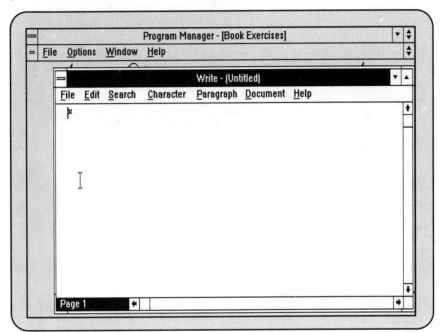

Figure 6.1. Write initially displays a blank editing screen.

The Write Menus

As is true of all Windows accessories, Write's command menus are neatly tucked away, where they won't interfere with your primary work area. Specifically, Write commands are accessed from the Write window's menu bar, which, logically enough, runs across the top of the Write window. As was true in previous chapters, use your mouse to display Write's pull-down command menus. Let's see how this works.

√ To Access the Write File Menu

▶ Choose File from the Write menu bar.

This displays a pull-down menu listing the various Write File operations, as shown in Figure 6.2. Some of these include starting a new document (New), loading an already existing Write file (Open), saving your current document to a disk file (Save or Save As), and printing a Write document (Print). We'll examine each of these File options. For now, let's look at some other Write command menus.

118

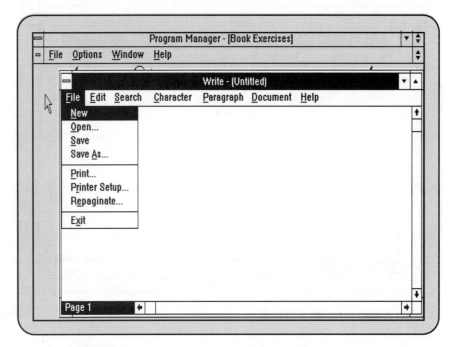

Figure 6.2. Like all Windows accessories, Write uses pull-down command menus.

√ To Display Edit Menu

▶ Press Right Arrow.

The arrow keys provide a quick method for moving between Windows menus, one that may be more convenient than using the mouse if you're already working at the keyboard. Each time you press the Right Arrow key, Write displays a different pull-down menu. As you've seen previously, each menu lists multiple options.

You may notice, as you move through the various Write menus, that only certain options are *active*—that is, displayed in clear, legible type—at any given time. For example, because no text currently exists in this Write file, none of the options on the Edit menu would accomplish anything. These options are, therefore, *disabled*—listed in light colored or, alternately, fuzzy type. The remaining Write menus will contain additional disabled options, depending on what you are doing at the time.

Go ahead and use the arrow keys to familiarize yourself with the various Write menus. After you're finished, pressing Esc will return you to the opening screen.

> ▶ **Tip:** Consistency between different programs is one of the biggest advantages of working in the Windows environment. Once you're familiar with how one program works, learning the other Windows accessories is greatly simplified.

119

Navigating a Write File

I've spent a lot of time extolling the virtues of using a mouse whenever possible when you're working within the Windows environment. Normally, this reliance on the mouse is quite helpful. Write is a little different, however. It's only natural that, as you create your Write documents, you'll be spending a lot of time entering text at the PC keyboard. For this reason, Windows provides several keyboard-based shortcuts for quickly moving from one location to another within a Write file, shortcuts that may actually be more convenient to use than their mouse-driven counterparts.

Keyboard shortcuts available in Write include:

Key(s)	Function
Left Arrow	Moves the cursor one character to the left.
Right Arrow	Moves the cursor one character to the right.
Up Arrow	Moves the cursor one line up.

Key(s)	Function
Down Arrow	Moves the cursor one line down.
Home	Moves the cursor to the beginning of the current line.
End	Moves the cursor to the end of the current line.
PgUp	Moves you one window up in your document.
PgDn	Moves you one window down in your document.
Ctrl+Right Arrow	Moves the cursor to the next word in the document.
Ctrl+Left Arrow	Moves the cursor to the previous word in the document.
Ctrl+Home	Moves the cursor to the beginning of the document.
Ctrl+End	Moves the cursor to the end of the document.

120

 Tip: Familiarizing yourself with these shortcuts will allow you to quickly navigate even the longest Write documents.

Okay, it's time to begin working on our sample Write document.

Defining Page Layout

The whole purpose of using Write is to write. That sounds logical, doesn't it? We'll start writing shortly. Before we do, however, let's define the most elementary aspect of a document's page layout and margin settings.

√ **To Define Margin Settings for the Sample Document**

▶ Choose Document.
▶ Choose Page Layout.

Choosing the Page Layout option displays the dialog box shown in Figure 6.3. Use the Page Layout dialog box to specify margin settings for the current document.

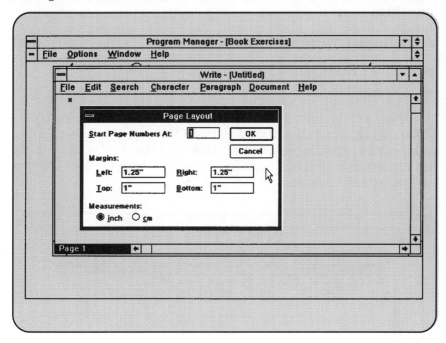

Figure 6.3. Use the Page Layout dialog box to specify margin settings for your Write documents.

Let's change the left and right margin setting to 1.5" each, acceptable margins for a business letter like the one we'll be writing for our sample document.

√ To Change the Left and Right Margin Settings

▶ Press Tab.
▶ Type **1.5**.
▶ Press Tab.
▶ Type **1.5**.
▶ Press Enter to accept the new values.

Before composing our sample letter, let's make one more modification to the default Write settings. Specifically, we're going to tell Write to display its on-screen ruler to simplify document formatting.

√ To Display Write's On-Screen Ruler

▶ Choose Document.

▶ Choose Ruler On.

This adds an on-screen ruler to the top of the Write display, as illustrated in Figure 6.4. As you'll see a little later in this chapter, using your mouse in conjunction with the ruler icons can simplify the process of formatting individual paragraphs and blocks of text within your document.

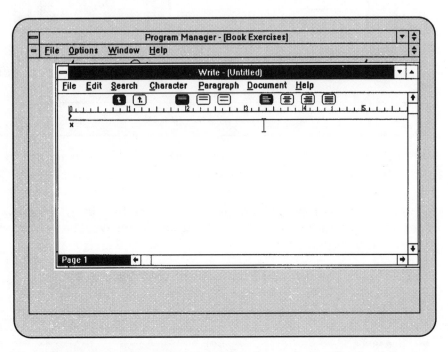

Figure 6.4. Mouse owners can use the various ruler icons to simplify document formatting.

With our initial page layout defined and the on-screen ruler easily accessible, we're ready to write with Write, if you'll forgive my redundancy.

> ▶ **Note:** Notice that the ruler displays a small marker about midway between 3 and 4. This identifies the actual width of the text comprising your document as being 5 1/2-inches wide, a figure arrived at by subtracting the two 1.5-inch margins you set earlier (or 3 inches) from the width of a standard 8 1/2-inch wide piece of typing paper. How Write uses this right margin setting will become clear in the next section.

Entering Write in a Write Document

Let's begin with the basics, by adding a couple of blank lines to the beginning of our new document and then typing in a simple salutation.

123

√ **To Begin the New Document**

▶ Press Enter twice.

▶ Type **Dear valued customer,** and press Enter twice.

As this simple beginning demonstrates, composing a document with Write is much like using a traditional typewriter. What you enter at the computer keyboard appears within the Write window. It's all straightforward and not radically different from the way you've written in the past—at least, at this stage of the game.

At this point, let's add some more text to our document.

√ **To Continue Entering Text into the Document**

▶ Type the following passage:
   We recently reaped the harvest of a substantial drop in the purchase price of materials used to manufacture our best-selling Wonderful Widgets. Consequently, we're able to pass these savings on to you, our customers, through a special price reduction on new orders.

▶ Press Enter.

> ▶ **Tip:** As you type in the first sentence of this passage, notice that Write automatically moves to a new line each time you reach the right margin. This feature, called *word wrap*, is one of the big advantages using a word processor has over using a traditional typewriter, where you have to anticipate where each line should end and manually press the Return key before you reach the right margin setting. When working in a word processor, the only time you need to press the Enter key to manually move to a new line is between paragraphs.

When you have completed these, your display should resemble that in Figure 6.5, which shows the document elements entered to this point. We'll add more to our sample document in a moment. But first, lets take a short detour to perform a very important operation.

124

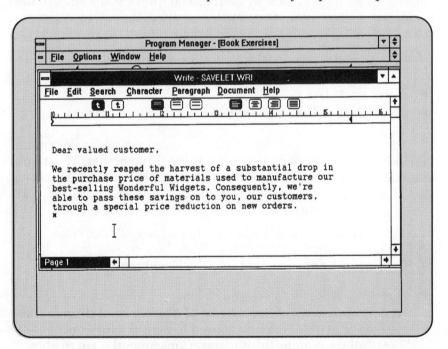

Figure 6.5. This screen shows how the sample Write letter should appear on your display.

Saving a File

While your personal computer is extremely dependable, it is not totally infallible. All kinds of things can happen to cause either real or potential problems, things over which you have no control. Suppose, for example, that the power goes out while you're composing and editing a letter in Write. Bye, bye, PC—at least temporarily. Also, bye, bye Write file—if you haven't saved it to disk. You should cultivate the habit of regularly saving your work-in-progress to a disk file. While working in Write, you accomplish this with the Save command, located on the File menu.

√ **To Save the Sample Letter**

▶ Choose File to access the File menu.

▶ Choose Save.

125

Because this is the first time you have saved the sample file, Windows displays a File Save As dialog box, as shown in Figure 6.6. Notice that this dialog box allows you to specify several items about the new file, including:

▶ A name for this file.

▶ The directory in which it should be stored.

▶ Whether or not Write should automatically maintain a backup copy as future modifications are made to this file.

▶ The file format in which the current file should be stored.

> ▶ **Note:** You need to specify this last item only if you want your document stored in a format other than the default Write format, a procedure generally used to share Write files with other applications. Specifically, if desired, you can save your document as an ASCII file (Text Only) or in a file format compatible with Microsoft's popular word processing program, Word (Microsoft Word Format).

We'll save this letter as a file called SAVELET in the WINBOOK subdirectory created in Chapter 5. While we're at it, let's have Write automatically maintain backup copies of the document, just for safe keeping.

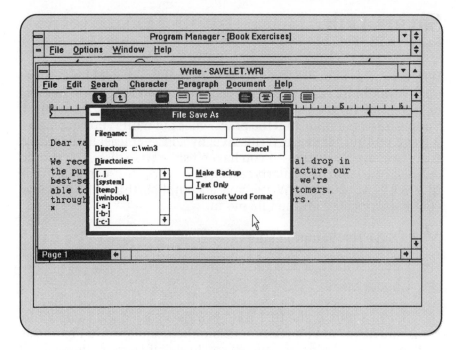

Figure 6.6. Saving your files regularly guards against lost data.

✓ To Backup and Save the New Document

► Type **WINBOOK\SAVELET**.

► Choose Make Backup.

► Press Enter or choose the OK button.

Notice that, whereas the top line of the Write screen previously indicated that the current file was "Untitled," it now lists the name assigned to the current file. Notice also that Write automatically added extension WRI to the file name you specified. Windows uses the WRI file extension to identify files created with Write. Because this file has been named, whenever you select the Save option from this point on, Windows will not take time to display the File Save As dialog box. Rather, it will automatically save your updated work to the file called SAVELET.WRI.

Now that we've protected the initial draft of our letter against accidental loss, let's go back to Write and begin adding some polish to its admittedly mundane appearance.

> ▶ **Tip:** It's always a good idea to name files in a way that allows you to identify their contents and/or purpose later. In this instance, for example, we named the letter announcing our impending price reduction "SAVELET." While it ain't the King's English, this representative name should remind us of what our sample letter is about.

Adding Formatting Elements to a Write Document

One big advantage to working in the Windows GUI, even when composing and editing a text document, is that its graphics-based display more precisely reflects the final appearance of your document. In computer parlance, this is referred to as the What-You-See-Is-What-You-Get (or WYSIWYG, pronounced "wis-e-wig") paradigm. How does working in a WYSIWYG environment differ from using more traditional DOS programs? I'm glad you asked.

127

Formatting Characters (Words and Phrases)

Suppose, for example, that you wanted the product name, Wonderful Widgets, to appear in boldface in our sample letter. If you were using a traditional text-based word processor instead of Write, you'd need to insert special codes in your file to indicate where you wanted certain formatting elements—boldface, italics, underlining, and the like—applied. Furthermore, you wouldn't see these enhancements until the document was actually printed. How would you accomplish this same thing using Write? Quite easily.

√ To Use Boldface

▶ Position the mouse cursor (now a vertical line) in front of the "W" in Wonderful.

▶ Depress and hold down the left mouse button.

▶ Drag the mouse to your right until "Wonderful Widgets" is highlighted—that is, displayed in reverse video.

▶ Release the left mouse button.

▶ Choose Character from the Write window menu bar.

▶ Choose Bold.

▶ Click the left mouse button.

This formats the selected text, Wonderful Widgets, to boldface, as shown in Figure 6.7.

128

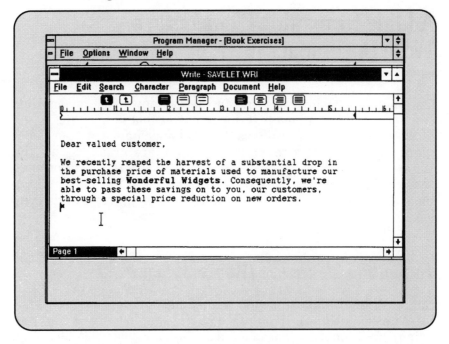

Figure 6.7. Window's WYSIWYG interface allows you to modify the appearance of a Write document.

Formatting Paragraphs

In the previous example, you altered the font for a selected passage. Write also allows you to modify entire paragraphs, using the formatting icons located above the on-screen ruler. To see how this feature works, let's reformat our opening paragraph so that both its left and right margins are fully justified.

√ **To Specify Full Justification**

▶ Make sure the mouse cursor is located somewhere within the body text of the first paragraph.

▶ Click on the Justify icon.

▶ **Note:** The Justify icon, a small box containing four equal lines, is located to the extreme right in the line of icons above the ruler line. (See Figure 6.8.)

Write reformats the selected paragraph to full justification, as illustrated in Figure 6.8.

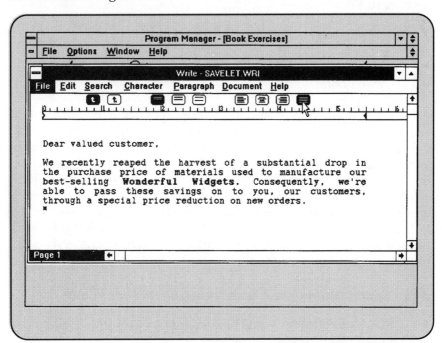

Figure 6.8. Use the ruler icons to reformat quickly entire paragraphs in your Write document.

> ▶ **Tip:** Each of the ruler icons represents a command available in the pull-down Paragraph menu. There may be times when selecting a menu option is more convenient than clicking on the corresponding ruler icon.

Creating Headers and Footers

Write allows you to create *headers* and *footers*—text that will appear on the top and bottom of each printed page, respectively—for your documents. Optionally, you can tell Write to number automatically the pages of your printout in either of these two areas. Let's use this last feature to see how you specify headers and footers when working in Write.

√ To Include Page Numbers Within a Footer

▶ Choose Document from the Write window menu bar.

▶ Choose Footer.

Choosing the Footer option displays a blank window and the Page Footer dialog box, as illustrated in Figure 6.9. It helps to think of headers and footers as being "subdocuments" to your main document. Use the blank portion of the Footer screen, for example, to enter any text that should appear in your footer. Furthermore, various menu options are available to format this text. Additional options located in the Page Footer dialog box allow you to indicate placement of your footer text, as well as specify whether it should include page numbering. We'll use the Footer screen to specify page numbering, centered on the document margins.

√ To Center Automatic Page Numbering in Your Footer

▶ Click on the Center icon (the third icon from the right).

▶ Choose Print on First Page.

▶ Choose Insert Page #.

▶ Choose Return to Document.

Write will now insert a centered page number on each page of this document at print time.

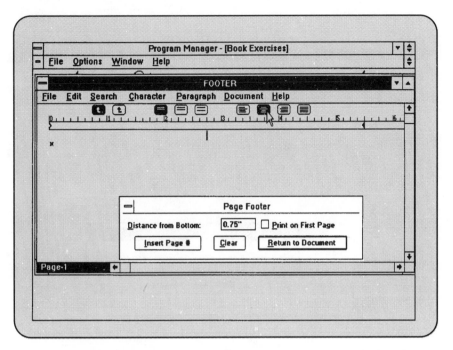

Figure 6.9. You can have Write automatically include headers and footers in your documents.

131

Replacing Text

One of the most convenient features associated with using a word processor like Write is that you can quickly find selected words and phrases, regardless of where they are located in your document. You can even tell Write to replace these passages automatically with something else. Let's see how this works by changing the phrase "price reduction" in our sample letter to another word, "discount".

√ To Initiate a Find-and-Replace Operation

▶ Choose Search from the Write window menu bar.

▶ Choose Change.

Choosing the Change option displays the dialog box shown in Figure 6.10. Use this dialog box to enter information about the current find-and-replace operation.

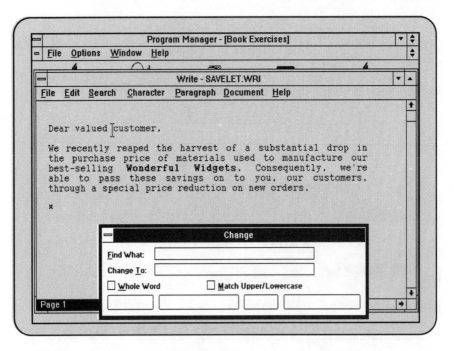

Figure 6.10. Find-and-replace (called "Change" in the Write vernacular) is one of the most convenient features associated with word processing.

✓ To Use Change

▶ Type **price reduction**.

▶ Press Tab.

▶ Type **discount**.

▶ Choose Change All.

Selecting the Change All option causes Write to automatically perform the Change operation across the entire file, finding all occurrences of the specified Find What text and replacing it with whatever you entered into the Change To field. When this process is completed, Write leaves the Change dialog box displayed for further use. Because we have no additional changes to make at this time, let's return to our sample letter.

✓ To Remove the Change Dialog Box and Return to Your Document

▶ Press Esc.

132

> ▶ **Tip:** Whereas find-and-replace may not seem like an extremely useful feature when used to revise a single-page letter like the one we've been working with here, it can be a real godsend when you need to convert text across a long document. (Remember that Ms. Brown to Mrs. Smith file conversion I mentioned earlier?) Believe me, if you do much writing, you'll soon learn to love Write's find-and-replace feature.

We're about finished with our initial examination of the Windows Write accessory. (We'll be coming back to this sample letter several times in the next few chapters.) Before we move on, however, I'd like to demonstrate one more powerful feature of Write, its Undo option.

Using the Undo Feature

133

Write keeps a record of the latest edit you have performed and allows you to use a special Undo option to reverse the results of the previous edit operation quickly. When selected, Undo restores your document to however it was before the most recent edit command was executed. Right now, for example, Undo would reverse the find-and-replace procedure from the previous exercise. You don't believe me? Okay, let's try this.

√ **To Reverse the Previous Operation**

- ▶ Choose Edit from the Write window menu bar.
- ▶ Choose Undo.

Notice that selecting Undo changed "discount" back to "price reduction." Stated simply, Undo reversed the previous find-and-replace operation and then marked any blocks of text affected by this procedure for additional processing, as illustrated in Figure 6.11.

Exiting Write

Although the letter is not yet finished, let's take a short break and end this introductory Write session. Use the Exit option in the Write File menu to return to the Windows Program Manager.

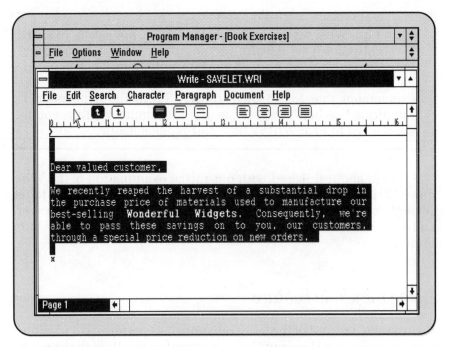

Figure 6.11. Write's Undo feature can be used to reverse previous changes to a document quickly.

✓ To End a Write Session

▶ Choose File from the Write window menu bar.

▶ Choose Exit.

Whenever you exit a Windows accessory, that program checks to see whether you've made any modification to the current file since the most recent Save operation. If changes have been made, Windows displays a prompt box similar to the one shown in Figure 6.12, asking whether the revised version of the file should be saved to disk. This safeguards against your inadvertently losing work by prematurely closing a Windows accessory.

✓ To Save the Latest Revisions and Exit Write

▶ Press Enter or choose the Yes button.

After storing the latest version of SAVELET.WRI on disk, Windows returns you to its Program Manager screen. As I mentioned earlier, we'll be returning to our sample letter in future chapters, when we look at how Windows allows elements created with several programs to be combined into a single file.

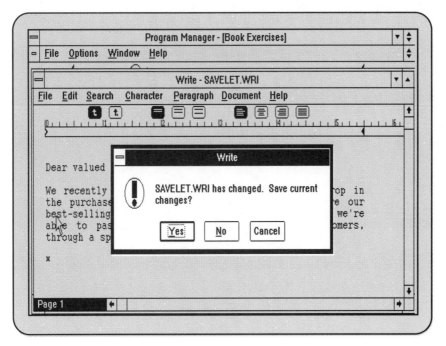

Figure 6.12. Like all Windows accessories, Write checks to see if you have saved the most recent revisions to your files before returning to the Program Manager.

What You Have Learned

▶ Write is the Windows word processor. You use Write to create, revise, and print documents.

▶ Working with a word processor like Write is much easier than using a traditional typewriter. For example, Write allows you to revise and even reformat a document without forcing you to retype that document's contents completely.

▶ The Windows GUI allows Write to run in so-called WYSIWYG mode, where changes you make to your document on-screen will reflect that document's final printed appearance.

▶ Write includes an advanced search-and-replace feature that can be used to make global changes in the contents of your text documents.

136

Chapter 7

Cardfile

In This Chapter 137

- ▶ *A definition of database management*
- ▶ *How to manage records in a Cardfile database*
- ▶ *How to design and create a Cardfile database*

What Is Database Management?

Database management typifies everything a personal computer does well. Managing the kinds of information a PC database generally contains is repetitive and tedious work—a chore not unlike tightening bolts on an automobile coming down one of Detroit's infamous assembly lines. We long ago realized the advantages associated with turning over such pedestrian work to computerized robots. Why should the dull and monotonous task of database management be any different? Why should you, an intelligent and creative human being, waste your time sifting through thousands of bits and pieces of information simply to find the one item you need when a computer can accomplish this so much faster, so much more reliably, so much more efficiently than you could, even on the best of days? So many other activities are so much more ideally suited to the unique abilities of the human intellect. Given this fact, why not turn the drudgery of database management over to your computer?

But what's involved in managing data in a PC database? How does database management work? What things will a database manager like Cardfile allow you to accomplish? And how do you use a database manager like Cardfile? We have many questions to answer. Never fear, the answers provide the foundation for this chapter's discussion of Cardfile, the database manager included as part of the basic Windows package.

Database Fundamentals

A *database* is a file, just like any other PC file. And like any other PC file, a database contains some kind of information. The information contained in a database file, however, is organized in a very precise manner, using specific data elements. A database contains *records*, each of which consists of one or more fields, with each *field* representing a particular piece of information. In a database designed to keep track of names and addresses, for example, all the information about a given individual would be a record. Within that record there would be several fields—first name, last name, address, telephone number, and so forth.

One other term you will encounter regularly in any discussion about database management—and Cardfile proves no exception to this general rule—is form. Basically, a *database form* is the screen you use to enter information into a database file. As such, a database form resembles the more traditional paper forms we've all grown familiar with in this age of burgeoning bureaucracy, where virtually every move we make must be meticulously recorded. As its name implies, Cardfile uses a form resembling your typical 5 x 7-inch index card to record information stored in your database files.

PCs, the Perfect Information Managers

As implied earlier, the personal computer is the ideal tool for keeping track of the types of information each of us must manage regularly. Consider for a moment the steps involved in extracting a particular piece of information from a manila folder stored in a traditional filing cabinet, an organizational technique with which most of us are intimately familiar.

138

Even relatively easy procedures become tedious and bothersome when done repeatedly. First, you must get up from your desk (or wherever you're working at the time) and walk over to the filing cabinet. Next, you must identify the drawer in which the folder you are seeking resides. After opening the correct drawer, there's still the little matter of tracking down the actual file folder containing the specific information you need. Transport this folder back to your desk and—Finally!—you're ready to review the information that you needed.

Even in the most ergonomically designed environment, keeping track of important information in this manner is bound to be inconvenient. Worse still, it's highly inefficient. If, as the old adage implies, time is money, then think of all the money you've wasted down through the years, wearing tracks in your carpet.

Wouldn't a more ideal situation be to have all the information you need readily available and easily found? Quite literally at your fingertips, whenever you needed it? When you use a PC database like Cardfile, it is.

139

PC databases are not only convenient, they're also flexible. Going back to our previous example, let's consider for a moment some different methods you might use to organize those manila folders stored within that imaginary filing cabinet, the one designed to keep track of names and addresses. Do you arrange your folders alphabetically? This would work. Providing, of course, that you always planned to look up information based on some alphanumeric value—for example, a person's last name. But suppose that instead you needed to track down information about someone living at a specific address? In this case, having your file folders organized alphabetically by last name provides no help at all. Or what if you needed to find the names and addresses of everyone living within a particular state? Now you're really facing an organizational nightmare, if you still depend on an old-fashioned record keeping method like a filing cabinet stuffed full of manila folders.

The Advantage of Using Cardfile

Using an electronic database like Cardfile eliminates all these hassles. To begin with, you can enter information (individual records) into a Cardfile database in totally random order. Cardfile couldn't care less. In fact, Cardfile doesn't even worry about organizing the individual records its databases contain, unless and until you tell it to. Only then does Cardfile concentrate on arranging the records a database contains into some structured order. Furthermore, it arranges these records in the precise order you specify at the time. If the next time you go to look up information you request a completely different organizational structure, that's okay. Cardfile won't complain. It simply goes about its assigned task, fulfilling your latest request quietly and, as I implied earlier, much more efficiently than you ever could.

Ask Cardfile to print out an alphabetical listing of names and addresses contained in a customer database, arranged by company name, and it will do so. If 5 minutes later you ask Cardfile to generate this same list, but this time grouping your customers together by their respective ZIP Codes, it would comply with your new request. And Cardfile would do so quickly—more quickly than you ever could, if your only alternative was to pull a pile of paper folders out of a traditional filing cabinet and then manually rearrange them.

Now that we've outlined some of the things Cardfile's various database management functions allow you to do, let's look at how to do them. We'll begin by using Cardfile to design and create a sample database.

140

Using Cardfile

Cardfile is Windows' generic database manager. Using Cardfile, you can store and manage information on a wide range of topics. Some specific applications for which you might use Cardfile include:

▶ Maintaining sales and inventory records—an invaluable tool for anyone who runs a small business.

▶ Organizing your collection of record albums or compact disks—who recorded them, what style of music they are, when they were recorded, which songs they contain, where they are located, and so forth.

▶ Keeping track of your critical tax records. (Who, facing this nightmare, hasn't wished they could simply sleep through midnight, April 15th?)

▶ Keeping a recipe file.

Because you design each Cardfile database to contain only the information you want, this list could be several pages long. In fact, the number and types of items you can organize using Cardfile are limited only by your personal data management needs, and your own imagination. Perhaps more than any other potential use of a personal computer, database management is the most personal. Given this fact, my goal in this chapter is to discuss the basic steps involved in creating and using a Cardfile database. How will you ultimately apply this elementary information to your personal database management activities? In this respect, the sky's the limit.

Starting Cardfile

By now, you should be very familiar with this particular step of working within the Windows environment.

141

√ **To Start the Cardfile Accessory**

▶ Double-click on the Cardfile icon located in your Book Exercises program group.

After a few seconds you'll see the Cardfile display, shown in Figure 7.1. Admittedly, this display does not look overly impressive. In this case, however, looks are definitely deceiving.

Notice that, as was true with Write, Cardfile creates an Untitled file the first time you start it. We'll name our new database in a few minutes. Before we do, though, let's provide some information for it to manage.

Adding Records to a Cardfile Database

As I mentioned earlier, the Cardfile screen is designed to emulate a traditional 5 x 7-inch index card. To create individual records in a Cardfile database, simply enter information into these cards by selecting the Add option from Cardfile's Card menu.

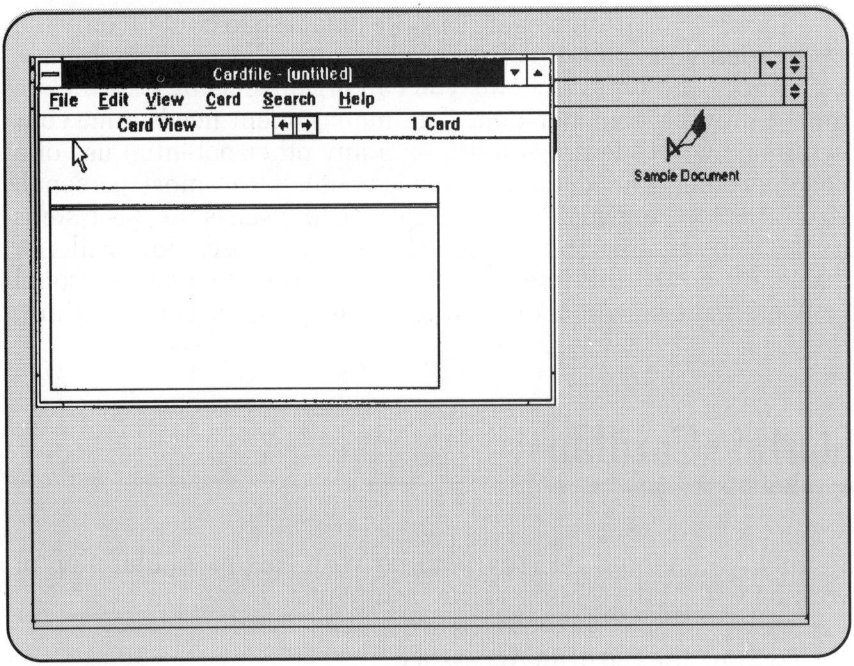

Figure 7.1. Cardfile's display is deceptively unsophisticated.

√ To Add a Record to a Cardfile Database

▶ Choose Card from the Cardfile menu bar.

▶ Choose Add.

This displays the Add dialog box shown in Figure 7.2. Use this dialog box to enter information that will appear on the first line of a Cardfile card—information that in turn will serve as the primary index for that card within its database file.

▶ **Tip:** Like Write, Cardfile is another keyboard-intensive application. Consequently, it is often more convenient to use the F7 function key—the keyboard Add command—rather than its mouse alternative, to initiate an Add operation.

Selecting an Effective Index

Expanding on an earlier analogy, Cardfile uses its *index field* (the first line of each record) in much the same way you would depend on

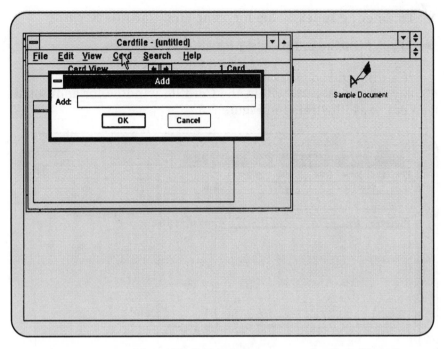

*Figure 7.2. Use the Add dialog box to enter the first line of a
Cardfile record.*

folder tabs within a traditional filing cabinet. This field provides
Cardfile with a method for quickly scanning a database in order to
locate a specific record, a procedure similar to your scanning the tabs
on folders in a file drawer to find the one you want. Consequently,
you should design a Cardfile database so that, whenever possible,
the value you will use most often to access records within that
database will be stored in its index field.

Suppose, for example, that you owned a manufacturing company and wanted to set up a Cardfile database to record information
about the customers to whom you regularly sell the bread-and-butter
of your product line, the Wonderful Widget. In such a case, a logical
choice for the index field would be the individual company names
of these customers. In fact, this is exactly the type of information that
will be recorded in the sample Cardfile database you're going to
create in the following exercises.

Entering the Index Line

The first step in adding a new record to a Cardfile database is to enter
that record's index value in the Add dialog box.

✓ **To Enter an Index Value for Your First Cardfile Record**

▶ Type **MiniCorp, Inc.** and press Enter.

Cardfile adds a new card to the current file and automatically displays this new card within the Cardfile window for additional data entry, as illustrated in Figure 7.3.

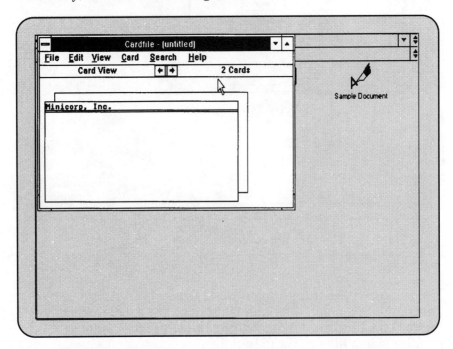

144

Figure 7.3. Entering an index value creates a new card in the current Cardfile window.

Completing a New Card

Once you specify the Add field, complete the new record just as if you were typing information on a typical 5 x 7-inch index card.

✓ **To Complete The First Record**

▶ Type **1234 First Avenue** and press Enter.
▶ Type **New York, NY 10012** and press Enter.
▶ Type **1-212-555-1234** and press Enter.
▶ Type **Contact: James Doe** and press Enter.

When you've finished, your screen will resemble Figure 7.4, which shows the information entered above. All that remains now is to save this information as a new record in the Cardfile file.

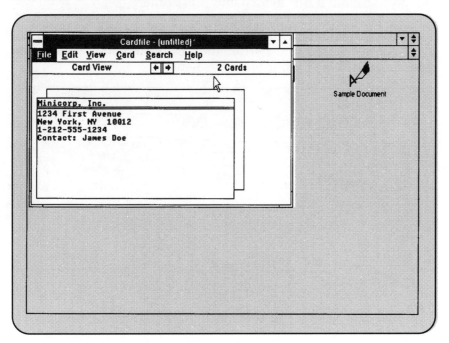

Figure 7.4. Use Cardfile to record important information about your business contacts.

145

Let's go ahead and add a few more entries now, so that we'll have some sample records to work with later.

√ **To Add Additional Records to the Cardfile File**

▶ Press the F7 function key to access the Add dialog box.

▶ Type **Conglomerate, Inc.** and press Enter.

▶ Type **456 Second Street** and press Enter.

▶ Type **Anywhere, USA** and press Enter.

▶ Type **555-3456** and press Enter.

▶ Type **Contact: Betty Brown** and press Enter.

▶ Press the F7 function key to access the Add dialog box.

▶ Type **The Buyer's Club** and press Enter.

▶ Type **3333 Third Street** and press Enter.

▶ Type **Cincinnati, Ohio 45255** and press Enter.

▶ Type **1-513-555-4567** and press Enter.

▶ Type **Contact: Bill Brown** and press Enter.

Your display should now resemble Figure 7.5, which shows the three cards you just created within the Cardfile window. These three records will suffice for our purposes here.

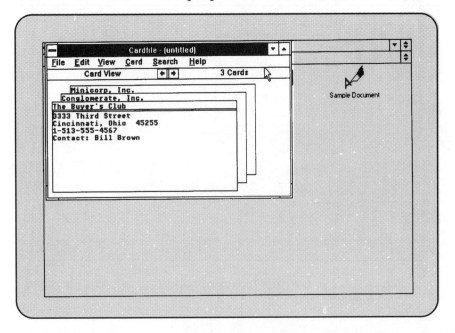

Figure 7.5. Cards are added to the Cardfile display each time you record a new entry.

Viewing Cardfile Records in List Mode

Information in your Cardfile databases can be viewed in one of two ways. Until now, we've been working exclusively in Card mode, where records are displayed using the simulated index cards alluded to earlier. Cardfile also allows you to examine a database's contents in List mode. Let's switch over to this second mode and see what information is available there.

√ To Switch to List Mode

▶ Choose View from the Cardfile menu bar.

▶ Choose List.

Your screen should now resemble Figure 7.6, which shows the Cardfile List display. When running in List mode, Cardfile displays the first line of any records stored in the current file, its index line.

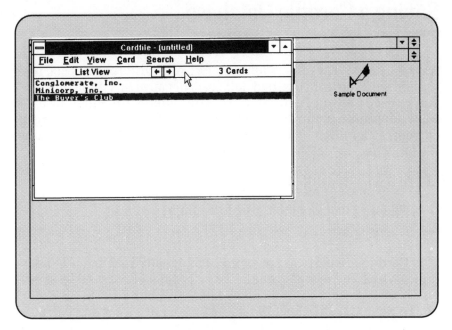

Figure 7.6. List mode displays the first line of records in the current Cardfile database.

If you look carefully at Figure 7.6, you will notice several items that provide information about how Cardfile works.

1. Records in a Cardfile file are automatically organized in alphabetical order, based on the initial character in the first line of each record. (Notice, for example, that even though you entered information for Minicorp, Inc., first, it is the last line displayed in Figure 7.6.)

2. The status line indicates the number of records stored in the current database. (Figure 7.6, for instance, shows that you have added three records to this file.)

3. Whenever you work in Cardfile, the record on which the previous operation was performed remains the active record. (For example, the line containing The Buyer's Club should be highlighted on your display, since that was the last record added to the current file.)

Saving a Cardfile Database

As was true in Write, unless told otherwise, Cardfile begins each new session working in an untitled database. Because this is the first time you've used Cardfile, none of the records entered up until now have been identified with a named file. The file you're working is currently identified as Untitled on its title bar. Let's go ahead and assign your new database a file name.

148

√ **To Save a Cardfile File**

▶ Choose File from the Cardfile menu bar.

▶ Choose Save As.

Cardfile displays a dialog box, asking you to enter a file name under which the records comprising this database should be saved.

√ **To Save Cardfile Records**

▶ Type **WINBOOK\PRACTICE** and press Enter.

Notice that the specified filename, PRACTICE.CRD, now appears in the title bar of the Cardfile window.

> ▶ **Note:** Should you enter any new records and then attempt to exit Cardfile without first saving those records to a file, you will be asked whether you wish to do so before returning to the Windows Program Manager.

Before looking at some of the specific activities you can perform with Cardfile, let's examine the various keyboard commands that program takes advantage of to simplify its use.

Cardfile Key Commands

As mentioned earlier, when you're working in Cardfile you will rely heavily on keyboard input. For this reason, Cardfile provides a number of keyboard commands to simplify entering and finding records in the current file without forcing you to switch over to the mouse for menu selection. These include:

Key(s)	Function
Ctrl+Home	Brings to the first entry in the current database to the front of the Cardfile window
Ctrl+End	Brings to the last entry in the current database to the front of the Cardfile window
PgDn	In Card mode, scrolls forward one card in the current file; in List mode, moves forward one page (window) group of records
PgUp	In Card mode, scrolls backward one card in the current file; in List mode, moves backward one page (window) group of records
Down Arrow	Scrolls forward one card in List mode
Up Arrow	Scrolls backward one card in List mode
F4	Used to initiate a Search from the keyboard

149

> ▶ **Tip:** Clicking on the Right and Left Arrows displayed in the status of the Cardfile window allows you to move forward and backward one record at a time within the current database. These scroll arrows provide a convenient method for quickly scanning individual cards within a Cardfile database.

Working in Cardfile

As I've mentioned several times already, the key to understanding how Cardfile works—and, therefore, learning how you can best put Cardfile to work for you—is to think of each record you enter in your Cardfile database as resembling an index card. As you finish filling out a new card, that card is placed into an imaginary drawer, the current Cardfile file. Furthermore, as I mentioned earlier, Cardfile automatically organizes all of these cards in alphabetical order, based on the initial character on its first line. Once you have this index card metaphor in your mind, figuring out what the various Cardfile commands accomplish is relatively easy.

Scanning a Cardfile File

150

Scanning the records in a Cardfile file is analogous to thumbing through our imaginary file drawer when it's filled with index cards. Pressing Ctrl+End in Card mode, for example, is comparable to flipping all the way back to the last index card in that drawer. Conversely, pressing Ctrl+Home would be like pulling out and looking at the first card the drawer contains. The other Cardfile keyboard file scanning commands work in similar ways. Let's use our three sample records to demonstrate what I mean. But first, we'll switch back to the Card view.

√ To Switch to Card View

▶ Choose View from the Cardfile menu bar.
▶ Choose Card.

Your Cardfile window should show the record for The Buyer's Club, the last record we entered into this database. Go ahead and press Ctrl+Home. This should bring the first card (record) in our PRACTICE.CRD file, the record for Conglomerate, Inc., to the front of the display window. Now, let's quickly move to the end of the file.

√ To Display the Last Record in the Current File

▶ Press Ctrl+End.

The record for The Buyer's Club reappears. (And, yes, pressing Ctrl+Home right now would just as quickly redisplay the record for Conglomerate, Inc.) Admittedly, this isn't a very impressive feat with only three records in a file, but you can use the Cardfile command keys to navigate just as quickly a file that contains hundreds of names, addresses, phone numbers, and other information. And best of all, Cardfile doesn't limit you to linear scans. As is true of any PC application program, Cardfile's real strength lies in the ease with which it allows you to find a specific piece of information located in one of its records.

Searching a Cardfile's Index

You can use Cardfile's Search command to find specific records in a file quickly. We're going to see how this works, but first let's make the first record in our PRACTICE file the active record.

151

√ To Move Back to the Beginning of the Current File

▶ Press Ctrl+Home.

Suppose, for example, that you had a large Cardfile database and needed to look up the name of your contact at Minicorp, Inc. Scanning this Cardfile file alphabetically, therefore, would be impractical. So, what could you do? We'll attempt to use the Cardfile Search command to see if we can find the record containing the name of our sales representative contact at MiniCorp, Inc.

√ To Find a Record Quickly

▶ Choose Search from the Cardfile menu bar.
▶ Choose Go To.

Cardfile displays the Go To dialog box, shown in Figure 7.7. Use this dialog box to enter the index value you want Cardfile to find in the current file.

√ To Have Cardfile Display the Record

▶ Type **Minicorp** and press Enter.

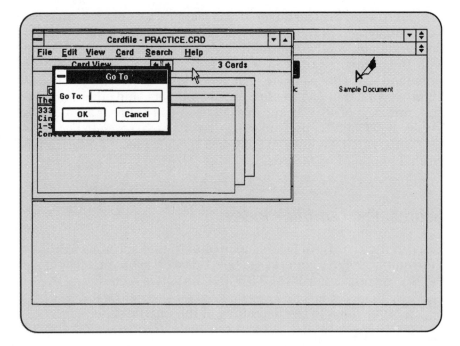

Figure 7.7. Use the Go To command to find a specific record in a Cardfile file.

Cardfile initiates a file search based on the criteria you specified—that is, with instructions to stop searching when it finds a record containing the text string "Minicorp" in the index field. In our sample file, therefore, this search brings the card containing information for Minicorp, Inc., to the front of your Cardfile window.

Searching for Non-Index Text

The Find command allows you to locate a specified text string within a database file, regardless of where that string exists within a Cardfile record. This feature is extremely useful if you need to perform a random search on your database for information you know is not contained in an Index field.

Suppose, for example, that you were planning a trip to Cincinnati and wanted to know which of the customers in our PRACTICE database were located in that city. Obviously, an index Search would be useless in this situation. Instead, you'd want to use the Find command.

√ To Initiate a Find Operation

▶ Choose Search from the Cardfile menu bar.

▶ Choose Find.

Cardfile displays a Find dialog box similar to the Go To dialog box shown in Figure 7.7. Use this dialog box to enter the text string you want Cardfile to locate within records in the current file. In this case, we want to find all customers located in Cincinnati.

√ To Have Cardfile Find Specific Information Within a Record

▶ Type **Cincinnati** and press Enter.

Cardfile initiates a file search based on the Find criteria you specified—that is, with instructions to stop searching when it finds the text string "Cincinnati" anywhere in a Cardfile record. Using our sample records, therefore, this search ends when Cardfile reaches the card containing information for The Buyer's Club as illustrated in Figure 7.8. Notice that Cardfile automatically highlights the specified text string within the display window.

153

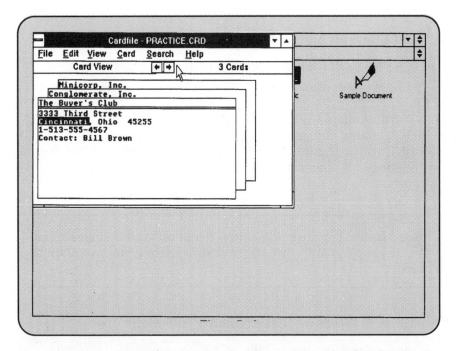

Figure 7.8. The Find command allows you to search a database for a text string located anywhere in a Cardfile record.

The Cardfile Autodial Feature

If you own a Hayes or Hayes-compatible modem, you can have Cardfile automatically dial phone numbers contained in a Cardfile database. Before testing the Cardfile autodial feature, however, perform the following steps:

▶ Press the F7 function key to add a new Cardfile entry to the PRACTICE database.

▶ Type the name of someone you know and press Enter.

▶ Type that person's phone number and press Enter.

Are you ready? Okay, here we go. Let's see how the autodialer works.

154

 Tip: You may want to manually call your friend first and let him or her know they're about to become part of a small experiment in automation.

√ **To Initiate an Autodial Operation**

▶ Choose Card from the Cardfile menu bar.

▶ Choose Autodial.

Cardfile displays the dialog box screen shown in Figure 7.9, which contains the phone number associated with the current record. If you configured Windows to recognize your modem during installation, all that remains now is to have Cardfile dial this number.

▶ **Note:** Of course, the actual telephone number shown in your Cardfile display will differ from the one shown here.

√ **To Have Windows Dial a Number Automatically**

▶ Press Enter or choose OK.

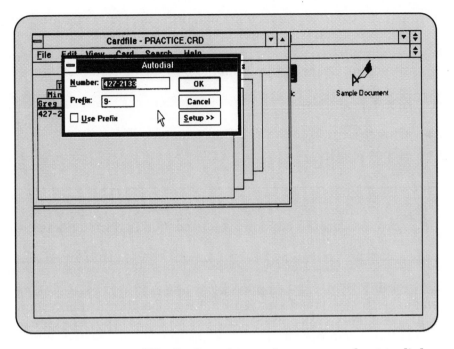

Figure 7.9. Cardfile displays the number you are about to dial.

You will hear a series of beeps coming from your modem's speaker. These beeps are the same tones a touch-tone phone system would use to dial the number previously displayed in your Cardfile window. A few seconds later, you should hear the sound of your friend's voice on the phone.

> **Tip:** If Windows is not configured to recognize and use your modem automatically, choosing the Setup button in the Autodial dialog box allows you to specify modem setting for the current call.

Deleting Records from a Cardfile Database

Now that we're finished with the special card we created to test the Autodial command, let's get rid of it. Deleting a record from a Cardfile database is a simple two-step operation:

155

1. Using a Go To or Find command, bring the card containing the record you want to delete to the front of the Cardfile window.
2. Select the Delete option from the pull-down Card menu.

√ To Delete a Record

▶ Choose Card from the Cardfile menu bar.
▶ Choose Delete.

> ▶ **Note:** Because your friend's record was already displayed in the Cardfile window, you needed to perform only the second step listed above.

Cardfile displays the option box shown in Figure 7.10, asking you to verify that you do indeed want to delete the current record. Notice that the default option in this box is Cancel. Choosing Cancel aborts the Delete operation and leaves the current record within

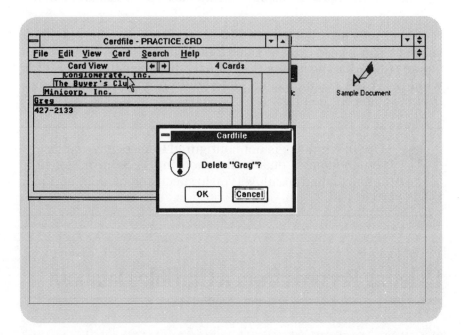

Figure 7.10. Windows guards against your accidentally deleting records in a Cardfile database.

√ **To Complete the Delete Operation**

▶ Choose OK.

Quitting Cardfile

Let's go ahead and quit the Cardfile application. We'll return to Cardfile in Chapter 12, "Putting It All Together."

√ **To Quit Cardfile**

▶ Choose File from the Cardfile menu bar.
▶ Choose Exit.

Because you modified the contents of this database since it was saved earlier in this chapter, Cardfile asks if your changes to that file should be saved to the PRACTICE.CRD file before it closes the current window.

157

√ **To Update a Changed File Before Closing It**

▶ Press Enter or choose Yes.

Cardfile updates the PRACTICE.CRD file and returns you to the Program Manager, from which you can select more Windows programs. That's exactly what we'll do in the next chapter, when we look at another Windows accessory, Calendar.

What You Have Learned

▶ Database management is an extremely powerful PC application. It allows you to keep track of large amounts of information quickly and efficiently, drawing on those types of operations computers perform best.

▶ Cardfile is the Windows database manager. You can use Cardfile to record, manage, and analyze virtually any type of information, on any subject. Furthermore, Windows' pull-down menus make using even the most advanced features of Cardfile, like the ability to find records based on their contents, easy to learn and use.

▶ Cardfile includes an Autodial command that allows anyone owning a Hayes or Hayes-compatible modem to dial phone numbers stored in a Cardfile database automatically.

158

Chapter 8

Calendar

▶ *How to keep track of important dates and appointments with the Windows Calendar*

▶ *How to set a Calendar alarm*

Time, Your Most Precious Resource

Time is the one thing we never seem to have enough of. If you take on too many duties and assume too many responsibilities, inevitably you will forget something, somewhere. Even if you do manage to remember everything you've already planned, you're still not out of the woods. There's always one more project knocking at your door, one more co-worker, relative, or friend demanding a little piece of your time. There are times when it all seems overwhelming. Those are the times you may catch yourself thinking, "If only I could add an hour to each day."

Although Windows can't give you that extra hour, it will help organize the 24 hours you do have. How? With Calendar, a Windows accessory that combines a month-at-a-glance calendar and a daily appointment book into a single time-management tool.

Calendar Features

As its name implies, Calendar is Windows' electronic answer to the traditional appointment calendar. Like its paper predecessor, the Windows Calendar can be used to record appointments, remind you of upcoming commitments, and even to jot down a quick note to make sure you don't forget important events like your mother-in-law's birthday or your own anniversary. (Name a haggard husband or woeful wife who hasn't let this one slip by at some time or another down through the years.) Furthermore, Windows enhances your ability to track such information by integrating Calendar into the total Desktop environment, thus making its advanced time-management features available to you at the push of a key or click of a mouse button, at anytime during a Windows session.

Features of the Windows Calendar accessory include:

160

▶ The ability to view and analyze your scheduled appointments on a daily or monthly basis.
▶ Appointment entries that are easily edited to reflect changes in your schedule.
▶ A built-in alarm that reminds you of planned events and appointments before they happen.
▶ An on-screen scratch pad that allows you to incorporate notes about your appointments into the Calendar display.
▶ A Mark option that lets you quickly mark special days in Calendar's Monthly view.

As you can see, using the Calendar application can give an entirely new meaning to the old phrase, "time on your hands." So let's start using Calendar.

Adding Calendar to the Book Exercises Program Group

As you've probably noticed, Calendar has not yet been added to your Book Exercises program group. Let's correct that oversight now. On the way from here to there, we'll look at still another example of the flexibility of the Windows GUI.

Minimizing a Program Group Window

To prepare for this exercise, let's temporarily close the Book Exercises program group and minimize it to a group icon. There are two ways to minimize an individual window in your Windows workspace:

1. By selecting the Minimize option from a window's Control menu.
2. By clicking on a window's Minimize box until it becomes a small icon on your workspace.

We'll use the first method described here to familiarize you with the Control menu options associated with individual windows.

√ **To Access a Program Group's Control Menu**

▶ Choose the Control menu box of the Book Exercises.

161

> ▶ **Note:** This is the menu box just to the left of File on the Book Exercises menu bar. Do not choose the Control menu box on the title bar.

This displays the pull-down menu shown in Figure 8.1. You use a window's Control menu to specify operations you want performed on that window only, rather than your total Windows environment.

√ **To Minimize the Program Group to a Group Icon**

▶ Choose Minimize.

This shrinks the Book Exercises program group to a group icon, which Windows positions with the other inactive icons across the bottom of your Windows workspace. It also, by the way, exposes the Accessories program group, which has been active but obscured behind our full-screen Book Exercises program group window throughout the last few chapters.

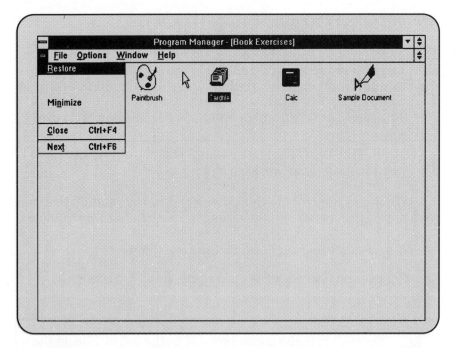

Figure 8.1. Each window on your workspace has a Control menu from which you can select commands that affect that window only.

Copying an Accessory to a Group Icon

Previously, we've only copied accessories into open windows—as was the case when we first created our Book Exercises program group in Chapter 5. But a program group does not have to be open for you to modify it. To demonstrate this, let's copy the Calendar application into our Book Exercises group icon.

√ To Copy Calendar into a Program Group

▶ Position the mouse cursor over the Calendar icon in the Accessories program group.

▶ Depress the left mouse button.

▶ Press and hold down the Ctrl key.

▶ Drag the mouse until the duplicate Calendar icon is sitting over the Book Exercises group icon.

▶ Release the left mouse button and the Ctrl key.

162

It doesn't really look like much happened, does it? Don't worry. Something did. We'll reopen the Book Exercises program group to see what. But rather than simply double-clicking on the Book Exercises group icon, which would work, let's try something else. This time, let's use a Restore command to return that program group to its previous full-screen display.

Restoring a Group Icon

But, you may be asking, how do you specify a Restore command, which is located on the Control menu, when the Book Exercises program group's Control menu box is not visible? I'm glad you asked.

√ To Access a Group Icon's Control Menu

▶ Choose the Book Exercises group icon.

Clicking on a group icon has the same effect as choosing the Control menu box when that group is displayed in a window—that is, it calls up the Control menu, as illustrated in Figure 8.2. Notice that the Restore option on this menu is displayed in clear print, indicating it can be selected.

163

√ To Restore a Program Group

▶ Choose Restore.

The Restore command returns a program group to its previous size and location—that is, restores that program group to however it was before you issued the most recent Minimize command. In this case, the Book Exercises program group was restored to a full-screen display, as illustrated in Figure 8.3. And guess what? The Calendar accessory is now included in this group.

As I said, I took this little detour to demonstrate one more example of the flexibility built into the Windows environment. Now that we have Calendar available from within our Book Exercises program group, let's see how it works.

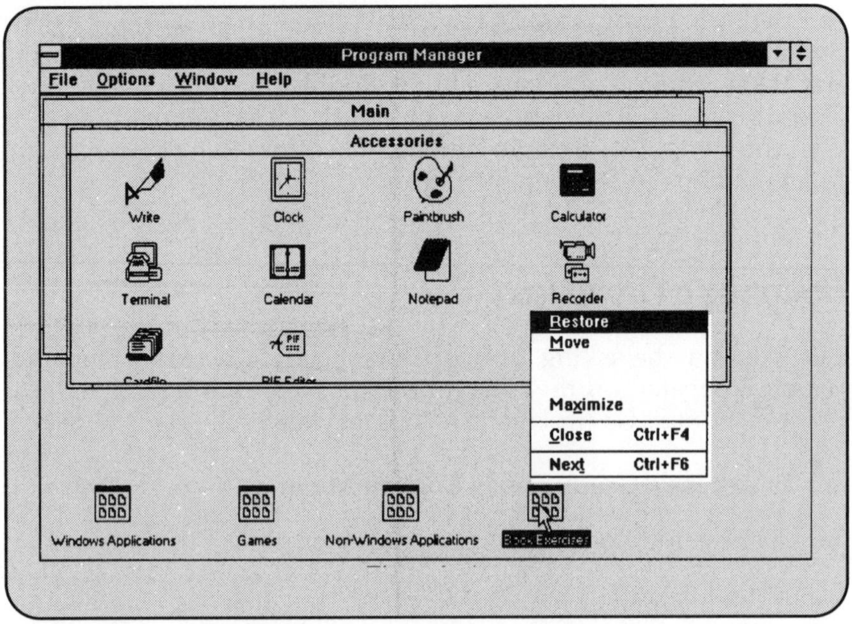

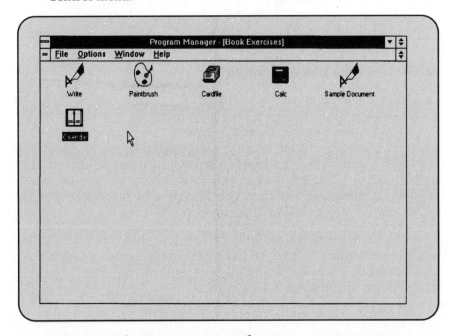

Figure 8.2. Clicking on a group icon displays that group's Control menu.

164

Figure 8.3. The Restore command restores a program group exactly as it was displayed before you issued the previous Minimize command.

Starting Calendar

√ **To Start the Calendar Accessory**

▶ Double-click on the Calendar icon located in your Book Exercises program group.

After a few seconds you'll see the Calendar display, shown in Figure 8.4. The first time you start Calendar, it displays a window resembling a typical page from a more traditional daily appointment book.

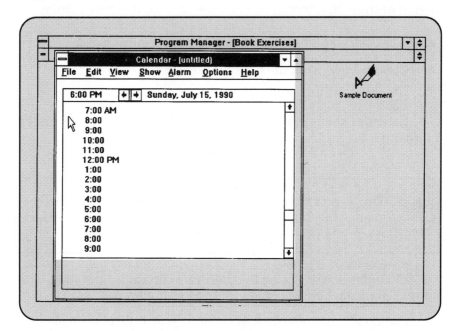

Figure 8.4. Calendar's initial display resembles a page from a daily appointment book.

 Note: Your display will show a different date, the current date, which Calendar reads from your system clock.

Notice that, as was true with Write and Cardfile, Calendar creates an Untitled file the first time you start it. We'll name our new Calendar file in a few minutes. Before we do, though, let's take a look at some rudimentary Calendar operations.

Displaying Calendar's Monthly View

Calendar offers an alternative to the appointment book display shown in Figure 8.4. This second display option, the Month view, allows you to use Calendar to examine your schedule over a longer period of time than would be convenient with its Daily display.

√ To Switch Calendar to a Month View

▶ Choose View from the Calendar menu bar.
▶ Choose Month.

Calendar changes its display to the Month view, as illustrated in Figure 8.5.

▶ **Tip:** If you're working at the keyboard and need to quickly change the Calendar view, you can do so by pressing the F8 (Day) or F9 (Month) function key.

Calendar makes it easy to determine certain information with a quick glance when displayed in its Month view:

▶ Notice that one date is highlighted. This indicates the active date. When you first start Calendar, it automatically makes the current date active (July 15, 1990, in Figure 8.5—providing, of course, that your system clock is set correctly. You can change the active date, as you will see later in this chapter.

▶ Use the two horizontal scroll buttons located at the top of the Calendar display to "thumb through" different months sequentially, a procedure not unlike turning the pages of a

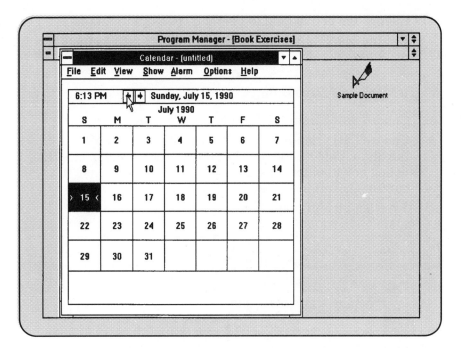

Figure 8.5. The Month view lets you use Calendar to analyze more than a single day's schedule.

167

traditional calendar. Mouse users can access this feature simply by clicking on the appropriate action button. The corresponding keyboard commands are PgUp (the previous month) and PgDn (the next month).

▶ Calendar includes the familiar Windows menu bar across the top of its display window.

Since we're in the Month view, let's examine the various Calendar features there.

Marking a Date

Remember how I told you Calendar could guarantee that you never again forget your wedding anniversary (or, for my unmarried readers, any other important annual event)? We'll start there by adding a subtle reminder on June 15 to our sample Calendar. In Calendar's terminology, this would involve *marking a date* in the current file. Marking a date is a two-step process:

1. Change the active date to the date you want to mark.
2. Use the Mark command in the Options menu to attach a mark to that date.

√ To Mark an Active Date

▶ Choose Show from the Calendar menu bar.

▶ Choose Date from the pull-down Show menu. This displays the Show Date dialog box, as shown in Figure 8.6. Use this dialog box to enter the date you want to make active in the current Calendar display.

▶ Type **6/5/90** and press Enter.

168

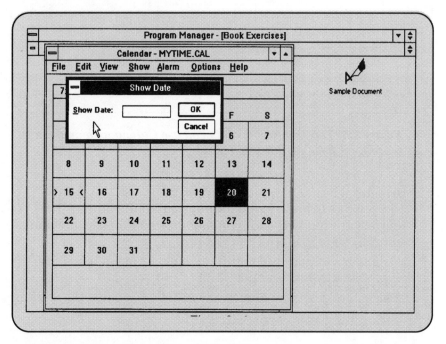

Figure 8.6. Use the Show Date dialog box to enter the date you want to make active in the current Calendar display.

Now that June 15 is the active date, we can mark it as a special occasion.

✓ **To Mark the Active Date in Your Calendar File**

▶ Choose Options from the Calendar menu bar.
▶ Choose Mark.

This displays the Day Markings option box shown in Figure 8.7. Use this option box to specify which of five symbols you want assigned to the active date. Associating a different symbol with different types of special events allows you to organize your Calendar files so that a quick scan of a month will give you an idea of your schedule for that month. You could, for example, use Symbol 1 for personal events, Symbol 2 for business meetings, Symbol 3 for project deadlines, and so forth. In this case, we'll choose Symbol 4.

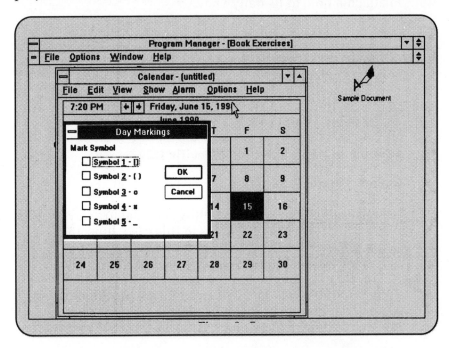

169

Figure 8.7. Assigning different symbols to different types of special events helps you organize your Calendar files.

✓ **To Assign a Special Symbol to an Active Date**

▶ Choose Symbol 4.
▶ Press Enter or choose OK.

Calendar returns you to the Month view of the currently active month. Notice, however, that a small x (Symbol 4) has been placed in the date box for June 15.

Adding Notes to a Calendar File

Admittedly, a small x in a date box doesn't tell you much. But it doesn't have to. Remember, that mark only serves as a reminder of some important event. To specify what that event is, you'll probably want to attach a note to its daily view.

Switching from a Month to a Day View

170

Earlier we accessed the View menu on the Calendar menu bar to switch between the Month and Day view. There is a simpler way to call up a Day view of June 15.

√ **To Switch to a Day View of a Specific Day**

▶ Double-click on June 15.

Calendar switches from the monthly calendar to a Day view for the date on which you double-click—in this case, June 15.

> ▶ **Tip:** Double-clicking on the status bar anywhere to the right of the scroll bars will switch back to a Month view from a daily appointment book display.

Using Calendar's Scratch Pad

You can use the scratch pad to hold reminders about specific events and appointments recorded in your Calendar file. Let's use the Calendar scratch pad to attach a reminder of our imaginary wedding anniversary to the daily calendar for June 15.

√ **To Add a Reminder to an Active Date on the Scratch Pad**

► Position the mouse cursor anywhere in the blank box at the bottom of the Calendar window.

► Click the left mouse button.

► Type **Wedding anniversary**.

That takes care of our general reminder. Next, let's enter an individual appointment in our June 15 daily calendar—lunch reservations arranged to celebrate this special day.

Recording Individual Appointments in a Daily Calendar

171

Let's assume that you've arranged to meet your spouse for lunch at 12:45. Rather than appending this information to that day's scratch pad, it makes more sense to record this appointment for the actual time it's scheduled to take place. There's only one problem. Calendar's default daily display divides the day into 60-minute increments. To record a 12:45 appointment, therefore, you'll first need to insert a special line into June 15 for that time.

Specifying a Special Time

The Special Time command allows you to specify an appointment for a time other than Calendar's default values.

√ **To Access the Special Time Command**

► Choose Options from the Calendar menu bar.

► Choose Special Time.

This displays the Special Time dialog box, shown in Figure 8.8, which you use to insert an appointment line for times other than the Calendar default values.

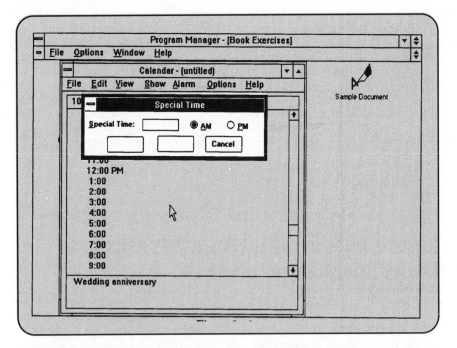

Figure 8.8. Calendar allows you to specify special times for your appointments.

√ **To Insert an Appointment Line into the Currently Active Date**

▶ Type **12:45**.

▶ Choose PM.

▶ Press Enter or choose Insert.

Calendar inserts a new line for the specified time and returns you to its daily view. Now that this line exists, you can use it to record your special anniversary plans.

√ **To Record Specific Information on the Current Appointment Line**

▶ Type **Anniversary luncheon date**.

At this point your Calendar display should resemble Figure 8.9, which shows both the scratch pad note and the individual appointment added to the June 15 record.

172

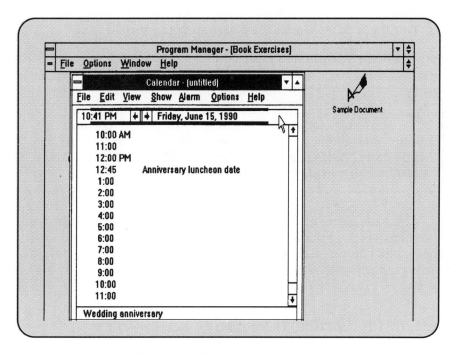

Figure 8.9. In this screen, both the scratch pad note and appointment record remind you of this special day.

For many people, this might be enough to ensure continued marital bliss. Others may need a little extra reminder. (I know myself too well.) I'll take all the help Calendar can give me. Luckily for me, and others like me, Calendar still has one more trick up its electronic sleeve.

173

The Calendar Alarm Feature

Setting an alarm is a logical and effective way to make certain you don't forget appointments recorded in your Calendar file.

Setting an Alarm

This one's so simple, we're going to breeze right through it.

√ **To Attach an Alarm to the Current Appointment Line**

▶ Press the F5 function key.

> ▶ **Note:** There is a menu alternative to this command. It's the Set option on the Alarm menu. But why perform two mouse operations when a single keystroke accomplishes the same thing? As good as a graphical interface is, there are times when nothing beats the reliable old PC keyboard.

This places a small bell icon next to the current appointment line. Now you might imagine that anyone would feel fairly secure in their ability to remember this luncheon date. Secure, maybe. But, quite possibly, still not positive.

174

Setting an Alarm to Ring Early

You want positive? I'll give you positive, by showing you how to set this alarm to ring 10 minutes early.

√ **To Set Your Alarm to Ring Early**

▶ Choose Alarm from the Calendar menu bar.
▶ Choose Controls.

This displays the Alarm Controls dialog box, as shown in Figure 8.10. The number you enter into the Early Ring field determines how long prior to a recorded appointment Calendar will begin sounding its alarm.

√ **To Have Your Alarm Ring 10 Minutes Early**

▶ Type **10**.
▶ Choose OK or press Enter.

As these few examples illustrate, Calendar provides some impressive time-management tools. And all these features come bundled with the basic Windows package. Before we end our discussion of Calendar, allow me to point out one more advantage of organizing your schedule electronically, rather than depending on more traditional methods.

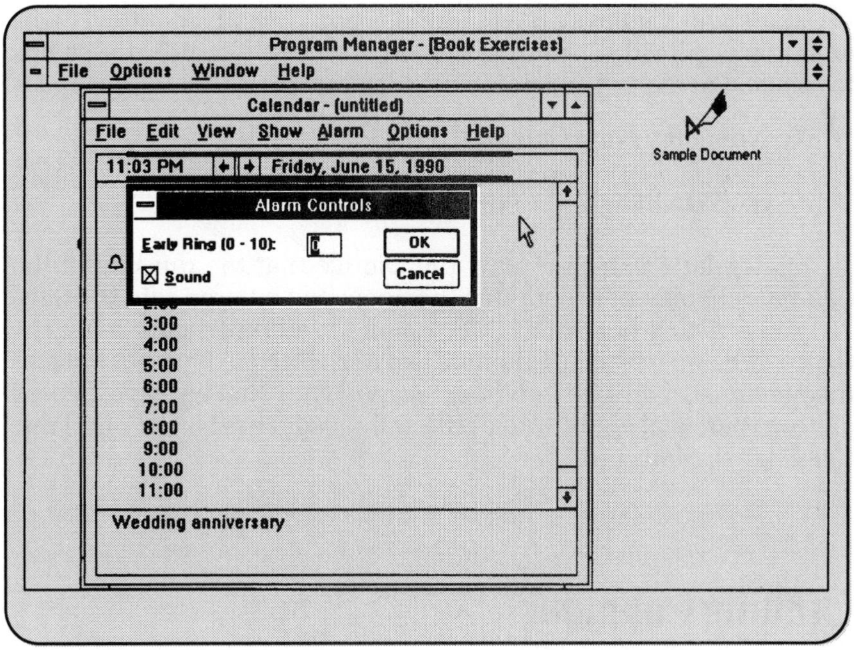

Figure 8.10. With the Alarm Controls dialog box, you can set the alarm to ring early.

Creating a Personal Calendar File

I don't know how it is with your family, but here at Chez Nims everyone uses the same calendar—a free gift from the local pharmacy that's magnetically clamped to the side of our refrigerator—to keep track of important events. Consequently, by the time the last day of a given month rolls around, its calendar page contain more notes, reminders, quickly scribbled phone numbers, and general graffiti than a New York subway train. Calendar solves this problem by allowing you to create and manage multiple Calendar files. Therefore, each person with access to your Windows environment can set up a different Calendar on which to keep track of his or her schedule.

√ To Create a Personal Calendar File

▶ Choose File from the Calendar menu bar.

▶ Choose Save As.

Calendar displays a Save As dialog box virtually identical to the ones you've already seen in Write and Cardfile. Use this dialog box to assign a name to your new Calendar file.

√ **To Name the New Calendar File**

▶ Type **WINBOOK\MYTIME** and press Enter.

Calendar creates the new file. Notice that the top line of the Calendar display now contains the name you entered into the Save As Name dialog box, MYTIME. Calendar automatically adds the CAL extension to this file name. (The MYTIME.CAL name replaces the previously Untitled Calendar legend.) Now that we have created our own personal appointment file and saved it to disk, let's end this Calendar session.

176 Quitting Calendar

√ **To Quit Calendar**

▶ Choose File from the Calendar menu bar.
▶ Choose Exit.

Because you just saved your most recent activity to a disk file, Calendar bypasses the cautionary prompt box encountered in earlier chapters and immediately returns you to the Calendar Program Manager.

What You Have Learned

▶ The Windows Calendar accessory helps you organize and manage time, perhaps your most precious resource. Calendar allows you to record planned activities and then review your schedule by day or month.

▶ Calendar recognizes two distinct types of activities: date-related events and appointments assigned to specific times. You mark dates to remind you of special dates, such as birthdays and anniversaries. Individual appointments represent activities planned within a specific date, such as business meetings and luncheon dates.

▶ Once an event is recorded in Calendar, you can use that program's Alarm feature to make certain you don't forget it.

177

178

Chapter 9

Paintbrush

In This Chapter

179

- ▶ *A definition of Paintbrush and what it does*
- ▶ *How to start Paintbrush*
- ▶ *How to access and use the Paintbrush Toolbox*
- ▶ *How to include text in a graphic file*
- ▶ *How to mix text and graphics with Paintbrush*

What Is Paintbrush?

We've been busy over the course of the previous eight chapters. So far, we've examined how your PC works and how Windows works on that PC. We've also devoted several chapters to instructions on how you perform specific tasks using a trio of Windows accessories—Write, Cardfile, and Calendar. Now is a good time to lighten up a bit. In this chapter, therefore, we're going to look at Paintbrush, a Windows accessory that can be as much fun as it is functional.

Paintbrush is the Windows graphics program. Based on the popular PC Paintbrush program from ZSoft Corporation, Paintbrush lets you easily create a variety of graphic images using its special drawing tools. Having Paintbrush installed in your Windows environment is much like having an electronic Etch-A-Sketch sitting on your desktop, constantly at your beck and call. Doodlers will love Paintbrush. (Almost everyone I know is a closet doodler. I still sneak in a few minutes on my four-year-old son's Etch-A-Sketch every week—usually after he's safely tucked in bed and can't accuse me of hogging his toys.)

Paintbrush is useful for more than mere doodling, however. A well-designed graphic can enhance the appearance of virtually any document, including something as potentially boring as a form letter announcing an upcoming reduction to the purchase price of widgets. Let's put Paintbrush through its paces by designing a stationery logo for Wonderful Widgets, Inc.

180

▶ **Note:** In addition to adding an element of fun to our examination of the Windows environment, this chapter will provide you with your first taste of how the various Windows accessories complement one another, thus creating a gestalt work environment where the total output of your PC activities can be greater than the sum of its parts.

Starting Paintbrush

You run Paintbrush by double-clicking on its screen icon, a stylized artist's palette and paintbrush. Since Paintbrush already exists in our Book Exercises program group, let's start it from there.

√ **To Start the Paintbrush Accessory**

▶ Double-click on the Paintbrush icon located in your Book Exercises program group window.

This loads Paintbrush and displays its opening screen, as shown in Figure 9.1.

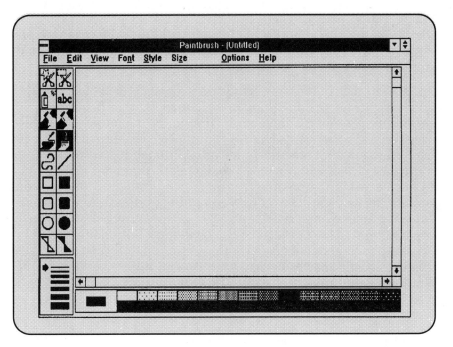

Figure 9.1. The opening Paintbrush screen.

It's not much to look at, is it? The initial Paintbrush screen shouldn't be anything fancy.

> ▶ **Note:** Your Paintbrush display may look a little fancier, in that it probably includes color. One of the major drawbacks to writing about a program like Paintbrush is that color screens do not reproduce well in black and white. Consequently, I've set up my copy of Paintbrush to run in monochrome mode—that is, using a black-and-white display. Rest assured, however, that this won't interfere with our investigating the various Paintbrush features and functions.

Think of your Paintbrush display as being the electronic analog of an artist's canvas. If you think about it, even the greatest masterpiece ever painted began life as an empty canvas. Over time, the artist transformed this emptiness into meaningful images. That's exactly what you'll do with the Paintbrush display. And recognizing that an artist requires special implements to create his or her art (a palette, paint, paintbrushes, and the like), Paintbrush provides a number of tools to simplify life for the budding PC Picasso—tools you'll learn about as this chapter progresses. But first, a word about everyone's favorite electronic rodent, the mouse.

Paintbrush is the one Windows accessory in which using a mouse represents more than mere convenience. In addition to serving as a pointing device, as it does in all other Windows accessories, the mouse assumes the role of paintbrush once you begin filling in your electronic canvas. Although it may be possible to run Paintbrush without a mouse, I don't recommend it. Attempting such a feat is comparable to trying to replicate the Mona Lisa on a typewriter keyboard. I won't say it couldn't be done; there's always someone, somewhere, willing to attempt something that is nearly impossible, simply for the sake of a challenge. But I doubt whether the final product would be worth the effort. A paintbrush simplifies creating artistic masterpieces; a mouse simplifies working in the Windows Paintbrush accessory. It's as simple as that.

182

The Paintbrush Tools

The drawing tools are accessed from the set of icons running down the left-hand side of the Paintbrush display, the area of the screen referred to as the Toolbox. Each tool serves a different function, and you can use the tools to create and edit your Paintbrush images.

These tools are listed in the order of their appearance, from left to right and from top to bottom of the Paintbrush display. The functions that these tools allow you to perform are also noted.

Scissors	Selects an irregularly shaped area of your picture, which you can then manipulate with the various Paintbrush commands located in the Edit and Action menus.
Pick	Selects a square or rectangular shaped area of your picture, which you can then manipulate using your mouse or the various Paintbrush commands located in the Edit and Action menus.

Airbrush	Produces a circular pattern of dots in the current foreground color.
Text Tool	Adds text, using several different fonts and type sizes, to your Paintbrush pictures.
Color Eraser	Changes selected foreground colors under the Eraser icon to a background color or, alternately, automatically changes every occurrence of one color in the drawing area to another.
Eraser	Changes any areas it touches into the currently selected background color.
Paint Roller	Automatically "fills"—that is places colors or patterns within any closed shapes you create.
Brush	Adds freehand sketch elements to your Paintbrush pictures.
Curve	Generates curved lines, resembling portions of a circle or other rounded object.
Line	Draws a straight line between two specified points.
Box	Draws squares and rectangles outlined in the foreground color.
Filled Box	Draws squares and rectangles that are filled in with the foreground color.
Rounded Box	Draws squares and rectangles having rounded corners and outlined in the foreground color.
Filled Rounded Box	Draws squares and rectangles with rounded corners that are filled in with the foreground color.
Circle	Draws circles and other rounded (or elliptical) shapes outlined in the foreground color.
Filled Circle	Draws circles and other rounded (or elliptical) shapes that are filled in with the foreground color.

183

Filled Polygon	Generates triangles or other multi-sided, irregularly shaped (polygonal) objects outlined in the foreground color.
Filled Polygon	Generates triangles or other multi-sided, irregularly shaped (polygonal) objects that are filled in with the foreground color.

Now that you know what each Paintbrush tool is designed to accomplish, let's see how they can be used.

Selecting a Paintbrush Tool

184

You activate a Paintbrush tool by clicking the mouse cursor on its corresponding icon. Let's see how this works by selecting the Filled Circle tool.

√ **To Select a Tool**

▶ Move your mouse until the mouse cursor is pointing to the Filled Circle icon (the second icon from the bottom in the right-hand column of the Toolbox).

▶ Click the left mouse button.

This highlights the Filled Circle icon within the Toolbox, identifying it as the currently active tool. Once a tool is active, you can use it to create or modify elements within the drawing area, that currently blank portion of the Paintbrush display in which you'll create your pictures and graphic images.

Before we begin creating our letterhead logo, however, let's add one element to the Paintbrush display that will make it easier to coordinate the following exercise.

Displaying Cursor Coordinates

As you perform operations within the Paintbrush drawing area, you're actually manipulating the individual picture elements (or *pixels*, the dots on the video screen) your PC uses to generate its display. You can use the Cursor Position command, located on the View menu, to tell Paintbrush to display coordinates indicating the current position of the mouse cursor within its drawing area. Doing so simplifies such activities as lining up objects, drawing straight lines, and the like.

√ To Display the Cursor Coordinates

▶ Choose View from the Paintbrush menu bar.

▶ Choose Cursor Position.

Your screen should now resemble Figure 9.2. Notice that the current cursor coordinates appear in a small box near the top-right corner of the Paintbrush display. (In this figure, the cursor is located 60 pixels in and 80 pixels down from the left and top border of the Paintbrush drawing area, respectively. The actual numbers shown on your screen may be different.)

185

Go ahead and move the mouse cursor around the drawing area for a few seconds. As you do, notice how the coordinates listed in the cursor position box change to reflect this movement.

Using a Drawing Tool

Now that we can establish common reference points for the mouse cursor, let's draw a filled circle.

√ To Draw a Filled Circle

▶ Position the mouse cursor at coordinates 265, 125.

▶ Press and hold the left mouse button.

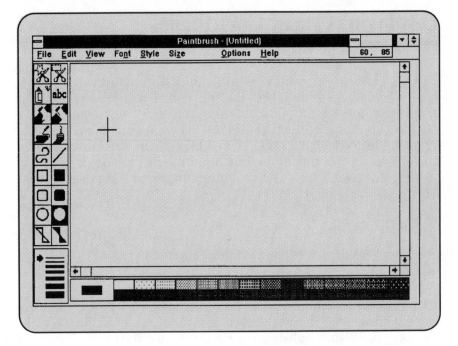

*Figure 9.2. Displaying the cursor position simplifies such Paint-
brush activities as lining up objects and drawing straight lines.*

▶ Drag the mouse down and to the right until the mouse cursor
is located at coordinates 350, 200.

▶ Release the left mouse button.

Your display should now resemble Figure 9.3, in which Paintbrush has drawn a filled circle, using the specified cursor coordinates.

> ▶ **Note:** Depending on the type of monitor you use, this
> circle may appear slightly more elliptical—that is, elon-
> gated—on your display.

All of the Paintbrush tools operate in basically this same
manner. That is, you use the mouse to activate the tool you want to
use, then move the mouse cursor into the Paintbrush drawing area
and perform the operation associated with whatever tool you selected. You'll see several more examples of what specific tools

186

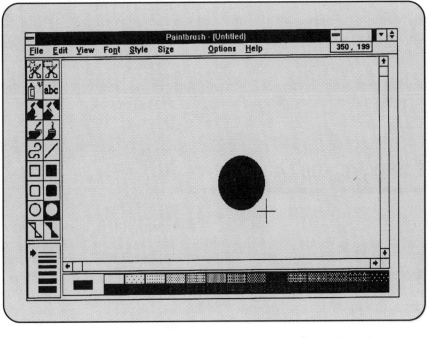

Figure 9.3. Dragging your mouse with an activated tool automatically creates the shape associated with that tool within the Paintbrush drawing area.

187

accomplish later on in this chapter, as we go about the task of creating a corporate logo for our imaginary company, Wonderful Widgets, Inc. Before beginning this project, however, let's get rid of the filled circle we drew in the previous exercise.

The easiest way to erase an object is to use the Eraser tool to change that object to the background color. This is similar to using an eraser to eliminate pencil marks and return a page to the color of the paper underneath.

√ **To Select the Eraser Tool**

▶ Move your mouse until the mouse cursor points to the Eraser icon (the third icon from the top in the left-hand column of the Toolbox).

▶ Click the left mouse button to activate the Eraser tool.

Next, move the mouse cursor back into the drawing area. A small white square appears representing the size of the area that will be erased each time you press the mouse button or, alternately, drag the mouse over a portion of the Paintbrush display. The operative word in the previous sentence is "small." That's a small square, and we have a big circle to erase. We can, however, change the size of the square so that we can erase the circle more quickly.

Changing the Drawing Width

Use the Linesize box, located in the bottom-left corner of the Paintbrush display, to change the size of the area affected by a Paintbrush tool or, alternately, the thickness of the border around any objects you draw. Selecting a larger Linesize, for example, would increase the area affected by the Eraser tool, something that will come in handy as we erase the circle.

√ To Increase the Linesize

▶ Move your mouse until the mouse cursor is pointing to the bottom line in the Linesize box, the widest Linesize available.

▶ Click the left mouse button to select the widest Linesize.

Now move the mouse cursor back into the drawing area. This time you should see a much bigger square representing the size of your eraser. (Notice, also, that the arrow that previously indicated the thinner Linesize now points to the one you just selected.) It should be big enough, in fact, to make erasing the circle a relatively easy task.

Using the Eraser

To use the Eraser tool, press and hold the left mouse button then drag the Eraser icon (the white square) across the area to be eliminated.

√ **To Use the Eraser**

▶ Move the eraser icon until it partially obscures the circle.

▶ Press and hold down the left mouse button.

▶ Drag the mouse back and forth over the circle until it has all been erased.

Voilà! We have a blank screen—a virgin palette, so to speak. So, let's take advantage of this virgin palette and get down to the nitty-gritty of designing our Wonderful Widgets corporate logo, checking out some additional features of Paintbrush on our way.

Adding Text to a Picture

189

Even admitting the validity of that old adage, one picture is worth a thousand words, there are times when only words will suffice. For example, it doesn't make sense to design a company letterhead that does not include your company's name. Ideally, then, we'd want to incorporate "Wonderful Widget, Inc." into the Paintbrush file we'll be creating. As luck would have it, Paintbrush's Text tool allows us to accomplish this with relative ease.

√ **To Enter Text in the Drawing Area**

▶ Position the mouse cursor over the Text icon (the second icon from the top in the right-hand column of the Toolbox).

▶ Click the left mouse button to activate the Text tool.

▶ Position the mouse cursor at coordinates 150, 80.

▶ Click the left mouse button.

▶ Type **Wonderful Widgets, Inc.**

Don't click the left mouse button at this point. I will explain the reasons behind my issuing this caution shortly. Your screen should now resemble Figure 9.4, which shows the name of our imaginary company added to the Paintbrush drawing area.

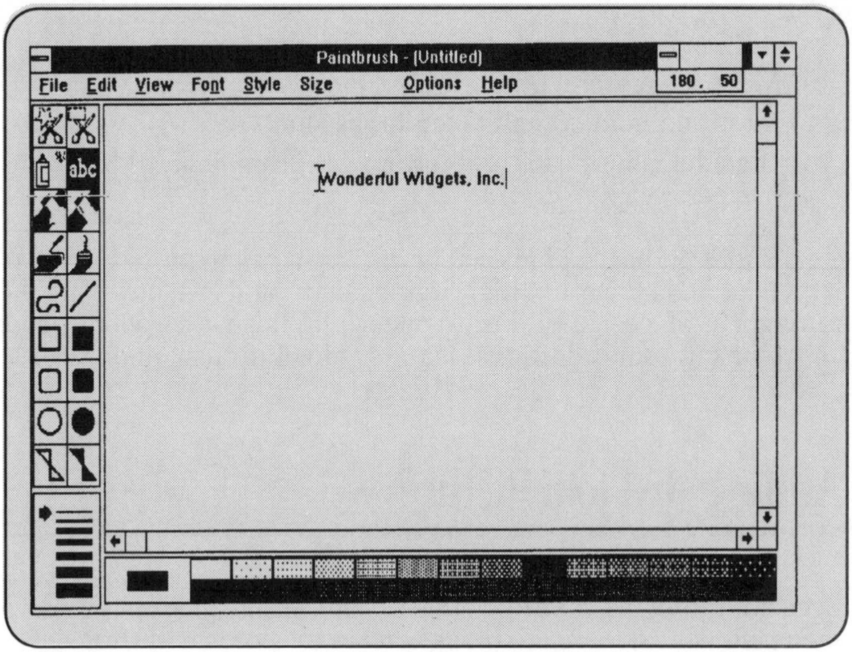

Figure 9.4. Use the Text tool to include text in a Paintbrush graphic.

190

Changing Text Attributes

The company's name is there, to be sure. But it's not very dramatic, is it? I can't imagine many people going out of their way to read a piece of paper topped by such a mundane letterhead. Let's add a little spice to our corporate name by using a different kind of lettering. We'll begin by making our text a little larger.

√ To Change the Size of the Current Text

► Choose Size from the Paintbrush menu bar.

► Choose 24.

That looks better. The larger type is more apt to attract someone's attention. It's still rather uninspiring, though, isn't it? Let's try using a different *font*, or lettering design, for the company's name.

√ To Select a Different Font

▶ Choose Font from the Paintbrush menu bar.

▶ Choose Roman.

Now we're getting close. The Roman font is certainly fancier than Paintbrush's default System lettering. It adds a little class to our letterhead. As my father used to say, however: "Close only counts in horseshoes and hand grenades." Something's still missing. What we need is some style. Talk about a coincidence, there just happens to be a Style option on the Paintbrush menu bar. Let's see what options this menu includes.

√ To Add "Style" to Your Text

▶ Choose Style from the Paintbrush menu bar.

This displays the Style menu shown in Figure 9.5. Use the Style menu to specify any visual enhancements (boldface, underline, italics, and the like) you want applied to your Paintbrush text. Let's pick several of these and really "gussy up" our corporate logo.

191

√ To Enhance the Corporate Logo

▶ Choose Bold.

▶ Choose Style.

▶ Choose Italic.

▶ Choose Style.

▶ Choose Underline.

Your display should now resemble Figure 9.6, which shows how Paintbrush has modified the appearance of the company logo, based on the Style options you specified. Now we have the beginnings of an attractive letterhead.

I should explain the caution I issued earlier. Changing size, font, and style attributes affects only the current text, which Paintbrush defines as any letters entered prior to the last time you used the mouse cursor to select a text input location. If you had clicked the left mouse button earlier, the new values we've selected here would not have been applied to our Wonderful Widgets logo.

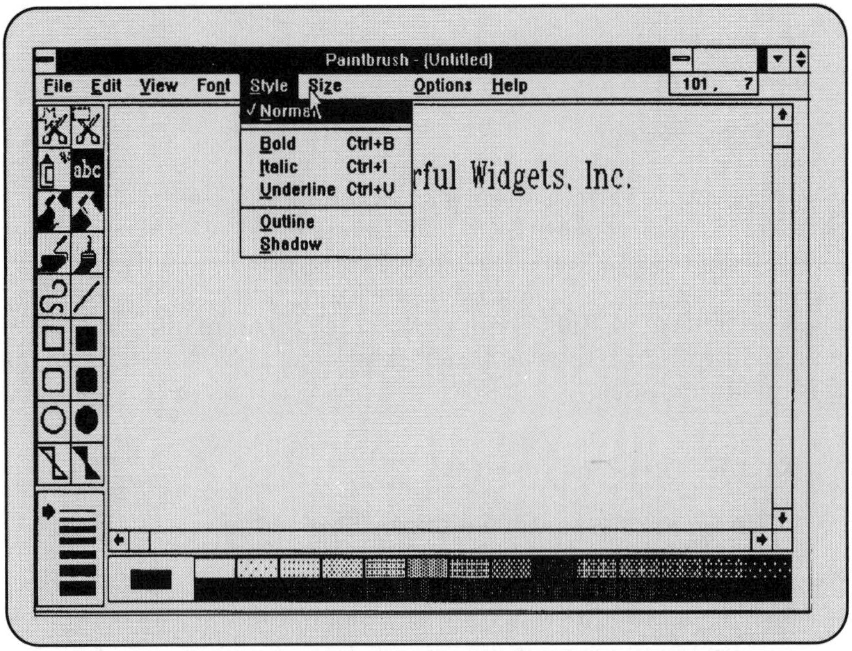

Figure 9.5. The Style options allow you to enhance the appearance of text in a Paintbrush file.

Figure 9.6. Style attributes are applied immediately to the current text.

Additionally, any subsequent text you enter at this time will be printed in the current type style, unless and until you use the various Paintbrush menu options to once again modify the font attributes. Before we go much further, let's return the Size, Font, and Style options back to some less ostentatious settings.

√ **To Reset Text Values for Subsequent Input**

► Click the left mouse button to "deactivate" the current text.

► Choose Size.

► Choose 12.

► Choose Font.

► Choose System.

► Choose Style.

► Choose Normal.

193

► **Tip:** Choosing Normal from the Style menu automatically removes any font enhancements currently in effect—in this case, Bold, Italic, and Underline.

Now that we're on a roll, let's fill in the rest of the address that we want to include in the company letterhead.

√ **To Add an Address to the Company Letterhead**

► Position the mouse cursor at coordinates 235, 75.

► Click the left mouse button.

► Type **4321 Corporate Drive** and press Enter.

► Type **New York, NY 10012** and press Enter.

► Press Spacebar five times.

► Type **(212) 555-1234** and press Enter.

When you've finished, your display should resemble Figure 9.7, which shows address information added to the previous screen. The only element missing from our letterhead now is some type of graphic that will draw the reader's attention to the stationery and, therefore, whatever message it contains. Before doing so, however, let's relocate our letterhead address to make room for this graphic.

Figure 9.7. Paintbrush's System font works well for standard text.

Using the Cutout Tools

Use the Paintbrush cutout tools to select a segment of the drawing area for additional processing. The two available cutout tools include:

Scissors   Selects an irregularly shaped section of the Paintbrush display.

Pick   Selects a square or rectangular shaped section of the Paintbrush display.

After defining a cutout, you can use commands from the Edit menu to cut, copy, paste, and save the cutout section. Options in the Pick menu can also be applied to cutout sections. We won't be doing anything quite this fancy. Instead, we'll use the Pick tool to select and then move our address information to a different location within the drawing area.

√ **To Move the Address Information**

▶ Position the mouse cursor over the Pick icon (the first icon on the right-hand column of the Toolbox).

▶ Click the left mouse button to activate the Pick tool.

▶ Position the crosshair just above and to the left of your address block (at about coordinates 135, 60).

▶ Press and hold down the left mouse button.

▶ Drag diagonally across the address until it is entirely surrounded by a dotted line.

▶ Release the left mouse button.

▶ Position the mouse cursor within the address block.

▶ Press and hold down the left mouse button.

▶ Drag the mouse cursor to coordinates 275, 170.

▶ Release the left mouse button.

This moves the selected cutout to a new location lower on the screen, thus freeing up space on top of our address information for a graphic image.

195

Mixing Text and Graphics

Because no one really knows what a widget looks like, I can design and draw any graphic I please to complement the letterhead address. I plan to keep this simple. (Be grateful for small favors; my artistic talents rank right up there with that of an average two-year-old.) Before starting, let's do two things:

▶ Reduce the Linesize back to a more manageable width.

▶ Save the address information to a Paintbrush file in order to protect the work we've done so far.

√ **To Decrease the Linesize**

▶ Move your mouse until the mouse cursor is pointing to the second line in the Linesize box.

▶ Click the left mouse button to select the thinner Linesize.

√ To Save the Address Information to a Disk File

▶ Choose File from the Paintbrush menu bar.

▶ Choose Save As.

▶ At the Save As dialog box, type **WINBOOK\LOGO** and press Enter.

Now we're ready to create our graphic—a nice, simple image, the primary purpose of which is to represent our imaginary widget. (Pay attention here because I'm gonna move fast.)

√ To Draw a Widget

▶ Position the mouse cursor over the Filled Rounded Box icon (the third icon from the bottom in the right-hand column of the Toolbox).

▶ Click the left mouse button to activate the Filled Rounded Box tool.

▶ Position the mouse cursor at coordinates 240, 70.

▶ Press and hold down the left mouse button.

▶ Drag the mouse cursor to coordinates 310, 110.

▶ Release the mouse button.

▶ Position the mouse cursor over the Line icon (the fourth icon from the top in the right-hand column of the Toolbox).

▶ Click the left mouse button to activate the Line tool.

▶ Position the mouse cursor at coordinates 230, 120.

▶ Press and hold down the left mouse button.

▶ Drag the mouse cursor to coordinates 325, 60.

▶ Release the mouse button.

When you've completed these steps, your screen will resemble Figure 9.8, which now contains an admittedly primitive image of a widget above our address information.

That's all there is to it. We've now designed a corporate logo and company letterhead for the Wonderful Widgets company. Before quitting Paintbrush, you'll want to save this image because we'll be using it in a later chapter.

√ To Save the Current Image

▶ Choose File from the Paintbrush menu bar.

▶ Choose Save.

196

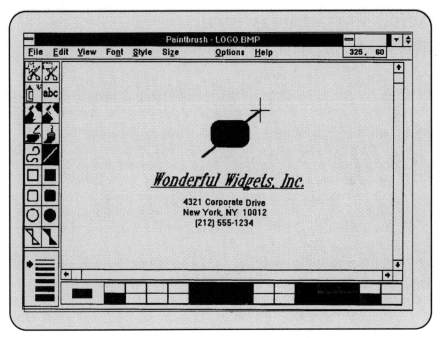

Figure 9.8. You can use the various Paintbrush tools to create graphic images as simple or complex as the situation demands.

Now we're ready to close down Paintbrush and end this chapter.

Quitting Paintbrush

√ To Quit Paintbrush

▶ Choose File from the Paintbrush menu bar.

▶ Choose Exit.

Because you just saved your most recent activity to a disk file, Paintbrush bypasses the cautionary prompt box encountered in earlier chapters and immediately returns you to the Windows Program Manager.

197

What You Have Learned

▶ Paintbrush is the Windows graphics program. Using Paint-brush, you can create pictures consisting of geometric shapes, freehand drawings, and other graphic images.

▶ Paintbrush provides several drawing tools to simplify the process of designing and creating your graphic images. With these tools you can quickly draw circles, boxes, rectangles, and even irregular polygons, all with a few simple mouse movements. These geometric shapes—or tools, as they are called in the Paintbrush vernacular—can then be enhanced using additional Paintbrush features such as color and fill patterns.

▶ Paintbrush includes a Text tool that allows you to enter text in the drawing area. These text passages can be printed in a variety of type sizes and font attributes to add emphasis to your Paintbrush graphics.

198

Chapter 10

Terminal

In This Chapter

▶ *A definition of telecommunications*
▶ *How to configure the Windows Terminal application to run properly on your PC system*
▶ *How to use Terminal*

What Is Telecommunications?

I love telecommunications. I could ramble on for pages about the enjoyment inherent in telecommunications—that is, the process of using my PC, a modem, and telecommunications software to hook my PC up with another computer anywhere in the world, at virtually any time of the day or night. In fact, I write two monthly columns on telecommunications for two computer magazines in which I do discuss the value of telecommunications. Of all the PC applications I work with, telecommunications is my hands-down favorite. Furthermore, I'm not alone in my excitement.

How popular is telecommunications? Popular enough that CompuServe, only one of more than a dozen on-line information services currently doing business in this country, claims over

500,000 subscribers. (An *on-line information service* is a clearing house of sorts that dispenses a variety of telecommunications-related services to its subscribers.) That I and my fellow PC enthusiasts are hooked on telecommunications should be obvious. But what exactly is telecommunications? How does telecommunications work? What will the ability to telecommunicate allow you to accomplish? And, perhaps most important, what will you need to do, should you decide to use Terminal, the Windows telecommunications accessory?

A Telecommunications Primer

I'm not going to let this discussion get very complex. Several well-written books explain telecommunications in much more detail than I have the luxury of going into here. (Not ironically, I wrote a couple of these books.) Consequently, we'll keep this overview of telecommunications relatively simple.

I offered a fundamental definition of telecommunications in my introduction to this chapter. Specifically, telecommunications is the process of using your PC, a modem, and special software to communicate with another, similarly equipped computer, over standard telephone lines. Get it? Telephone communications between two computers. Telecommunications.

Beyond this simple definition, many technical considerations come into play, if and when you decide to use your PC to access another computer in a different location. (As you'll soon see, however, the Windows Terminal accessory virtually eliminates the need to worry about such minutia.) That explains what telecommunications is. Next, let's address how telecommunications does this. To understand that, you'll need to know a little about one specific piece of PC hardware: a *modem*.

The word "modem" is derived from the expression modulate/demodulate, which is precisely what a modem does. At one end of the telecommunications link, it *modulates* the digital signals a computer generates into analog tones compatible with a standard telephone line. Conversely, on the other end of this link, a modem *demodulates* the analog tones transmitted over a standard telephone line into the digital signals your computer requires to work properly. The electronic principles governing how this occurs are complex but, within the parameters of our current discussion, unimportant.

What is significant is that this series of events must happen, if two computers are to be able to communicate successfully with one another over a telephone hookup. You must have a modem to use the Windows Terminal application. If you don't own a modem, you may want to skip ahead to the next chapter. If your PC system does include a modem, however, read on. Because the next thing you'll learn is what that modem—and, by extension, the telecommunications capabilities that modem supports—will allow you to do, the third point I promised we'd get into.

Quite simply, telecommunications allows you to electronically explore the world, without ever leaving the confines and comfort of your own home or office. Once you attach a modem to your PC, that modem becomes a gateway to virtually anywhere in the world— from Miami to Moscow, Newark to Nepal, Washington to Warsaw. Ignoring for a moment the expense of long-distance telephone charges, miles mean nothing to someone who is telecommunicating. Your PC can be hooked up to a computer next door or to one on the next continent. You won't know the difference. Furthermore, aside from adding the few extra numbers required to dial into a foreign exchange, making an international connection is no more difficult than getting in touch with someone on the next block. And once you make that connection, the types of on-line activities you can perform are similarly diverse.

201

Sending and receiving electronic mail, transferring files, researching arcane information, conferring with other PC users who share your interests, shopping for a new car or computer, even playing games—these represent but a few of the activities you'll be able to participate in, once you've learned how to use Terminal. You can pursue these activities at your convenience, any time of the day or night. You see, your computer is as ignorant of minutes as it is of miles. I've run across European callers using the various on-line services to which I subscribe at three or four o'clock in the morning, my time—which only makes sense, because it was late afternoon or early evening in their part of the world. From this perspective, telecommunications has helped shrink the world, to bring us all a little closer.

That, in a nutshell, is what telecommunicating is all about. And Terminal, the Windows' application that we'll concentrate on for the remainder of this chapter, is designed to help you telecommunicate. So, let's get started. After all, there's a whole world out there waiting for you.

Starting Terminal

I knew we wouldn't be combining your on-line activities with any other exercises in this book, so I did not have you incorporate Terminal into the Book Exercises program group. Consequently, you'll need to access the Accessories program group before you'll be able to start Terminal. One of the quickest and easiest ways to accomplish this is with the Cascade command.

√ To Rearrange Your Program Manager Display

▶ Choose Window from the Book Exercises menu bar.

▶ Choose Cascade.

202

Windows automatically rearranges all windows currently active in Program Manager. In the process, the Book Exercises window is reduced from its previous full-screen display to a size that leaves portions of the other active windows unobscured.

√ To Switch to the Accessories Window

▶ Position the mouse cursor on any visible portion of the Accessories window.

▶ Click the left mouse button.

The Terminal icon, a picture of a PC with a telephone in front of it, should be visible within the Accessories window.

√ To Start Terminal

▶ Double-click on the Terminal icon.

If this is the first time you've started Terminal, Windows will need to request a critical piece of information about how your hardware is configured for telecommunications. Specifically, Windows needs to know the serial port (COM port) to which your modem is attached, as shown in Figure 10.1.

√ To Specify a Serial Port for Your Modem Operations

▶ Choose the COM number corresponding with the serial port to which your modem is attached

▶ Choose OK or press Enter.

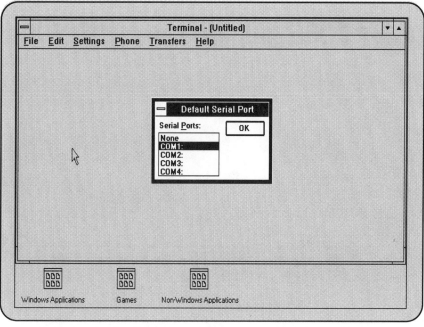

Figure 10.1. The first time you start Terminal, you'll need to tell Windows about your hardware setup.

▶ **Tip:** Unless you know differently, it's safe to assume your modem is attached to COM1, the first serial port installed on your PC. If you are unsure of your modem port, take the necessary steps to find out. Terminal will not work properly if you specify an incorrect COM port with this dialog box.

After specifying your modem port, you will be advanced to the main Terminal screen, which is shown in Figure 10.2.

Before outlining the steps required to have Terminal connect your PC to another computer, we need to discuss how you set up Terminal for a given on-line session, beginning with how the two computers involved will communicate with one another.

203

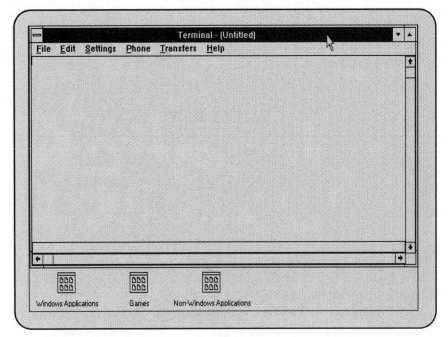

Figure 10.2. The Terminal screen.

204

Setting Communication Parameters with Terminal

For telecommunications to be successful, both computers involved in an on-line session must speak the same "language." Think of this as resembling normal, human conversations, wherein two people generally use a single language (for example, English) in order to communicate with one another. When working with a modem, this language consists of several special settings called *communication parameters*. Communication parameters determine how Terminal formats your data prior to transmitting it across the phone line.

The communication parameters you must be aware of to configure Terminal properly for telecommunications include:

Baud Rate This is the transmission rate at which your computer sends and receives information during a Terminal session. You can set Terminal to operate at any one of several popular baud rates, including 110, 300, 600,

> ▶ **Note:** Some of the terms that follow may seem somewhat confusing at this point in your telecommunications career. (And, in truth, several of them do represent fairly technical concepts.) Don't worry about this. Although understanding precisely what each setting accomplishes helps you comprehend exactly how telecommunications works, it's not a prerequisite to using Terminal. What is critical is realizing that these settings must be configured properly for your PC to communicate with another computer.

	1200, 2400, 4800, 9600, and 19,200 baud. The type of modem you have will determine which baud rates you can use.
Data Bits	This setting represents the number of *bits* (BInary digITS, the individual 0 and 1 settings stored in memory) used to send a single character during a Terminal session. Terminal supports five word-length settings, ranging from 4 to 8 bits.
Stop Bits	This setting specifies the number of bits Terminal will append to the end of each character to indicate that the entire character has been transmitted. Terminal allows you to choose between using 1, 1.5, or 2 stop bits.
Parity	This determines how the receiving computer verifies the accuracy of any data you transmit during a Terminal session. Available parity settings supported by Terminal include None, Odd, Even, Mark, and Space.
Flow Control	This setting determines how your PC and the remote computer will coordinate data transfers—that is, how one computer will know when the other computer is waiting for data and vice versa.
Parity Check	Activate this setting if you want Terminal to display the byte in which any parity check errors are encountered. Normally, you'll leave the Parity Check option inactive.
Carrier Detect	How you set this option depends largely on what type of modem you have. If your modem is 100% Hayes-compatible—that is,

205

it fully emulates modems manufactured by the Hayes Corporation, the closest thing to a modem standard in the PC marketplace— you should turn Carrier Detect (CD) on. This tells Terminal to use your modem's internal electronics to determine when a connection is made. If you have trouble making connections and have checked to see that all other Terminal settings are correct, try disabling CD. This tells Terminal to bypass a modem's CD circuitry and use its own internal methods for detecting a carrier signal.

Individual settings for these parameters may vary, depending on the remote system you plan to contact during a given on-line session. The best rule of thumb I can give you as to how these settings should be configured for a specific on-line session is that they should match the parameters the computer you are connecting with uses to establish a connection over the telephone line.

206

Use the Communications dialog box to set the proper parameters for an on-line session.

√ To Access the Communications Dialog Box

▶ Choose Settings from the Terminal menu bar.

▶ Choose Communications.

This displays the Communications dialog box shown in Figure 10.3. The various options in this dialog box correspond to the parameter setting outlined in the previous section. Use the Communications dialog box to specify the appropriate parameters for the remote system you will be contacting with Terminal.

√ To Return to Terminal after Specifying the Appropriate Communication Parameters

▶ Press Enter or choose OK.

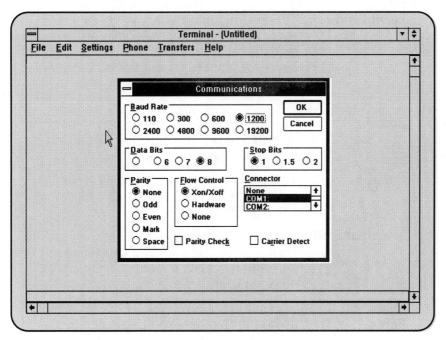

Figure 10.3. The Communications dialog box.

Setting Terminal Preferences

The parameters set in the previous section define how Terminal communicates with the outside world—that is, to whatever remote system you are connected. You can also specify the internal procedures Terminal should use during a communication session, how Terminal itself should handle any data exchanged between it and another computer during a remote session. In the Windows vernacular, these settings are called your *Terminal preferences*.

Terminal preferences you can specify include:

Line Wrap   Activating Line Wrap causes Terminal to automatically format incoming data to fit within the column width of your Terminal configuration. (See Columns box.)

207

208

Local Echo	This setting tells Terminal whether it should send any characters you type directly to your display monitor or allow the remote system to "echo" these characters back over the phone line after it has received them.
Sound	This setting activates or deactivates the system bell (or, more likely, beep) for the remote system.
Columns	This setting lets you specify whether Terminal should format your data for an 80- or 132-column display.
Terminal Font	This setting lets you select the display font Terminal should use. You can select any font that has been installed in your Windows environment.
Show Scroll Bars	This setting lets you tell Terminal whether it should display scroll bars. Displaying scroll bars simplifies the process of reviewing data that has already scrolled out of the Terminal display window.
CR to CR/LF	This setting tells Terminal whether it should add a line feed to each carriage return received from the remote system.
Cursor	Use this option to tell Windows what style of cursor you want displayed in your Terminal window.
Translation	You will need to use this option only if you plan to have Terminal connect with a remote system that uses a foreign language.
Buffer	Terminal uses a temporary storage area called a *buffer* to store incoming data. The Buffer option allows you to specify a size for this buffer, ranging from 25 to 400 lines of information. If you specify a buffer amount exceeding the amount of available memory, Terminal automatically reduces its buffer to an appropriate size.

Use the Terminal Preferences dialog box to specify settings for these items.

√ **To Access the Terminal Preferences Dialog Box**

▶ Choose Settings from the Terminal menu bar.

▶ Choose Terminal Preferences.

This displays the Terminal Preferences dialog box shown in Figure 10.4. The various options in this dialog box correspond to the parameter setting outlined in the previous section.

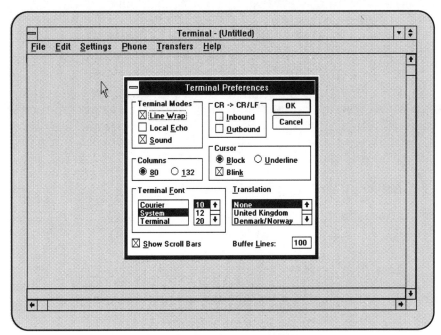

Figure 10.4. The Terminal Preferences dialog box.

209

√ **To Return to Terminal after Specifying Your Preferences**

▶ Press Enter or choose OK.

Specifying Terminal Emulation

All computers are not created equal. Not only are computers not equal, they also are not the same. Different systems use different standards to communicate with the outside world. I'm not discussing telecommunications between two computers here. Rather, I'm talking about the procedures a single computer employs to transmit instructions from a user to its central processing unit. Without getting too technical, this boils down to the type of terminal settings a specific computer recognizes.

> ▶ **Note:** In this context, the word "terminal" indicates the type of keyboard and display monitor a specific computer uses, as opposed to the Windows Terminal program.

210

For your PC to communicate successfully with another system, it must be able to emulate the type of terminal that system recognizes. Terminal (the Windows accessory) provides a simple method for specifying the type of terminal emulation you want in effect during an on-line session.

√ To Specify Terminal Emulation

▶ Choose Settings from the Terminal menu bar.

▶ Choose Terminal Emulation.

This displays the Terminal Emulation dialog box shown in Figure 10.5. Use this dialog box to specify the type of terminal (keyboard/display) Terminal (the Windows accessory) should emulate for a given system.

√ To Return to Terminal after Specifying the Appropriate Emulation

▶ Press Enter or choose OK.

> ▶ **Tip:** You have an emulation mismatch if the remote system does not respond to commands issued from your PC. As a rule, you should use DEC VT-100 (ANSI) emulation when connecting to a commercial on-line service or another PC. Many mainframe computers, on the other hand, used DEC VT-52 terminals. If all else fails, try TTY, the most generic emulation Terminal supports.

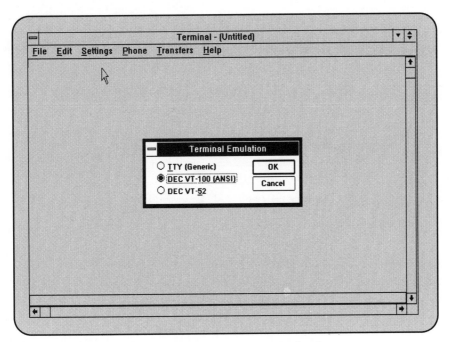

Figure 10.5. The Terminal Emulation dialog box.

Specifying a Phone Number

Of course, before Terminal can call a remote system, it needs to know the telephone number at which that system can be reached.

√ To Specify the Telephone Number of a Remote System

► Choose Settings from the Terminal menu bar.

► Choose Phone Number.

This displays the Phone Number dialog box shown in Figure 10.6. Use this dialog box to specify the phone number Terminal should use to connect with the remote system you want to call.

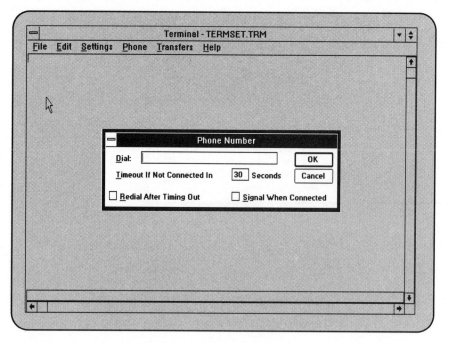

Figure 10.6. The Phone Number dialog box.

Additional information you can specify with the Phone Number dialog box includes:

Timeout	Use this field to specify the number of seconds you want Terminal to wait for a connection to be made successfully with the remote system.
Redial	Activating this option tells Terminal that, if no connection is made within the number of seconds specified in the Timeout field, it should automatically try to redial the number.
Signal When Connected	Activating this option tells Terminal to sound an audible tone once a connection is established.

√ **To Return to Terminal after Specifying These Items**

▶ Press Enter or choose OK.

212

Saving a Terminal Configuration

The good news is that, after your parameters and terminal options are set properly, you're ready to have Terminal call a remote system. The better news is that you don't need to repeat all these steps each time you want to make an on-line connection. Windows allows you to save the current settings to a disk file. Once this file exists, loading it back into memory automatically prepares Terminal to contact any system that uses the settings it contains.

√ To Save Your Current Terminal Settings to a Disk File

▶ Choose File from the Terminal menu bar.

▶ Choose Save As.

▶ Enter the name you want assigned to the current settings.

▶ Choose OK or press Enter.

213

> ▶ **Tip:** Whenever possible, select a filename that will indicate the task for which specific file settings are used. You might, for example, assign the filename CSERVE to a Terminal file containing the correct settings for connecting with CompuServe. Unless you specify a different file extension during the Save operations, Windows automatically assigns a TRM file extension to Terminal files.

Making a Connection with Terminal

Once you specify the proper settings for a given session—or, alternately, use the File Open command to load a disk file containing the appropriate settings into RAM—you're ready to begin telecommunicating. Do that by telling Terminal to dial the remote system.

√ To Dial a Remote System

▶ Choose Phone from the Terminal menu bar.

▶ Choose Dial.

Terminal dials the specified number, using the current communications settings. Notice that as Terminal performs the steps required to make this connection, the commands associated with those steps are displayed within the Terminal display, as illustrated in Figure 10.7.

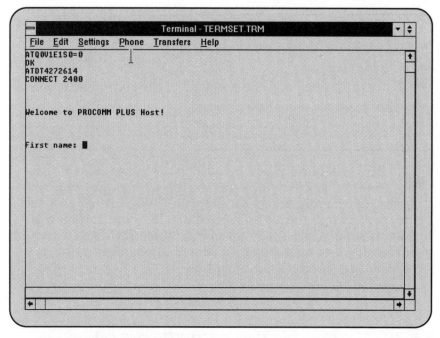

Figure 10.7. Terminal automatically performs all steps required to call the remote system.

What happens after Terminal makes a connection depends on the specific remote system you have called. Figure 10.7, for example, shows the sign-on prompt you would see if you called a PC that was running Procomm Plus in Host mode.

Each remote system you access with Terminal will use different procedures. For this reason, I'm not going to go any further on the system I called than this opening prompt. Instead, we'll use the Hangup command to drop this connection and return to the main Terminal display.

√ **To Disconnect Terminal from a Remote System**

▶ Choose Phone.

▶ Choose Hangup.

This causes Terminal to send a hangup string to your modem. As a result, Terminal drops the previous connection and returns to its standard display.

> ⊘ **Caution:** With certain on-line services, you must first sign off that system (using a command identified as Exit, Goodbye, or some similar option) before disconnecting the Terminal line, or they will continue to bill you for on-line time. Check to see if this is true of any services you use, before you issue a Hangup command to end a remote session.

215

Quitting Terminal

Now we're ready to quit Terminal and return to the Windows Program Manager.

√ **To Quit Terminal**

▶ Choose File from the Terminal menu bar.

▶ Choose Exit.

If you've saved your most recent Terminal settings to a disk file, Terminal immediately returns you to the Windows Program Manager. If your telecommunications configuration has changed since the last Save operation, Windows displays a cautionary prompt box asking whether you want to save the current settings before exiting Terminal.

√ **To Save the Current Settings**

▶ Choose Yes or press Enter.

This concludes our tour of the Windows Terminal accessory. Admittedly, we've only mentioned a few of Terminal's assets. The program includes enough features and functions to keep you excited about telecommunications for years to come. My main hope is that this chapter has communicated some of the reasons I personally find telecommunications to be such an exciting activity. Additionally, it's given you enough information to see how easy telecommunicating with Terminal can be.

What You Have Learned

216

▶ Telecommunications is the process of using your PC, a modem, and special software to communicate with another, similarly equipped computer, over standard telephone lines. Terminal is the Windows telecommunications accessory.

▶ You use interactive dialog boxes to configure Terminal to run properly with your PC hardware—specifically, your computer and modem. Additional dialog boxes allow you to set up Terminal to connect with a remote system, using the communication parameters that system requires to telecommunicate successfully.

▶ Terminal further simplifies telecommunications by allowing you to save specific communication settings to a disk file, which can then be reloaded into memory each time you want to contact the remote system to which those settings apply.

Chapter 11

Additional Windows Accessories

In This Chapter

▶ *A discussion of the remaining Windows accessories and how they are used*

▶ *How Recorder can be used to automate your Windows operations*

The Remaining Windows Accessories

We've accomplished much over the past few chapters. We've composed a letter with Write, started organizing an address file with Cardfile, created the beginnings of a time-management system with Calendar, designed a corporate logo with Paintbrush, and learned how to put your PC in touch with the rest of the world with Terminal. Certainly, the capability to do all of this, plus the advantages associated with working in a graphics-based operating environment, more than justify adding Windows to your PC arsenal. And we're not done yet!

Although you'll do most of your work with Write, Cardfile, Calendar, Paintbrush, and Terminal, Microsoft includes several other less powerful accessories in the basic Windows package. Call these additional items miniaccessories. The remaining Windows accessories include:

▶ Calculator.

▶ Clock.

▶ Notepad.

▶ Recorder.

▶ PIF Editor.

In this chapter we'll look briefly at each of these remaining accessories, and see how each works within the total Windows environment.

Calculator

218

As its name implies, the Windows Calculator is similar to the hand-held calculator many of us keep within arm's reach throughout the workday. Although hardly appropriate for pulling together an annual budget, the Windows Calculator is ideal for those types of quick-and-dirty calculations all of us have to perform with surprising regularity. (My own battery-powered, manual calculator—which I picked up for $6 at a local yard sale several years ago—has had so much use, half its keys are worn down to bare plastic.) Furthermore, because it's an integrated part of the Windows workspace, Calculator is always available—literally a keystroke away—at any time during a Windows session. Finally, you can use the Windows Clipboard to transfer the results of your calculations into other Windows applications.

Starting Calculator

Since we're currently sitting in the Accessories window, let's start Calculator from there.

√ **To Start Calculator**

▶ Double-click on the Calculator icon.

This displays the Windows Calculator, as shown in Figure 11.1. As you can see, the Windows Calculator resembles a credit card-sized calculator. Not surprisingly, it also works in much the same way.

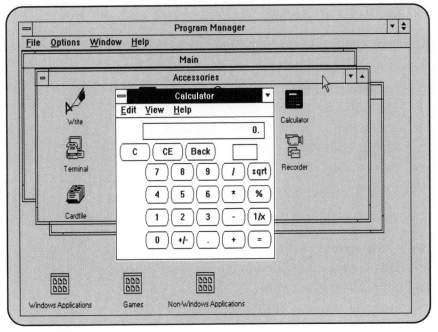

Figure 11.1. The Windows Calculator.

Using Calculator

To "push" a Calculator button, position the mouse cursor over that button and press the left mouse button. Calculator entries also can be made using either the row of number keys running horizontally across the top of your keyboard or the numeric keypad, which is probably located to the far-right of your keyboard.

> ▶ **Note:** If you plan to use your PC's numeric keypad, you must first activate Num Lock. Depending on what type of keyboard you have, this may be the default setting following system startup. Pressing a special key marked Num Lock toggles the keypad between its "normal" cursor control functions (the arrow keys, PgUp, PgDn, and so forth) and the ability to enter numeric values and perform mathematical operations (using 0–9, +, and –).

Calculator Functions

Calculator supports seven mathematical functions:

- ▶ Addition (+).
- ▶ Subtraction (–).
- ▶ Multiplication (* or x).
- ▶ Division (/).
- ▶ Square root (sqrt).
- ▶ Percentages (%).
- ▶ Reciprocal (1/x).

Additionally, Calculator supports four memory functions:

- ▶ Clear memory (MC).
- ▶ Display the current content of memory (MR).
- ▶ Store the current value in memory (MS).
- ▶ Add the current contents of memory (M+).

220

There are four remaining Calculator operations, each of which is performed by pressing the corresponding key icon on the Calculator display:

- ▶ Clear the current calculation (C).
- ▶ Clear the current entry (CE).
- ▶ Clear the rightmost digit of the current number (Back).
- ▶ Change the sign of the currently displayed number (+/–).

A Sample Calculator Session

Using Calculator is so straightforward, it really doesn't require any extensive explanation. Just to get your feet wet, however, let's calculate 12% of 260.

√ To Find a Percentage

- ▶ Type **260** (or, alternately, press these buttons with the mouse cursor).
- ▶ Choose – (the minus sign).
- ▶ Type **12** (or, alternately, press these buttons with the mouse cursor).

► Choose % (the percent sign).

► Press = (the equal sign).

When you have completed this simple calculation (260 minus 12% of 260), your screen should resemble Figure 11.2, which shows a result of 228.8 in the Calculator display. Using Calculator really is this easy; there's not much to it—unless you want more power.

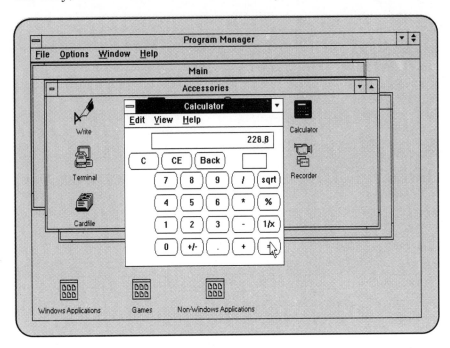

Figure 11.2. The Windows Calculator works much like a standard calculator.

Accessing the Scientific Calculator

In addition to simplifying the kinds of rudimentary mathematical operations listed earlier, Windows also responds to the needs of those people who look for real clout when performing calculations. It's hard to imagine a situation that could not be accommodated by Windows scientific calculator.

√ To Access the Scientific Calculator

► Choose View from the Calculator menu bar.

► Choose Scientific.

Selecting the Scientific view calls up the Windows scientific calculator, as shown in Figure 11.3.

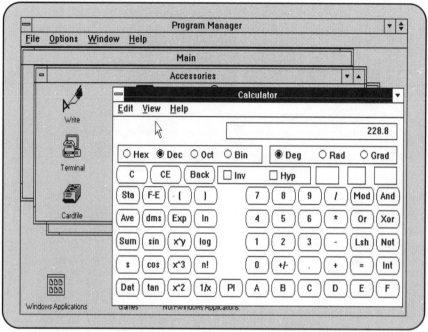

Figure 11.3. The Windows scientific calculator places true math power at your fingertips.

If you don't understand how a scientific calculator works, don't use it. If you do understand scientific calculations, on the other hand, then you certainly don't need any help from little, ol' math-anxiety-ridden me. So, let's get back to the standard calculator.

✓ To Return to the Standard Calculator

▶ Choose View from the Calculator menu bar.
▶ Choose Standard.

> ▶ **Note:** Windows preserves your previous calculations whenever you change calculator views, as a quick glance at Figure 11.3 discloses.

Now that I've diplomatically avoided having to reveal my total lack of math skills, let's tuck Calculator away and move on.

Exiting Calculator

You may have noticed that there is no File option on the Calculator menu bar. Up until now, we've always used an Exit command within the File menu to close the Windows accessories. So, are you stuck in Calculator? Of course not.

√ To Exit Calculator

▶ Position the mouse cursor over the Minimize box in the top-right corner of the Calculator window.

▶ Click the left mouse button.

223

> ▶ **Tip:** Exiting the Windows Calculator accessory is like turning off a traditional hand-held calculator. All previous work, including any values or calculations stored with the Calculator memory functions, will be lost. If you plan on incorporating the results of a Calculator session into work you'll perform in another Windows accessory, therefore, you should save that result to the Windows Clipboard before closing down Calculator. Clipboard is discussed in Chapter 12.

Clock

The Windows Clock accessory is...well...a clock. That really says it all. But let me show you what I mean.

√ To Display the Windows Clock

▶ Double-click on the Clock icon.

The first time you start Clock, it uses a traditional analog display format, as shown in Figure 11.4. About the only other feature associated with Clock is the option to change this display to a more modern, digital format.

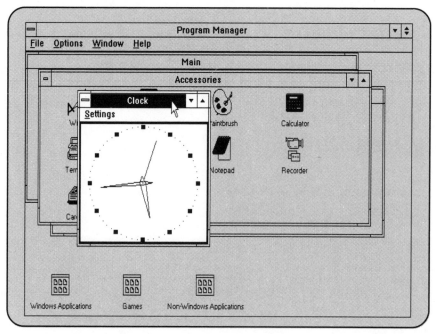

Figure 11.4. The first time you open Clock, it uses a traditional analog display.

√ **To Switch Clock to a Digital Display**

▶ Choose Settings from the Clock menu bar.
▶ Choose Digital.

The Clock display changes to a digital format, as shown in Figure 11.5.

Like any window, you can resize Clock so that it takes up minimal space on your display. If you want, therefore, you can place a small display containing Clock in a corner of your workspace for reference during your Windows session.

224

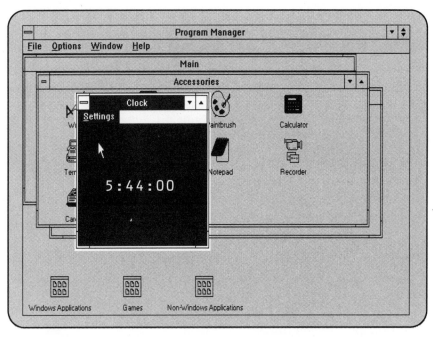

Figure 11.5. You can change your Clock display to a digital format.

√ To Exit Clock

▶ Position the mouse cursor over the Control menu in the top-left corner of the Clock window.

▶ Click Close.

▶ **Note:** Windows remembers the last Clock display option used. If you restart the Clock accessory now, for example, it would automatically open in digital mode.

Notepad

It helps to think of Notepad as resembling a "baby" Write. If you keep this comparison in mind, you should have no trouble understanding what Notepad is and how it's used. (For example, Notepad supports none of the advanced formatting features found in Write—you can't specify justification or use multiple fonts in a Notepad file.)

Like Clock, Notepad is exactly what its name implies: a simple notepad. This doesn't mean, however, that Notepad suffers from a lack of empirical uses. Whereas Write is appropriate for documents of almost any size, Notepad is more useful for jotting down short notes. Another task for which Notepad is ideally suited is creating and editing ASCII files, such as your CONFIG.SYS file and batch files. And there is one task at which Notepad excels, as you'll see a little later on in this section. Right now, though, let's get Notepad up and running in your Windows workspace.

Starting Notepad

226

√ **To Start Notepad**

▶ Double-click on the Notepad icon.

This calls up the opening Notepad screen shown in Figure 11.6. As was true in Write, Notepad initially presents you with an empty window, the electronic equivalent of a blank piece of paper.

Although admittedly less powerful than Write, Notepad does support several useful features. For starters, when you activate its Word Wrap feature, Notepad can automatically take words that will not fit within its document margins and move them down to the next line. Notepad also supports full search capabilities, but it does not include a find-and-replace feature. In addition to supporting the normal methods for marking text, a Select All command lets you quickly mark an entire Notepad document for additional processing. This last feature is especially useful when copying a Notepad document to the Windows Clipboard for subsequent transfer to another application. And then there's that task I mentioned earlier, the one at which Notepad excels—its ability to automatically maintain a log file of your activities.

Creating a Log File with Notepad

You can use Notepad to create a file that, each time it is opened, automatically appends the current time and date to its contents.

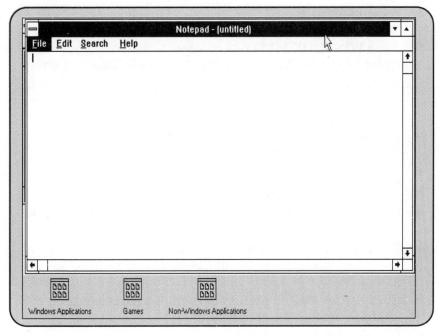

Figure 11.6. Starting Notepad is like sitting down with a blank piece of paper.

Used properly, this file represents the perfect tool for keeping track of what you are doing and when you are doing it.

✓ To Create a Notepad Log File

► Type **.LOG** and press Enter twice.

 Note: You must enter .LOG in capital letters for Notepad to recognize this as a time-log file.

Now, try the following experiment:

► Choose File from the Notepad menu bar.
► Choose Exit. Because you have not yet saved the current Notepad file to disk, Windows displays a prompt box asking whether it should save your changes.

▶ Press Enter or choose Yes. Windows displays a File Save As dialog box.

▶ Type **WINBOOK\MYLOG** and press Enter. Windows exits Notepad and returns you to the Accessories program group window.

Now, let's get really fancy:

▶ Position the mouse cursor over the Notepad icon in your Accessories program group.

▶ Press and hold down the Ctrl key.

▶ Press and hold down the left mouse button.

▶ Drag the mouse cursor to any visible portion of your Book Exercises program group window.

▶ Release Ctrl and the left mouse button. This adds a copy of the Notepad accessory to your Book Exercises program group.

228

▶ Click on any visible portion of the Book Exercises program group to make it the active window.

▶ Choose the Notepad icon.

▶ Choose File from the Program Manager menu bar.

▶ Choose Properties.

This displays the Program Item Properties dialog box shown in Figure 11.7. You can use this dialog box to customize the text associated with an on-screen icon and the command executed whenever that icon is selected.

√ **To Modify the Properties of the Current Notepad Icon**

▶ Press Backspace to erase Notepad from the Description prompt.

▶ Type **Activity Log**.

▶ Position the mouse cursor at the end of NOTEPAD.EXE in the Command Line prompt box.

▶ Press Spacebar.

▶ Type **C:\WIN3\WINBOOK\MYLOG.TXT**.

▶ **Note:** If you installed Windows in a location other than the WIN3 directory on drive C or are using a different directory for your book exercises, adjust the filename entered into the Command Line prompt accordingly.

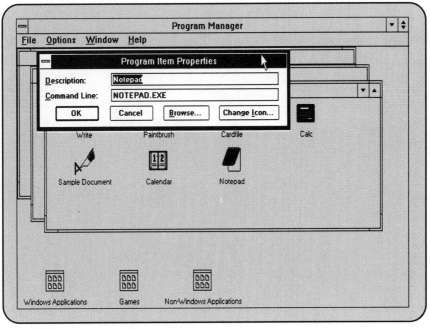

Figure 11.7. The Program Item Properties dialog box.

When you've finished, your screen should resemble Figure 11.8, which shows the specified information entered into the Program Item Properties dialog box.

√ To Complete This Exercise

▶ Choose OK or press Enter.

Your Book Exercises program group should now contain an icon marked Activity Log. Let's see what selecting this icon accomplishes.

√ To Open Your Activity Log

▶ Double-click on the Activity Log icon.

Windows starts Notepad and automatically opens your MYLOG file. Furthermore, because the MYLOG file begins with the .LOG command, Notepad appends the current time and date to the end of this file, as illustrated in Figure 11.9. Type an entry into MYLOG identifying whatever you were doing at the time it was opened and, voilà, you have an instant activity log.

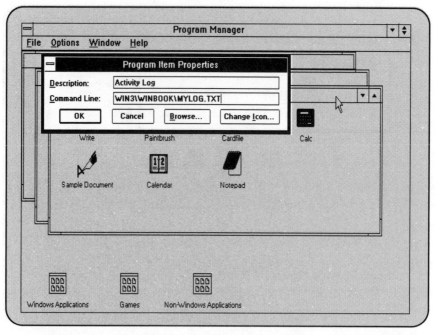

Figure 11.8. The File Properties option allows you to customize how Program Manager treats your on-screen icons.

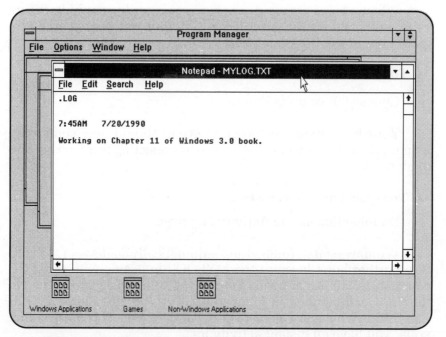

Figure 11.9. The .LOG command tells Notepad to enter the date and time in a file each time that file is opened.

> ▶ **Note:** Notepad reads the time and date from your system clock.

√ **To Close Your Time-Log File After Making an Activity Entry**

▶ Choose File from the Activity Log menu bar.

▶ Choose Exit.

▶ Choose Yes or press Enter when the Save current changes prompt appears,

Using Notepad in this way automates the process of keeping track of your activities, an especially useful feature for anyone who needs to document their time for customer billing, tax records, and so forth. But Windows can automate much more than a time log. In a modern twist on the old injunction, "Physician, heal thyself," you can tell Windows to automate virtually any of its operations, using another accessory, the Windows Macro Recorder.

231

Macro Recorder

In computer jargon, a *macro* is a series of keystrokes that has been assigned to a single command, keystroke, or key combination. Macros were first popularized in that granddaddy of all electronic spreadsheets, Lotus 1-2-3. Since then, companies have jumped on the macro bandwagon like lobbyists on a Congressional candidate. These days it's customary to incorporate a macro feature into almost all DOS programs. Windows proves no exception to this general rule.

The Windows Macro Recorder allows you to record a sequence of keystrokes and mouse actions for future use. Once a macro is recorded, it can be *played back*—that is, the keystrokes and commands it contains can be re-executed—at virtually any time during a Windows session. In this section, you'll create a simple macro, just to get a feel for how the Windows Recorder accessory works.

Starting Recorder

In order to record a macro for later play back, you first need to open the Recorder accessory.

✓ To Start the Recorder Accessory

▶ Position the mouse cursor on any visible portion of your Accessories program group.

▶ Click the left mouse button to bring the window forward.

▶ Double-click on the Recorder macro.

This opens an untitled Recorder window, as shown in Figure 11.10. Unlike other Windows applications, which display the actual keystrokes you enter, the Recorder window will contain only a listing of those macros you create and assign to a given Recorder file.

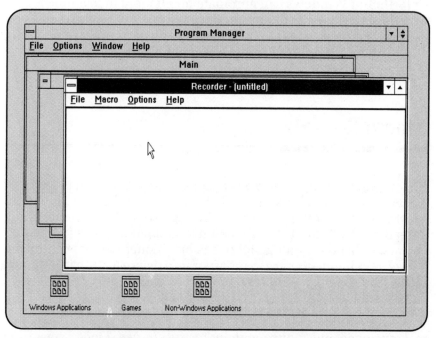

Figure 11.10. The Recorder window is used to display a listing of macros assigned to a given Recorder file.

Before creating a macro, however, let's open a Notepad window. You'll use this window in a few moments to enter the keystrokes our sample macro will contain.

√ To Open a Notepad Window

▶ Use the mouse to shrink the Recorder window to a small window near the bottom of the workspace.

▶ Position the mouse cursor on any visible portion of your Accessories program group.

▶ Click the left mouse button.

▶ Double-click on the Notepad icon.

Creating a Macro

Once the Notepad accessory is running and a Recorder window has been opened, you can start creating a new macro.

√ To Begin a New Macro

▶ Position the mouse cursor on any visible portion of your Recorder window and click the left mouse button.

▶ Choose Macro from the Recorder menu bar.

▶ Choose Record.

233

Whenever you create a new macro, Recorder displays the Record Macro dialog box shown in Figure 11.11. Use this dialog box to enter information about the new macro and how it will work.

√ To Tell Recorder About the Sample Macro

▶ Type **Name/Address** and press Tab.

▶ Type **Insert**.

▶ Choose the down arrow box next to the text Same Application in the Playback To: field.

▶ Choose Any Application.

▶ Choose the down arrow box next to the Record Mouse: field.

▶ Choose Ignore Mouse.

▶ Position the mouse cursor in the Description box and click the left mouse button.

▶ Type **Automatically enter name and address in any application**.

▶ Choose Start or press Enter.

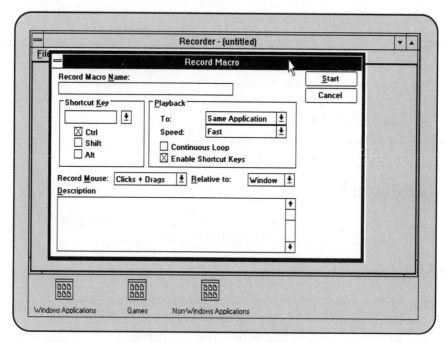

Figure 11.11. The Record Macro dialog box.

Windows closes the Recorder window and returns you to the Accessories program group. (Recorder is still running in the background.)

✓ To Enter the Actual Keystrokes That Will Comprise Your Macro

► Position the mouse cursor on any visible portion of the Notepad window and click the left mouse button. Windows makes the Notepad window active.

► Type in your name and address, using the format shown in Figure 11.12.

► Press Ctrl+Break to tell Windows that it should stop recording the current macro.

Windows displays the Recorder prompt box shown in Figure 11.13. Use this box to tell Windows what you want to do with the current macro.

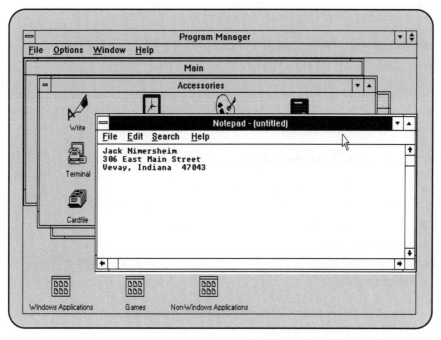

Figure 11.12. Enter your name and address for the sample macro.

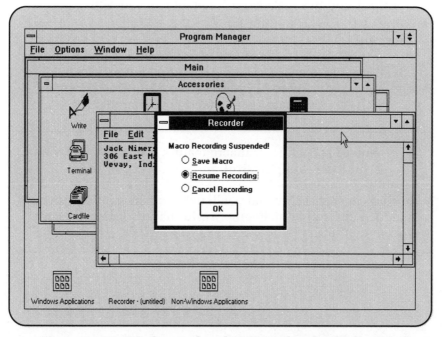

Figure 11.13. Windows asks what Recorder should do with the current macro keystrokes.

235

√ To Save Your Previous Keystrokes to a Macro

▶ Choose Save Macro.

▶ Choose OK or press Enter.

Windows stops recording your keystrokes and returns you to the untitled Notepad window. At this point, you can reopen the Recorder window and save this macro to a disk file.

√ To Save This Macro to a Disk File

▶ Position the mouse cursor on any visible portion of your Recorder window and click the left mouse button.

▶ Choose File from the Recorder menu bar.

▶ Choose Save.

▶ When the Save dialog box appears, type **MYMACS** and press Enter.

So, what happened? To answer that question, let's return to the untitled Notepad window.

▶ Position the mouse cursor on any visible portion of the Notepad window and click the left mouse button. Once again, Windows makes the Notepad window active.

▶ Press Ctrl+Ins (the Shortcut Key you assigned to your new macro).

If all went as planned, Windows should automatically enter a second copy of your name and address into the untitled Notepad file. Congratulations! You have just created your first macro.

> ▶ **Note:** The Windows macro feature is an extremely powerful tool—too powerful, in fact, for me to cover all its capabilities in this book. I simply wanted to introduce you to the Recorder accessory that you'll use to create macros for your Windows environment. For more information on how Recorder works, refer to the *Windows User's Guide*.

PIF Editor

There's one Windows accessory we haven't discussed yet, the PIF Editor. And guess what? I'm not going to discuss it now, beyond telling you that there will be times when you'll need to use the PIF Editor to create a special file containing information about how Windows should handle standard DOS programs—that is, application programs not designed to run exclusively under Windows. If you've glanced through the table of contents, you already know that we'll be discussing DOS in Chapter 14. Consequently, and given that we've already covered quite a bit of technical material in the last few pages, I'm going to wrap up this chapter and defer examining the PIF Editor until then.

What You Have Learned

237

- ▶ Rounding out your Windows package are several miniaccessories that can be used for a variety of special activities within a Windows session.
- ▶ The Windows Calculator can be used for simple mathematical operations. Alternately, Windows provides a scientific calculator option for complex computations.
- ▶ Notepad is a simple text editor, less powerful than the Windows Write accessory. One special feature of Notepad is that it can be used to create and maintain a time-log file of your activities.
- ▶ The Windows Recorder accessory can be used to record keystrokes, commands, and mouse operations for subsequent playback. The Recorder accessory resembles the macro feature included in many PC applications.

Chapter 12

Putting It All Together

In This Chapter

239

- ▶ *How to manage multiple Windows*
- ▶ *How to use the Windows Task List*
- ▶ *How to use the Windows Clipboard to transfer data between windows*

The Many Faces of Windows

Until now, all our discussions of Windows have involved a single application. We've seen how Write lets you compose documents, Cardfile allows you to manage information, Paintbrush allows you to create pretty pictures, and the like. But as I stated earlier, Windows is more than just a gathering of individual programs. It is a total, and totally integrated, operating environment that allows you to link the various Windows parts into a whole greater than the sum of its parts. In this chapter, we're going to examine some of the tools and features Windows provides to accomplish this.

Working With Multiple Windows

DOS is the operating system PC users love to hate. Although there are literally thousands of DOS programs currently available—programs that allow you to do everything from write a simple memo to project the annual operating budget of a multi-million dollar corporation—DOS handcuffs you by not allowing you to load more than one of these programs into memory concurrently. That's like buying a new house with dozens of big, bright, beautiful windows and then discovering that only one of them can be open at any given time. Under such conditions, your house would start to feel stuffy and cramped very quickly. And yet, millions of DOS users work under similarly cramped conditions almost daily. They keep trying to perform the many duties for which they are responsible with single-tasking DOS.

240

Windows eliminates this conflict by opening up stuffy old DOS to true multitasking. With Windows 3.0 running on your PC, each open window represents a different job that needs to be done and that can be done by running a different application or accessory or performing a different task.

This means you could, for example, prepare a letter announcing an upcoming price reduction in Write and have a Cardfile database containing the names and addresses of your important customers loaded in memory and available for reference, only a simple mouse click away. But rather than merely talk about Windows' multitasking capabilities, let's see how they work.

Write Revisited

In Chapter 6, you composed a letter announcing an upcoming price reduction to the Wonderful Widgets product line. At that time, I purposely omitted an opening section, the part of a letter that would normally contain the name and address of the company about to be offered this welcome relief. Finally, six chapters later, it's time to correct this oversight. We'll begin by reloading Write and calling up our sample letter, which we called SAVELET.

√ **To Load Write and a Document**

▶ Click on any visible portion of the Book Exercises program group to make it the active window.

▶ Double-click on the Write icon in the Book Exercises program group.

▶ Choose File from the Write menu bar.

▶ Choose Open.

▶ Double-click on the WINBOOK directory in the Directory area of the subsequent File Open dialog box.

▶ Double-click on SAVELET.WRI when this filename appears in the Files section of the File Open dialog box.

▶ Position the mouse cursor on the title bar of the Write window.

▶ Press and hold the left mouse button and drag the Write window down toward the bottom of your screen until the title bar of the Program Manager window is visible.

241

This starts Write and loads the SAVELET letter. Although informative, this letter currently looks pretty boring. Let's dress it up a little by adding a company logo and mailing address. In essence, we're going to transform our simple page of text into an impressive announcement on official letterhead.

On our way from here to there, we're going to introduce a couple of Windows features you've not yet encountered.

Preparing to Multitask

At this point, you should have a Write window that covers almost your entire workspace. Because we'll be opening multiple accessory windows soon, it makes sense to rearrange the display somewhat, in order to make more items more accessible. Let's begin by limiting the Program Manager window to the left half of the workspace, as it was a little earlier in this book.

√ **To Reduce the Program Manager Window to Half-Screen Size**

▶ Position the mouse cursor on the title bar of the Write window.

▶ Press and hold the left mouse button and drag the Write
window down toward the bottom of your screen until the
title bar of the Program Manager window is visible.

▶ Position your mouse cursor in the Restore box in the
top-right corner of the Program Manager window (the small
box with two arrows in it).

▶ Click the left mouse button.

At this point, your display should resemble Figure 12.1, which
shows the Program Manager window in the left half of the workspace,
partially obscuring the Write window opened in the previous exercise.

242

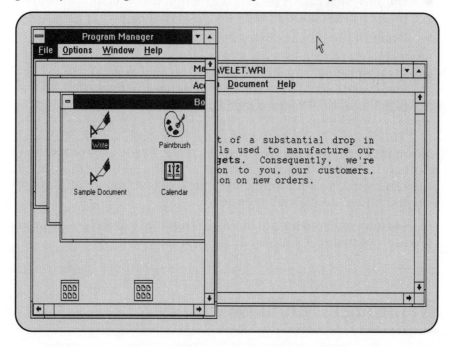

*Figure 12.1. You may find it convenient to rearrange your
workspace before opening multiple accessory windows.*

We're going to move quickly now as we open additional
accessory windows.

√ To Finish Setting Up Your Multitasking Workspace

▶ Double-click on the Paintbrush icon in the Book Exercises
program group.

▶ Choose File from the Paintbrush menu bar.

▶ Choose Open.

▶ Double-click on the WINBOOK directory in the Directory area of the subsequent File Open dialog box.

▶ Double-click on LOGO.BMP when this filename appears in the Files section of the File Open dialog box.

▶ Position your mouse cursor anywhere in the Program Manager box in the left half of your workspace.

▶ Click the left mouse button.

▶ Double-click on the Cardfile icon in the Book Exercises program group. (You may need to use the scroll bars to make this icon visible in the Program Manager window.)

▶ Choose File from the Cardfile menu bar.

▶ Choose Open.

▶ Double-click on the WINBOOK directory in the Directory area of the subsequent File Open dialog box.

▶ Double-click on PRACTICE.CRD when this filename appears in the Files section of the File Open dialog box.

243

Your workspace should now resemble Figure 12.2. Pretty crowded, isn't it—what with three accessory windows and all those icons associated with the Windows Program Manager still there? No problem. We can temporarily set aside the Program Manager window.

Minimizing Program Manager

We've been working almost exclusively in Program Manager since Chapter 5 of this book. Now that we've opened the accessory windows we'll need, let's temporarily set aside Program Manager by minimizing it to a workspace icon.

√ **To Minimize Program Manager**

▶ Position your mouse cursor in the Minimize box in the top-right corner of the Program Manager window (the small box with an arrow pointing downward).

▶ Click the left mouse button.

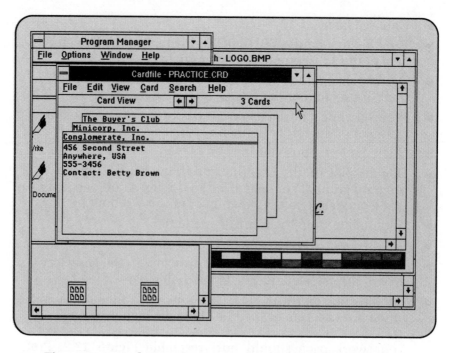

Figure 12.2. A cluttered screen can sometimes be confusing.

At this point, your display should resemble Figure 12.3 in which the Program Manager window has been reduced to a program icon at the bottom of the Windows workspace. Notice, however, that the individual accessory windows remain accessible. That's good because we're about to access them.

The Windows Task List

One problem associated with having multiple windows open concurrently is that some of them may, at times, be completely obscured. Because the normal procedure for making a window active is to click on a visible portion of that window, this could present a problem. It could, but it doesn't. The Windows Task List provides a convenient method for switching between open windows (tasks), regardless of whether they are currently visible within your workspace. To show you what I mean, try the following experiment:

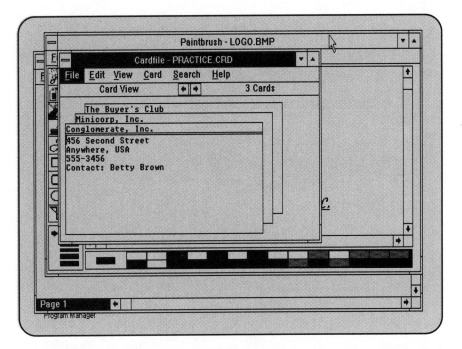

Figure 12.3. Reducing Program Manager to an icon clears up this confusion.

▶ Click on the Maximize box of your Write window (the small box with an arrow pointing upward in the right-hand portion of the Write title bar).

This causes your Write window (which, through no small coincidence, contains the sample letter we wrote earlier) to fill the entire workspace. So, how would you access Paintbrush if you needed to? You could reduce the Write window again, but this may be more trouble than it's worth. Instead, why not use the Windows Task List?

√ **To Access the Windows Task List**

▶ Choose the Control menu box of the Write window (the small box on the extreme left of the Write title bar).

▶ Choose Switch To.

This displays the Task List dialog box shown in Figure 12.4. Notice that this box lists all of the windows (tasks) that are open in the current session. As you've probably already guessed, accessing a different window is a simple matter of double-clicking on its corresponding task name.

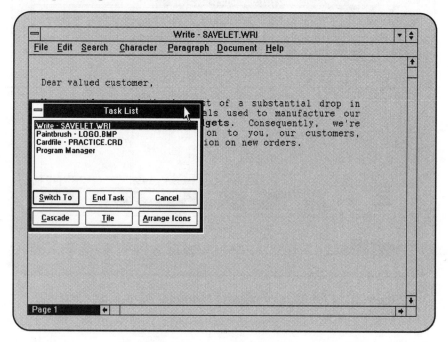

Figure 12.4. The Task List provides a convenient way to switch between windows in a complex workspace.

✓ To Access the Sample Memo

▶ Double-click on Paintbrush - LOGO.BMP.

This makes the Paintbrush window active and brings it back to the front of your workspace. Now that we're at Paintbrush, let's start pursuing some of that gestalt I mentioned earlier in this book.

> ▶ **Tip:** You may have noticed that Ctrl+Esc is listed on the Control menu as an alternate method for accessing the Task List. Depending on what you're doing at the time, you may find this keyboard shortcut even more convenient to use than choosing Switch To from the Control menu, as we did in the previous exercise.

Using the Windows Clipboard

If you've ever tried to take data created in one DOS program and transfer it to another DOS program, you'll quickly learn to love the Windows Clipboard. With Clipboard, exchanging data between two programs running in a Windows session is not only possible, it's virtually painless. In fact, using Clipboard is not that different from using the cut-and-paste feature found in many word processing programs. Again, however, rather than just talking about how easy a Windows feature is to use, let me show you.

Copying Items to the Clipboard

We'll begin by taking that corporate logo we created in Chapter 9 and copying it to Clipboard.

247

√ **To Copy Part of a File into the Clipboard**

▶ Click on the Maximize box of your Paintbrush window (the small box with an arrow pointing upward in the right-hand portion of the Paintbrush title bar).

▶ Choose the Pick tool (the top icon in the right-hand column of the Toolbox).

▶ Choose View from the Paintbrush menu bar.

▶ Choose Cursor Position.

▶ Position the mouse cursor at coordinates 100, 50.

▶ Press and hold the left mouse button.

▶ Drag the mouse cursor to coordinates 445, 220.

▶ Release the left mouse button.

This selects a rectangular section of your Paintbrush file, called a "cutout" in the Paintbrush vernacular, that includes the corporate logo created in Chapter 9. Once a cutout exists, you can copy it.

√ **To Copy a Cutout to the Clipboard**

▶ Select Edit from the Paintbrush menu bar.

▶ Select Copy.

It may look like nothing happened but, trust me, something did.To see what, let's return to our Write window.

√ To Switch to the Write Window

▶ Press Ctrl+Esc to display the Task List.

▶ Double-click on Write - SAVELET.WRI.

This redisplays the Write window containing our letter announcing the impending price reductions from Wonderful Widgets. Now, get ready to be impressed.

Pasting Items from the Clipboard into a Window

Use the Paste command to transfer items from the Clipboard into a second window. So, let's add that corporate logo to our sample letter.

248

√ To Paste a Graphic in Another Document

▶ Press Ctrl+Home to make sure the cursor is located at the beginning of the Write file.

▶ Choose Edit from the Write menu bar.

▶ Choose Paste.

Voilà! There's your corporate logo, sitting, if you'll forgive the pun, pretty as a picture at the top of our sample letter, as shown in Figure 12.5.

Things still don't look quite right. That corporate logo would look much better positioned in the middle of the page. Of course, I wouldn't suggest this if it weren't possible.

Moving Graphic Elements in a Write Document

To move an image in a Write file, you must first select that image. But there are no graphic tools in Write. So how do you accomplish this?

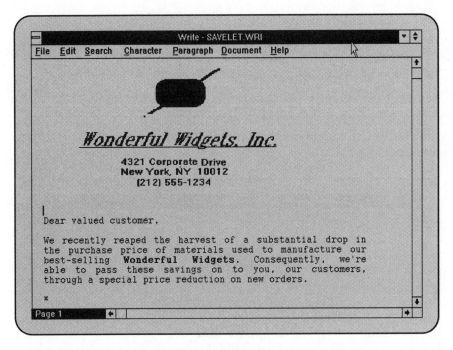

Figure 12.5. Objects in the Clipboard can be pasted into any Windows accessory.

✓ To Select the Logo Image

▶ Position the mouse cursor anywhere in the general vicinity of the logo or company address.

▶ Click the left mouse button.

That was simple, wasn't it. Placing the Write cursor within a graphic image selects that image for subsequent operations. Once you select an image, you can use the Move Picture command to move that image within your Write document.

✓ To Center the Logo in Your Write Document

▶ Choose Edit from the Write menu bar.

▶ Choose Move Picture.

▶ Slide your mouse to the right until the outline box identifying your Paintbrush image is centered on the Write text.

249

► Click the left mouse button.

► Position the mouse cursor before the word "Dear" in the salutation of our sample letter.

► Click the left mouse button.

Your display should now resemble Figure 12.6, which shows the Paintbrush image centered on the document text.within a Write document.

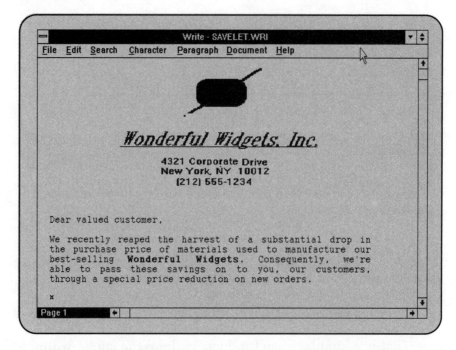

Figure 12.6. Selected images can be moved within a Write document.

The sample letter is beginning to shape up. About the only piece missing now is a mailing address, the specific customer to whom it will be sent. Adding this information will allow us to examine another way in which data can be exchanged between multiple applications running in a Windows session.

Marking and Copying Text to the Clipboard

Let's suppose you want to send this letter to Minicorp, Inc., one of the customers you entered earlier into the Cardfile database. Once again, we'll use the Task List to call up that accessory.

✓ To Switch from Write to Cardfile

▶ Press Ctrl+Esc to display the Task List.
▶ Double-click on Cardfile - PRACTICE.CRD.

This redisplays the Cardfile window containing the customer database records. Once this window is displayed, you can use Clipboard to mark and transfer text information from it to your Write document. Let's mark the address of Minicorp, Inc.

✓ To Mark an Address

▶ Position the mouse cursor on the Index line for the Minicorp, Inc. card.
▶ Click the left mouse button to bring this card to the front of the Cardfile display.
▶ Position the mouse cursor before the 1 in Minicorp's address line.
▶ Press and hold the left mouse button.
▶ Drag the mouse until the mouse cursor is sitting after the last number of Minicorp's ZIP Code, 10012.
▶ Release the mouse button.

251

This marks the specified block of text for further processing. As was true with Paintbrush, marked text in a Windows application can be copied to the Clipboard.

✓ To Copy Marked Text to the Clipboard

▶ Select Edit from the Cardfile menu bar.
▶ Select Copy.

Once again, the marked item—this time, the specified text from your Cardfile database record—is copied into Clipboard. All that remains now is to transfer this text into the sample letter.

Transferring Text from Clipboard

Before transferring Minicorp's address, you'll need to return to the Write file and prepare that letter for this information.

✓ To Return to Write and Prepare for the Text Transfer

▶ Position the mouse cursor before the word "Dear" in the salutation of our sample letter, which should be visible behind the Cardfile window.

▶ Click the left mouse button.

▶ Press Enter twice to insert two blank lines in the sample letter.

▶ Press Up Arrow twice to move the cursor up two lines.

▶ Type **Minicorp, Inc.**, and press Enter.

▶ Choose Edit from the Write menu bar.

▶ Choose Paste.

Windows automatically inserts Minicorp's address into the Write file. Before checking out one more Windows feature, let's save our polished letter as a new file and then clean up our desktop.

252

✓ To Save a Letter with a New Filename

▶ Choose File from the Write menu bar.

▶ Choose Save As.

▶ Press Backspace to remove the current filename when the File Save As dialog box appears.

▶ Type **SAMPLE.DOC** and press Enter.

Now that we have a new file containing our sample letter, let's close these accessories and return to the Program Manager.

✓ To Close the Open Windows

▶ Choose File from the Write menu bar.

▶ Choose Exit.

▶ Choose File from the Cardfile menu bar.

▶ Choose Exit.

▶ Choose File from the Paintbrush menu bar.

▶ Choose Exit.

 Tip: Double-clicking on the Control icon is an excellent shortcut for closing a window.

> ▶ **Note:** Although unlikely, it's possible that a file within one of these accessories was accidentally modified during the previous exercises. If this happens and Windows displays a caution box as you Exit a given accessory, simply respond No to the Save Changes prompt.

When all accessories are closed, your workspace will contain only the Program Manager icon we minimized earlier. Let's restore Program Manager to an active window.

✓ To Restore Program Manager to an Active Window

▶ Click on the Program Manager icon.

▶ Select Maximize from the subsequent Control menu.

This restores Program Manager to a full-screen window. Next, we're going to go all the way back to a special icon you created in Chapter 5 and see why we set it up as we did.

253

Automatically Loading Data Files with an Accessory

If you'll remember, the Sample Document icon in your Book Exercises is associated with both the Write accessory and a file named SAMPLE.DOC. Specifically, we entered the following Command line into the its Program Item Properties dialog box:

```
WRITE.EXE C:\WINDOWS\WINBOOK\SAMPLE.DOC
```

Associating a filename with a Windows program in this manner causes that file to be loaded automatically, each time its corresponding icon is selected.

✓ To Open Write and Automatically Load the Sample Document

▶ Double-click on the Sample Document icon in your Book Exercises program group.

A few seconds later and there it is—your polished letter, automatically loaded into Write and ready for further processing, as shown in Figure 12.7. Now we're talking fast, organized PC operations. And now you're getting a glimpse of the real power of Windows. But there's more to come. First, however, let's immediately close down our Sample Document window and get back to the basics of a workspace devoted to the Windows Program Manager.

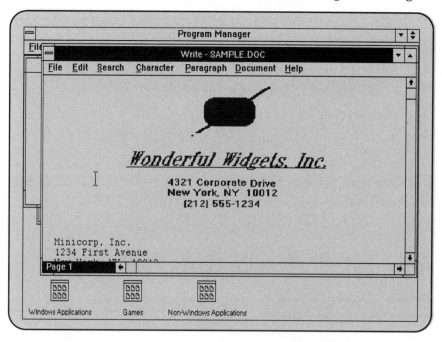

Figure 12.7. Organizing your Windows environment wisely can greatly improve the efficiency of your PC operations.

✓ To Close the Sample Document

▶ Choose File from the Write menu bar.

▶ Choose Exit.

This concludes our tour of Windows. Don't desert me yet, however. So far, we've looked only at Windows itself, the various features and accessories Microsoft includes with each copy of Windows it sells. Other companies also produce programs that are designed to take full advantage of the Windows GUI. Additionally, Windows is capable of helping you organize any standard DOS application programs you use. We'll look at these topics in Part Three, "Beyond Windows."

What You Have Learned

▶ Windows includes a number of special functions designed to allow its various applications to interact with one another. Chief among these is the Task List, which lets you switch quickly among several Windows programs running in a multitasking session.

▶ The Windows Clipboard lets you exchange data between different applications. Using the Clipboard, for example, you can incorporate Paintbrush graphics into a Write document. Once the image has been imported, Write allows you to modify that image's size and location to enhance your printed documents.

▶ You can set up special icons in Program Manager that not only run an application program but also automatically load a specified data file each time that icon is selected. This feature allows you to further automate your Windows-based operations.

255

256

Part Three

Beyond Windows

As mentioned several times throughout this book, the primary
function of the Windows GUI is to help you coordinate and manage
your PC activities. These activities can, and probably will, include
working in several application programs above and beyond the
various accessories shipped with the basic Windows package. In
this, the final part of *The First Book of Windows 3.0*, we'll examine
some of the alternatives available to you when you begin putting
together a comprehensive Windows environment. First, we'll review
several Windows-aware applications—that is, programs designed to
take full advantage of the Windows GUI. Finally, I'll provide information on how to run standard DOS applications—that is, programs
that do not directly support the Windows GUI—from within a
Windows session.

257

258

Chapter 13

A Windows Sampler

In This Chapter

▶ *A look at software that supports Windows*

▶ *How to install third-party software in your Windows environ-ment*

▶ *An overview of Windows-aware programs that are available in several different application areas*

Windows, Just the Beginning

As we've seen, Windows is a flexible yet friendly operating environ-ment. Furthermore, Microsoft did its best to help you become immediately productive in the Windows GUI by bundling several impressive miniprograms—Write, Cardfile, Calendar, and Termi-nal, to name but a few—with each copy of Windows it sells. In truth, you may find that the basic Windows package, as shipped by Microsoft, is all you'll ever need to turn your PC into the perfect productivity tool. Then again, you may not.

No PC program can be all things to all people; it's a fact of life. The key word in the phrase personal computer is "personal." My personal needs differ from your personal needs, and someone else's probably differ from both of ours. Luckily, Windows 3.0 has generated enough excitement within the PC community that everyone seems to be jumping on its bandwagon. Literally dozens of programs that are specially designed to take full advantage of the Windows GUI have been released. A partial listing of Windows-aware programs currently on the market include:

▶ Ami Professional (word processing).

▶ Microsoft Word for Windows (word processing).

▶ Micosoft Excel for Windows (electronic spreadsheet).

▶ Wingz (electronic spreadsheet).

▶ CrossTalk for Windows (telecommunications).

▶ DynaComm (telecommunications).

▶ Aldus PageMaker (desktop publishing).

▶ Ventura Publisher (desktop publishing).

▶ Corel Draw (graphics).

▶ Microsoft Project for Windows (project planning).

▶ PackRat (personal information manager).

▶ IBM Current (personal information manager).

▶ Grammatik for Windows (grammar and spell checker).

This represents only a few of the various third-party applications you can incorporate into your Windows environment. New names continue to be added to the list. Somewhere in this list—or perhaps among the scores of other Windows-aware programs out there—one almost certainly exists that's perfect for your personal situation.

Installing Programs for Windows

There is no universal way to install external programs into the Windows environment. As a rule, each program will include instructions on the procedures required for getting it up and running under Windows. Read these instructions carefully. With few exceptions, Windows applications cannot be installed by simply copying their files over to a hard disk directory. Quite often, a given program alters the WIN.INI initialization file to inform Windows of its presence and to establish certain operating parameters it needs to run properly within the Windows GUI. After performing the prescribed installation steps, it's a good idea to run the Setup accessory and use the Set Up Applications option to guarantee that your Windows environment recognizes the new program.

Product Profiles

For the remainder of this chapter, I'll profile some of the programs listed earlier, to give you an idea of just what's out there. Hopefully, the information contained in these product profiles will simplify the process of selecting the programs you want to include in your total Windows environment. To simplify matters even more, I've organized these product profiles by application type. If you're looking for a word processor, therefore, a quick look at the section on word processors should provide you with a basic idea of what options are available in this particular application genre.

261

> ▶ **Note:** New programs designed to take advantage of the Windows GUI are announced and released almost weekly. By definition, this chapter represents what's available; it is not a comprehensive compendium of the Windows software market. My goal is to hit the highlights. The basic information provided here, however, will help you know what to look for when you look for the Windows application best able to meet your personal needs. Also, the views and opinions expressed in this chapter are exclusively mine—and are admittedly subjective in nature.

Word Processors

Two programs, Microsoft Word for Windows and Ami Professional, entered the Windows word processing arena early and energetically. Each sports a list of features that should finally put to rest the ongoing debate of whether it's practical to process text in a graphics environment like Windows.

Both Word and Ami include an on-line spell checker and thesaurus, two items that are customary in today's word processing market. Each also includes a mail-merge module to simplify distributing your documents among a large audience, something lacking in the basic Windows package. Additional features common to both Word and Ami include context-sensitive help, automatic indexing, the ability to create easily a table of contents based on major document headings, multicolumn formatting, background printing, macro support, and rudimentary math functions, among others.

Ami Professional

Samna Corporation
5600 Glenridge Drive
Atlanta, GA 30342
(404) 851-0007
$495

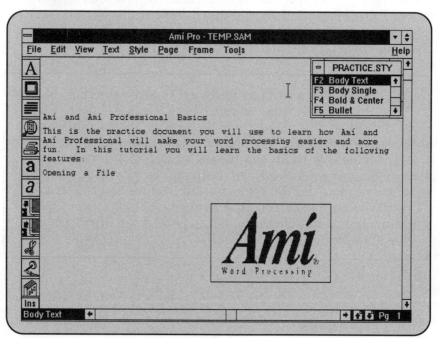

Figure 13.1. Ami Professional.

Ami straddles the fence separating word processing from desktop publishing (DTP) a little more comfortably than Word. It includes built-in Draw and Charting modules, two features Word lacks. While both programs import, size, and crop graphics, Ami also allows you to rotate any images you import into a document file. In fact, unless your printed pages tend to be complex, you may find that owning Ami eliminates the need to purchase a second, dedicated DTP package.

Operationally, Ami also resembles a desktop publishing program. As you enter text, your screen shows precisely how that text will appear as a printed document. Fonts, type styles, justification, line spacing, and margins, among other attributes, are accurately depicted on your display screen for you to review and adjust. A second way in which Ami resembles many desktop publishers is that it uses the paragraph as its basic formatting unit. You structure your document by assigning formatting characteristics to all the text in a given paragraph. Once your paragraph looks exactly as you want it to, you can assign a tag name to this basic design. From then on, any other paragraphs that you tag with this name will take on the same appearance. Of course, you can always alter the formatting characteristics of individual words or blocks of text within a given paragraph. For emphasis, you might elect to italicize a single word, for example. All tags for a given document can be saved to disk as a Style Sheet, which can in turn be used as the basic design for future projects.

263

If you've ever tried to mix text and graphics on the same page with a traditional, text-based DOS word processor, you'll quickly appreciate Ami's reliance on the Windows interface. Being in essence a graphics program itself, Ami handles graphics from other applications easily. Simply mark off the area in which you want your graphic to appear (called a *frame* in the Ami vernacular), select the Import File option, identify a file type, select a file, and it's done. A Graphics Scaling option allows you to size, crop, and even adjust the positioning of an image within its frame for greater visual impact. Ami Professional imports files in a number of graphic formats, including images in PC Paintbrush (PCX) format and scanned TIFF files. You can also use the Windows Clipboard to import graphics into an Ami document from virtually any other Windows application.

Microsoft Word for Windows

Microsoft Corporation
One Microsoft Way
Redmond, WA 98052
(206) 882-8080
$495

Word's text-editing features, on the other hand, are slightly more sophisticated than Ami's. Word, for example, allows redlining and document annotation, two popular editing tools missing from Ami

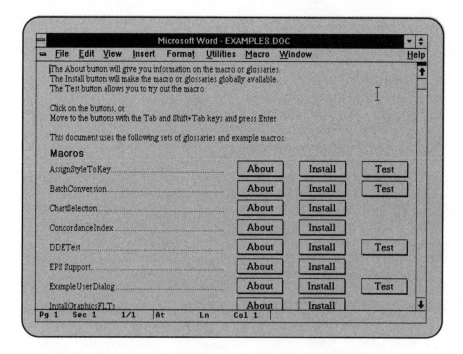

Figure 13.2. Microsoft Word for Windows.

Professional. Outlining is another area in which Word excels. Word for Windows also profits from its own electronic ancestry—Word for Windows is a direct descendent of earlier releases of Microsoft Word. Millions of people who already feel comfortable using Word in the standard DOS environment should have little trouble adapting to the Windows version.

Word for Windows adds a second option bar (called the *Ribbon*) below the standard Windows menu bar. You can use this option bar to specify quickly such formatting elements as font selection, line spacing, and justification. Below this formatting option bar sits a stylized ruler, which is used to specify a document's margins and tabs. Word for Windows' default display closely resembles Windows Write, when that accessory's Ruler is activated.

One of Word for Windows' most impressive features is the flexibility of its macro language. You should be aware, however, that some familiarity with programming is helpful, if you expect to take full advantage of Word's macro feature. When I say macro language, I mean macro *language*. Using Word's BASIC-like macro language, you can create custom menus and dialog boxes that automate any word processing activities you perform regularly.

Electronic Spreadsheets

When it comes to crunching numbers in the Windows environment, one program, Microsoft Excel (if you'll pardon the obvious pun) excels.

Microsoft Excel for Windows

Microsoft Corporation
One Microsoft Way
Redmond, WA 98052
(206) 882-8080
$495

265

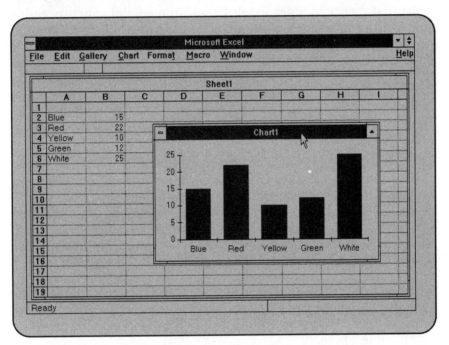

Figure 13.3. Microsoft Excel for Windows.

Excel's mathematical functions are comparable to any other spreadsheet program on the market, including Lotus 1-2-3. And the graphics it generates—bar graphs, pie charts, and the like—leave the competition standing in the dust. It's worth installing Windows 3.0 on your PC just to be able to use Excel. This program is that impressive.

Excel's graphics-based architecture permits incredible flexibility when specifying the screen appearance of your spreadsheets and charts. You can, for example, tell Excel to automatically display all entries below a certain value as red numbers on a white background, an easy way to identify potential problems in a budget projection. You can also adjust the height of individual rows within your spreadsheet and select from a variety of font styles for ranges, individual cells, or even single letters or numbers. Headers and footers, including automatic page count, can be added to an Excel spreadsheet at print time. Combine these formatting capabilities with a decent printer, and you can use Excel to generate reports of near-typeset quality.

Building spreadsheets in Excel's graphics-based environment is largely intuitive. Using either a mouse or Excel's alternate keyboard commands, virtually every feature any serious spreadsheet user might ever need sits at your fingertips. Without even opening a manual, you can start using Excel, immediately incorporating some of the program's more advanced features. Enter unfamiliar territory, and context-sensitive Help screens are available to provide assistance. Should you get lost, the program includes a comprehensive, on-screen tutorial, which you can run at any time during an Excel session. In an interesting tip-of-the-hat to two successful spreadsheet programs that have preceded it, Excel provides a special Help feature that allows you to enter a 1-2-3 or Multiplan command, and then see the Excel command sequence required to perform the same operation.

266

Excel makes it easy to convert your numbers into graphs—especially when you consider how convoluted this task is with traditional DOS spreadsheets. When you want to create a graph from numbers in an Excel spreadsheet, simply use the mouse to highlight the appropriate cell range, specify the Chart option, and then select one of Excel's 44 available chart types from the program's Gallery option. Your graph immediately appears in a second window. Excel automatically differentiates between text and numeric values in the specified range and places each in its appropriate place on the requested chart. Fine-tuning this initial chart to precisely the graphic you want is a breeze.

Once, when someone told me that they actually enjoyed working in their PC spreadsheet program, I laughed out loud. After using Excel for a while, I'm no longer laughing.

Wingz

Informix Software, Inc.
4100 Bohannon Drive
Menlo Park, CA 94025
(415) 926-6300
$495

Wingz is one of several Windows-aware programs born "on the other side of the tracks." Initially designed to run on the Macintosh, this graphics-based spreadsheet recently moved into the DOS community. One advantage inherent in this lineage is the fact that Wingz supports Informix's HyperScript application development language, a script language modeled after Hypercard and its programming language HyperText popularized on Macintosh systems. (Stated simply, Hypertext promotes the free-form association of diverse elements within an operating environment, allowing you to quickly jump from one task or operation to a second different, but related, task.) With HyperScript, it's possible to create a wide range of personal applications in Wingz, some of which can transcend the program's fundamental spreadsheet structure.

Telecommunications

While utilitarian, and certainly convenient for making quick-and-dirty connections, Terminal lacks some of the more advanced features traditionally found in stand-alone communications programs. However, two companies, Digital Communications and Future Soft Engineering Inc., have released Windows-based products that bring a wealth of telecommunications features to the Windows environment.

267

CrossTalk for Windows

> DCA
> 1000 Alderman Drive
> Alpharetta, GA 30201
> (800) 241-4762
> $195

CrossTalk for Windows is another application adapted from a successful DOS program to take advantage of the Windows GUI. Like its DOS ancestor, CrossTalk Mk.4, Crosstalk for Windows includes a powerful script language that you can use to automate your on-line activities.

Like virtually all Windows applications, CrossTalk's workspace is topped by the Windows menu bar. Top-level menu options in CrossTalk for Windows include File, Edit, Actions, Setup, User, and Help. Just below this menu bar is a status bar—not a universal Windows display element but rather a feature unique to CrossTalk for Windows. The status bar allows you to discern, at a glance, important information about your current CrossTalk session: the type of terminal emulation in effect, your communication param-

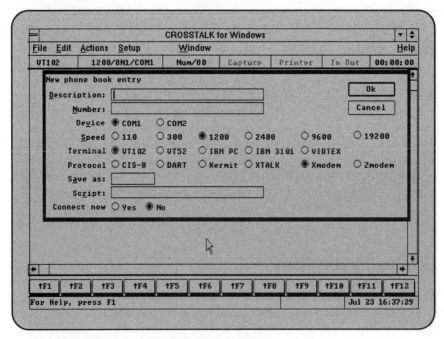

Figure 13.4. CrossTalk for Windows.

eters (baud rate, parity, data bits, stop bits, and the COM port your modem is using), whether you have opened a log file to capture this session, a "stopwatch" used to time on-line connections, and the like. In short, almost any information you may desire about the current status of your telecommunications session is readily available on the CrossTalk for Windows display.

You initiate on-line sessions by calling phone book entries. Before you can call a phone entry, you must create that entry with the "New phone book entry..." command, which you access from the Files option of the Windows menu bar. Selecting this command calls up a series of dialog boxes requesting the information CrossTalk needs to dial a specific remote system—access number, line settings, the terminal emulation it requires, and so forth. After supplying all the required information, you can place your call immediately or save this new phone entry for later use. Other File options let you open a previous phone entry, send terminal output to a system printer or file, initiate file transfers during an on-line session, and exit CrossTalk for Windows.

The Actions menu is where you initiate and coordinate most of your on-line activities. It includes the Connect option (used to call the current phone entry) and Dial, which displays a list of all phone entries you have created and then allows you to replace the currently active entry with a different one. The Actions menu also includes the

Script option, which lets you automate your on-line activities by executing a series of preprogrammed commands from a CrossTalk for Windows script.

Options in the Setup menu let you temporarily change the current program settings, without having to load a new phone entry. This is where you specify items like communication parameters and line settings, terminal emulation, file-transfer protocol, modem type, and the like. CrossTalk for Windows supports transmission rates of 110 to 19,200 baud. Emulation options include VT52, VT102, IBM 3101, and standard ASCII terminals. You can also specify terminal width and how line feeds and carriage returns should be handled during an on-line session. CrossTalk for Windows lets you choose from a wide range of file-transfer protocols, including XMODEM, YMODEM, CompuServe B, Kermit, and two protocols popularized by previous CrossTalk versions: DART and the proprietary CrossTalk protocol.

In short, CrossTalk for Windows packs telecommunications power into your Windows environment.

269

DynaComm

Future Soft Engineering, Inc.
1001 S. Dairy Ashford, Suite, 101
Houston, TX 77077
(713) 496-9400
$295

If you like Terminal, you'll love DynaComm, given that the former is actually a stripped-down version of the latter, which Microsoft licensed from Future Soft. DynaComm adds several impressive features to Terminal, including support for more file-transfer protocols and expanded terminal emulation options. DynaComm also includes a powerful script language that you can use to automate the majority of your on-line activities.

Future Soft almost completely redesigned DynaComm to take full advantage of the major changes Microsoft incorporated into Windows 3.0. DynaComm's previously spartan display—a major complaint, especially among neophyte users of previous releases—has been replaced with a much more attractive and informative user-interface, one that more closely resembles the icon-based design of Windows 3.0. This new release of DynaComm also employs the Windows 3.0 Help engine (a series of standard routines programmed into Windows that simplifies linking Windows-aware applications with their external Help files) to provide comprehensive information on virtually all aspects of its use.

Desktop Publishing

When Johann Gutenberg invented movable type in the 15th century, documents could be produced more quickly, more cheaply, and in greater quantities than ever before. As a result, information was more accessible. While the masses became a welcome market for the printed word, its actual production remained in the hands of a relative few—professional printers and major publishing houses like the one that produced this book.

The emergence of desktop publishing in the late 1980s changed all this. Suddenly, anyone who knew how to use a DTP program had the potential to produce a professional-looking document, providing access to the right PC and printer. The Windows graphics-based interface is ideally suited to DTP, which relies as much on coordinating the visual elements of a page as the creative writing that page contains. Two programs are currently duking it out for dominance in the high-end Windows desktop publishing arena: Aldus Page-Maker and Ventura Publisher.

270

Aldus PageMaker

> Aldus Corporation
> 411 First Avenue
> South Seattle, WA 98104
> (800) 333-2538
> $795

In many ways, PageMaker is the glue that held Windows together during the early years, back when the latter program was still struggling for acceptance. Desktop publishing in the Windows environment—even more specifically, desktop publishing with PageMaker in the Windows environment—lent validity to Microsoft's claim that the potential existed for a graphics-based user-interface to succeed within the DOS marketplace. That folks were willing to put up with earlier, admittedly clumsy versions of Windows, in many cases simply to use PageMaker, speaks highly of that program's popularity.

Basically, you start a PageMaker document by using important text and graphics elements that it has imported from your favorite programs. PageMaker can read files created by a wide range of Windows-aware and standard DOS applications. Once PageMaker converts these various elements, you can use that program to organize and arrange those elements into a fully formatted, professional-looking final printout.

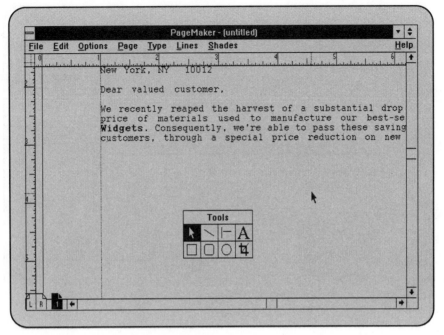

Figure 13.5. Aldus PageMaker.

Because PageMaker emulates an artist's paste-up board in your Windows workspace, it's ideal for creating and formatting short, graphics-intensive documents. If, on the other hand, you find yourself regularly creating longer documents with a greater emphasis on text—a book like this one being a prime example—then you may want to look at PageMaker's closest competitor, Ventura Publisher.

Ventura Publisher 3.0

Xerox Desktop Software
15175 Innovation Drive
San Diego, CA 92128
(619) 695-6416
$895

I've been a big fan of Ventura Publisher for years. Admittedly, this is more a consequence of the type of writing I do, rather than any objective analysis of how much more impressive Ventura may be than other DTP programs currently on the market.

Like PageMaker, Ventura works best when it's working with document elements created in other programs. (No DTP program is particularly adroit at creating text or images; this particular software

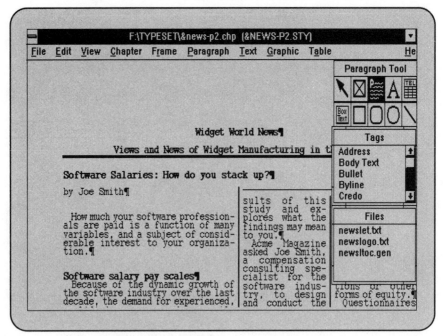

Figure 13.6. Ventura Publisher.

genre's forte is organizing and formatting what already exists.) Also like PageMaker, Ventura can import data from a number of popular DOS and Windows-aware programs. One advantage Ventura does have over PageMaker, which actually converts any data it uses into its own format, is that it preserves external files in their native format. If you need to revise the text of a Ventura document, therefore, you can return to your favorite word processor and perform these revisions. The next time you read that file into Ventura, the modifications you made are reflected in your DTP-formatted document. Given the lackadaisical word processing and graphics features built into most DTP programs—Ventura included—this feature can be a real godsend.

Judge desktop publishing programs wisely. The investment required for a truly useful DTP setup can be steep. In addition to the mandatory software (which doesn't come cheap), you'll want a printer capable of producing quality output. Also, a high-resolution display and a mouse are essential for DTP. When you're shelling out the kinds of bucks desktop publishing requires, you want to be extra careful in the DTP program you pick. Make sure the program you pick is well suited to your needs.

Database Management

Many database managers designed to run under Windows are programs that, like PageMaker and Wingz, initially were introduced in the Macintosh market. This isn't necessarily bad, however, because it means the folks "over there" have had time to refine their programs and eliminate the shortcomings and, in some cases, operational bugs that generally infest early versions of any application, prior to porting them over to the Windows environment.

Another phenomenon surfacing in Windows database programs is widespread support for Structured Query Language (SQL), an advanced technique for finding specific information in a data file developed for mainframe database applications. This may seem surprising, until you understand that numerous experts consider the Windows GUI to be a preliminary step in establishing a universal interface across all computer platforms—PC, minicomputers, and mainframes. Building SQL capabilities into Windows database managers now, it is believed, will simplify matters later, if and when such a universal interface standard emerges.

273

A number of Windows-aware database programs have emerged recently, as more and more companies realize that managing information in a visual environment like Windows represents a major advance over more traditional, text-based DOS database applications. Consequently, I'm not going to profile any individual packages, rather I'll list alternatives, including the address and phone number with each from which you can obtain more information.

PackRat
Polaris Software
1820 S. Escondido Blvd., Suite 102
Escondido, CA 92025
(619) 743-7800
$150

Omnis 5
Blyth Software Inc.
1065 E. Hillsdale Blvd., Suite 300
Foster City, CA 94404
(415) 571-0222
$795

Superbase 4
Precision Software, Inc.
844 Sterling
Irving, TX 75063
(800) 562-9909
$695

SQL Windows
Gupta Technologies
1040 Marsh Road
Menlo Park, CA 94025
(415) 321-9500
$1,295

Access SQL
Software Products International
10240 Sorrento Valley Road
San Diego, CA 92121
(800) 937-4774
$695

Thinx
Bell Atlantic Corp.
13100 Columbia Pike, Suite D37
Silver Spring, MD 20904
(800) 388-4465
$495

274

Miscellaneous Software

We have looked at profiles of several Windows-aware programs in five major software categories. Space considerations prohibit my covering every available program in all application categories. It would require an entire book to present a comprehensive compendium of all the Windows programs out there or planned for release in the near future. Therefore, I'll conclude this chapter by listing a few of the more intriguing Windows programs with which I am personally familiar. After each program's listing, I've included a very brief description on the type of program it is.

IBM Current
IBM Desktop Software
472 Wheelers Farms Road
Milford, CT 06460
(800) 426-7699
$395
Personal information manager

Microsoft Project for Windows
Microsoft Corporation
One Microsoft Way
Redmond, WA 98052
(206) 882-8080
$695
Project management software

SoftType
ZSoft Corp
450 Franklin Road, #100
Marietta, GA 30067
(404) 426-0008
$199
Screen and printer font generator

hDC First Apps & hDC Windows Express
hDC Computer Corporation
6742 185th Avenue N.E.
Redmond, WA 98052
(206) 885-5550
$99 each
Utility programs to enhance the Windows environment

275

Micrografx Designer
Micrografx, Inc.
1303 Arapaho
Richardson, TX 75081
(800) 272-3729
$695
Graphics program

Microsoft PowerPoint for Windows
Microsoft Corporation
One Microsoft Way
Redmond, WA 98052
(206) 882-8080
$495
Presentation graphics package

CA-Cricket Presents
Computer Associates
10505 Sorrento Valley Rd.
San Diego, CA 92121
(800) 531-5236
$495
Presentation graphics package

I may not have included your favorite program either through oversight or, worse still, because it was one of the many Windows applications I didn't receive in time to meet this book's deadline.

We're almost but not quite done. We still need to discuss briefly one topic that will bring us back full-circle to where we started—how Windows 3.0 handles standard DOS applications.

What You Have Learned

276

▶ Windows 3.0 has generated much excitement within the PC community. Consequently, dozens of programs are available that are specially designed to take full advantage of the Windows GUI.

▶ Installing a Windows-aware application generally includes several special steps, the main purpose of which is to inform Windows of what that program is and how it operates. As a rule, any Windows applications you buy will include specific instructions on how best to install that program to run properly in your Windows environment.

▶ The variety of Windows-aware applications entering the market is impressive. Specific programs are now available in all major software categories, with more appearing all the time. Consequently, it's possible to set up a comprehensive PC environment that runs exclusively under the Windows GUI.

Chapter 14

The Windows/DOS Connection

In This Chapter   277

▶ *How to access the DOS command prompt from within Windows*

▶ *How to run standard DOS applications from within Windows*

▶ *How Windows uses PIFs*

▶ *How to modify a PIF*

Windows Does DOS

Here we conclude our discussion with DOS—the operating system under which Windows runs. Although it's possible to manage all your PC activities from within the Windows GUI, there may be times when you'll find it to your advantage to initiate an operation directly from the DOS prompt. For someone familiar with DOS, issuing a command from the standard DOS prompt can often be an easier and more efficient way to accomplish something than choosing the corresponding Windows menu options.

Previous releases of Windows required that you close down any programs you had running within the Windows GUI and then exit that operating environment entirely, before you could execute a DOS command. Accessing DOS with Windows 3.0 is much easier.

Rather than forcing you to terminate the current Window session, Windows 3.0 includes a DOS icon that, when selected, suspends all Windows operations and accesses a special DOS shell—a temporary "opening" in Windows through which you can issue and execute standard DOS commands.

Accessing the DOS Command Prompt

During installation, the Windows Setup program automatically added a DOS icon in your Main program group. Accessing the DOS command shell is a simple matter of displaying this program group, then double-clicking on its DOS icon.

√ To Display the DOS Command Prompt

▶ Position the mouse cursor in any visible portion of the Main program group.

▶ Click the left mouse button.

▶ Double-click on the DOS Prompt icon.

Selecting the DOS Prompt icon temporarily suspends Windows and displays the DOS system prompt, as shown in Figure 14.1. (Notice that the DOS shell also reveals information about which version of DOS you are using, prior to displaying the system prompt.) Once this prompt is displayed, you may issue DOS commands and even execute DOS applications, just as you would if Windows were not running on your system.

⊘ Caution: Whenever you are working the Windows DOS shell, do not issue commands or run programs that modify file allocation tables. For example, if you issue a CHKDSK command from the Windows DOS shell, don't include that command's /F parameter, which causes DOS to convert any unallocated file clusters CHKDSK discovers to temporary files. Other examples of the types of programs that you should not run from within the DOS shell include so-called undelete programs and utilities that compress or optimize disk files. If you need to use such programs, exit Windows completely before running them.

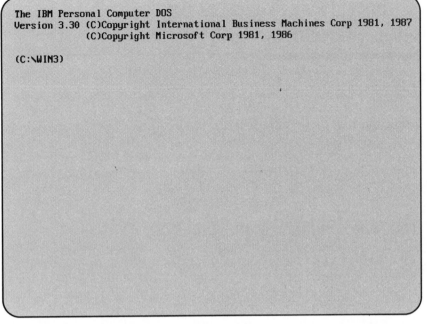

```
The IBM Personal Computer DOS
Version 3.30 (C)Copyright International Business Machines Corp 1981, 1987
              (C)Copyright Microsoft Corp 1981, 1986

(C:\WIN3)
```

Figure 14.1. Selecting the DOS Prompt icon suspends Windows and displays the DOS system prompt.

Exiting the DOS Shell and Returning to Windows

Once you're finished working in the DOS shell, use an exit command to reactivate the interrupted Windows session.

√ **To Exit the DOS Shell and Return to Windows**

▶ Type **EXIT** and press Enter.

Windows closes its DOS shell and returns you to whatever you were doing before you accessed the DOS system prompt.

> ▶ **Tip:** If you want to keep the DOS shell active while working in Windows, use an Alt+Esc key sequence to return to the interrupted Windows session. This places a minimized DOS Shell icon at the bottom of your Windows workspace. Double-clicking on this icon reactivates the DOS shell, without forcing you to once again access the Main program group.

Running DOS Programs from within Windows

Certainly, the ability to execute DOS commands and run programs from the DOS shell is a welcome convenience. In truth, however, it would be more convenient to include standard DOS programs in your total Windows environment—that is, without first having to suspend your current Windows activities and switch over to the DOS system prompt. (Remember, we're pursuing gestalt here.)

The Non-Windows Application Icon

280

Chances are you already have some non-Windows applications installed on your Windows workspace. One of the steps we performed in Chapter 3 was to have Setup scan all your disk drives and include any programs it discovered into your Windows environment. Any standard DOS applications that Setup recognized were automatically installed in a Non-Windows Applications program group, which was assigned its own icon on your Windows workspace.

✔ To Display the Non-Windows Program Group

▶ Double-click on the Non-Windows Applications icon.

Selecting the Non-Windows Applications icon opens a window containing individual icons for any standard DOS programs Setup discovered during installation. (See Figure 14.2.)

> ▶ **Note:** Your display will differ from Figure 14.2 in that it will contain icons for the specific DOS applications Setup found on your disks.

In many cases, Setup knows enough about a DOS application to assign it the appropriate icon, as was the case with my system, where Setup assigned a stylized telephone icon to Procomm Plus, a standard DOS telecommunications program it located on my drive D hard disk. WordStar, my word processor of choice, is another example of a standard DOS application with which Setup associated a suitable icon.

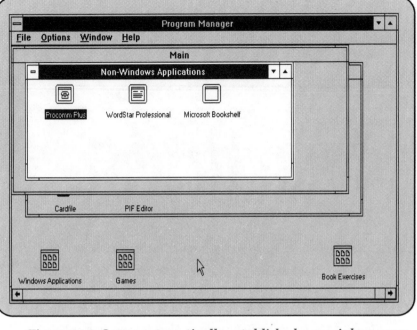

Figure 14.2. Setup automatically established a special program group for any non-Windows applications it discovered during installation.

Starting a Non-Windows Application

You start a non-Windows application just as you would any other program or accessory within your Windows environment, by double-clicking on its corresponding icon. In the following exercise, I'll open Procomm Plus, one of the programs listed in my Non-Windows Applications program group. (You may need to select a different DOS program, if Procomm Plus does not appear in your Non-Windows Applications window.)

√ To Start a Non-Windows Application

▶ Double-click on the Procomm Plus icon.

A few seconds later I see the initial Procomm Plus screen shown in Figure 14.3. I'm now running Procomm Plus from within Windows. Furthermore, when I'm done using Procomm Plus, exiting that program in the usual way will return me to the Windows GUI.

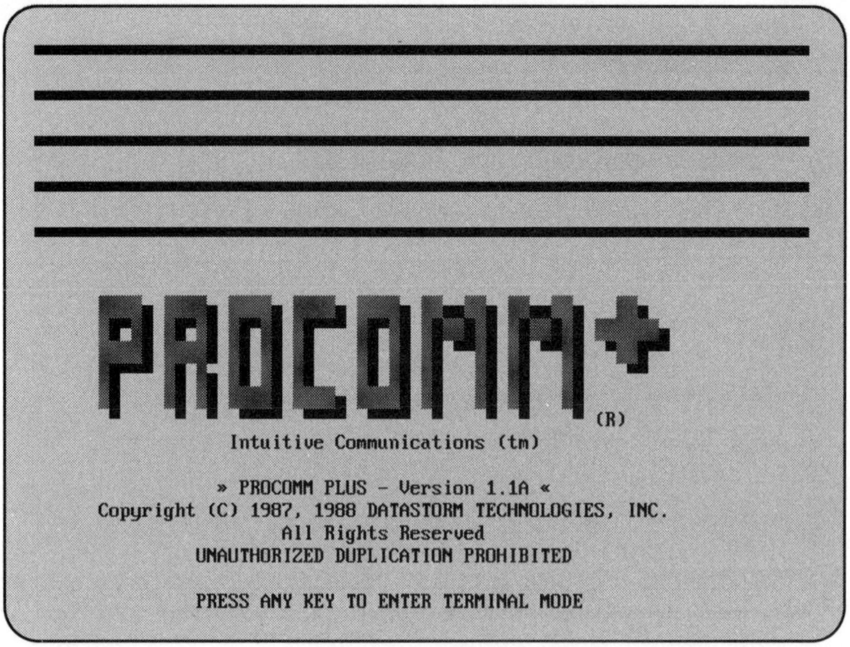

```
                    PROCOMM+
                              (R)
             Intuitive Communications (tm)

             » PROCOMM PLUS - Version 1.1A «
   Copyright (C) 1987, 1988 DATASTORM TECHNOLOGIES, INC.
                  All Rights Reserved
            UNAUTHORIZED DUPLICATION PROHIBITED

           PRESS ANY KEY TO ENTER TERMINAL MODE
```

282

Figure 14.3. Double-clicking on a Non-Windows Application icon runs the corresponding program from within Windows.

Windows' Strengths and Weaknesses

Windows is capable of doing some pretty nifty things while running standard DOS applications. But not all of these things can be accomplished in all PC environments. How many of Windows' advanced features you'll be able to take advantage of depends on what type of PC system you own and how you've configured Windows to run on that system. Specifically:

▶ When operating in Real or Standard mode, Windows runs standard DOS applications in a full-screen display, similar to the one shown in Figure 14.3.

▶ When operating in Real or Standard mode, Windows allows you to switch among any non-Windows applications running in a full-screen display. Windows suspends operations of all but the currently displayed non-Windows application, however, with this configuration.

▶ When operating in 386 Enhanced mode, Windows will be able to run most standard DOS applications in their own window—that is, a small window displayed as part of the Windows workspace.

▶ Depending on the DOS programs being run, Windows may also be able to multitask non-Windows applications when operating in 386 Enhanced mode.

▶ Running Windows in 386 Enhanced mode on an 80386- or i486-based PC may also allow you to cut and paste data from a non-Windows application into the Windows clipboard, depending on how you configure that application's PIF file.

How Windows Uses PIFs

Most non-Windows applications installed in your Windows environment have their own *Program Information File*, or PIF. A PIF is a special file that contains information Windows needs to run a standard DOS program successfully within the Windows GUI. The basic Windows package includes the PIF file for several popular DOS programs. When you use the Setup Applications option in the Windows Setup accessory, Setup automatically installs in your Windows environment any non-Windows applications for which it finds a PIF file. (That's how Procomm Plus, WordStar, and Microsoft Bookshelf made it into my Non-Windows Applications program group.)

283

If you try to start a standard DOS application for which no program information file exists, Windows attempts to run that program using its default PIF. In most cases, DOS applications will work just fine when loaded with this default PIF. There may be times, however, when a specific program requires customized PIF settings to peacefully coexist with the Windows GUI. Should this happen, you will need to either modify the current PIF settings or create a new PIF for the troublesome program, using the Windows PIF Editor accessory.

Working with PIFs

Windows needs to know certain information about every program it runs. For one thing, Windows has to be able to find that program, which means it needs to know the directory in which it is stored, called the Start-up Directory in Windows parlance. If Windows isn't told that your WordStar files are in a subdirectory called "WS," for example, how is it going to know where to look for the WS.EXE file to load that program's opening menu? The additional information that Windows needs includes a program's memory requirements, how that program handles writing to the screen, whether it can display graphics, what serial ports it uses (if any), and whether it should be given access to expanded memory. Beyond these critical items, there is additional information that can help Windows control how well a program runs within your Windows environment. So, where does Windows look for this information? In the PIF.

As mentioned earlier, Windows already knows this information about several popular programs. Consequently, all you need to do when you add one of these is to have Windows discover where that program is stored on your system. (This is basically what happens when you choose the Setup Applications option in the Windows Setup accessory.) Windows then appends the program's location with additional information in its PIF and assigns that PIF a program code associated with the appropriate program. On my disk, for example, is a file called WS.PIF, the program information file associated with WordStar.

Each time you start a program from the Open Window menu, Windows reads the corresponding PIF to determine how that program should be configured, as well as where it will be found on your system.

But how do you configure a program you use on a regular basis that is not automatically recognized by Windows? Or what if you need to change the default information about a program to make it more compatible with your Windows environment? To accomplish either of these two tasks, use the Windows PIF Editor accessory, which was automatically placed in the Accessories program group during installation.

The PIF Editor

Use the PIF Editor to edit the information contained in an application program's PIF. To study the information stored in a PIF, let's examine the contents of the PIF for WordStar on my system, WS.PIF.

√ To Access the PIF Editor

▶ Position the mouse cursor in any visible area of the Accessories program group.

284

▶ Click the left mouse button.

▶ Double-click on the PIF Editor icon.

If you are running Windows in Real or Standard mode, selecting the PIF Editor icon displays the PIF Editor dialog box shown in Figure 14.4.

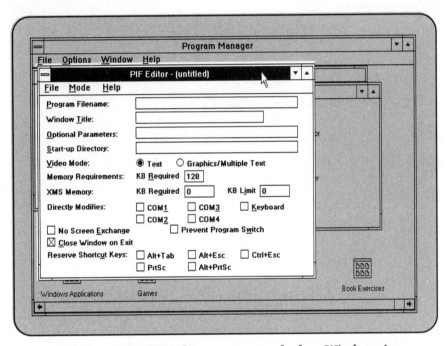

285

Figure 14.4. The PIF Editor screen used when Windows is operating in Real or Standard mode.

If you are running Windows in 386 Enhanced mode, you will see a different opening PIF Editor dialog box, the one shown in Figure 14.5.

▶ **Note:** When Windows is configured in 386 Enhanced mode on an 80386- or i486-based system, it can use the advanced memory management features built into those microprocessors to set up a virtual 8086 system in RAM for each application being run in a multitasking session. To accomplish this, Windows needs, and therefore requests, more information about non-Windows applications when it is running in 386 Enhanced mode.

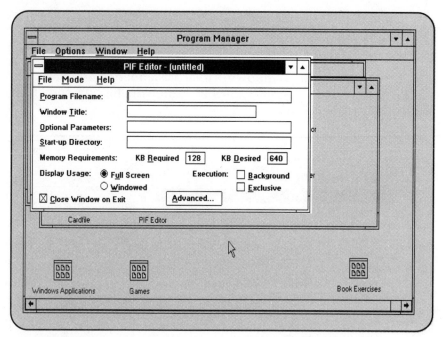

Figure 14.5. The PIF Editor screen used when Windows is operating in 386 Enhanced mode.

Regardless of the type of system you own and how you have configured Windows to run on that system, certain basic program information is stored in every PIF. We'll examine that information in the next section.

The Contents of a PIF

The information stored in a PIF can be broken down into five major categories:

▶ Information that identifies the program in a Windows program group.

▶ Information pertaining to how this program is normally accessed at the DOS level.

▶ Information about how Windows should allocate system memory for the program.

▶ Information about how the program should be configured within the Windows environment.

▶ Information about how Windows should handle this program during a multitasking session.

Some of the information contained in a PIF is self-explanatory. The "Windows Title" field, for example, contains the descriptive name you want displayed below its icon and in the Windows Title bar. Other obvious fields include "Program Filename" (the program's name—for example, "WS.EXE" for the WordStar executable program) and "Memory Requirements" (the program's published memory requirements). Other PIF information, however, is a little more technical and might require further explanation. To avoid confusion, let's start with the Real/Standard PIF dialog box.

Program Filename   This is the name of the executable program used to start this application. In most cases, this will be a file with an EXE or COM extension in its filename. You can also open an application window using a DOS batch file, which would have a BAT extension.

Window Title   This is the name assigned to this program, as it will be displayed below the corresponding icon. This name also appears in the title bar of any window into which you load this program.

Optional Parameters   This field contains any program parameters you would normally enter after the program name, were you typing this information on the DOS command line. For example, this could be a data file you want the program to load at startup, if the program normally allows entry of such an item when it is loaded from the DOS prompt. It could also be a DOS "switch" or command parameter (vis-à-vis, the "B:" in the DOS command "FORMAT B:") used to clarify or refine a program command.

Start-up Directory   This is the drive and directory you want Windows to make the current directory whenever this program is started.

Video Mode   Check Graphics/Multiple Text if a program ever uses graphics (that is,

287

288

a bit-mapped display) during execution. This instructs Windows to set aside the extra memory required to manage such a display. Specifying Text for DOS programs that use a character-based display makes more memory available for your total Windows environment.

Memory Requirements

This field specifies how many kilobytes of conventional memory must be available to start this application. As a rule, you should leave this value set to the 128 default value. (This is not the total amount of memory that will be allocated to an application. Windows itself determines that when a program is run. Rather, this is the amount of memory that must be free for Windows to even attempt to run this application.)

XMS Memory

The values in these fields represent the minimum (KB Required) and maximum (KB Limit) amount of expanded memory, EEMS or EMS 4.0, in kilobytes, that should be made available to this program. Leaving the latter field blank instructs Windows to place no limit on the amount of expanded memory this program can use.

> ▶ **Tip:** Some programs immediately grab all available expanded memory, if they are configured to do so when installed on your system. (Microsoft Excel is one such program.) To guarantee that some expanded memory remains available for your other Windows applications, enter a workable value in this field when configuring programs like Excel to run in the Windows environment.

Directly Modifies

Information in this field helps Windows eliminate conflicts resulting from multiple programs trying to access the same serial (COM) port concurrently. You should mark the box for any port this application uses. A communications program, for example, may use the second serial port for its modem connection. In this case, you would click on the COM2 box. You should also tell Windows when an application takes over the keyboard—that is, bypasses the standard keyboard I/O BIOS routines—during execution.

No Screen Exchange   Checking this box tells Windows to deactivate the Windows Clipboard while this application is running. Doing so makes more memory available for the application.

Prevent Program Switch   Checking this box tellsWindows to deactivate its Program Switch feature while this application is running. Doing so makes more memory available for the application. It also means, however, that you will need to quit this application completely to return to Windows or switch to another application running in a multitasking session.

289

Close Window on Exit   If an X appears in this box, whenever you exit this program to DOS (use the program's Quit or Exit command, for example), Windows automatically performs a Close Window operation. If no X appears in the Close Window on Exit box, quitting the program returns you to a DOS system prompt and leaves the application window open. You could then close the window manually by typing exit at the system prompt.

Reserve Shortcut Keys   As you've already seen, Windows uses several keystrokes to initiate special procedures during a multitasking session. Pressing Ctrl+Esc, for example, displays the Task List. But what if you run a DOS

290

application that also uses the Ctrl+Esc key combination to access for one of its functions? Normally, that application would never see this command, since Windows itself would intercept the Ctrl+Esc sequence for its own purposes. Checking the Ctrl+Esc box in the Reserve Shortcut Keys section of the PIF Editor dialog box tells Windows to pass that key combination onto the application. You should check all key combinations listed here that may conflict with a particular application.

Next, we'll describe the fields that appear on the 386 Enhanced PIF Editor dialog box. (See Figure 14.5.) Six of these fields should be familiar:

▶ Program Filename.
▶ Window Title.
▶ Optional Parameters.
▶ Start-up Directory.
▶ Memory Requirements.
▶ Close Window on Exit.

The values you enter into these fields are identical to those when you are running Windows in Real or Standard mode.

There are, however, two additional fields in the 386 Enhanced dialog box. These fields are used to enable features only available when Windows is running on a 386 or 486 system.

Display Usage

Checking the Full Screen option forces Windows to run this application in a full-screen display only. You may find it necessary to do this if a particular program misbehaves— that is, it bypasses the normal BIOS routines used to display information to your system monitor. If a program freezes (ceases to operate) or garbles your Windows display, try setting the Display Usage option to Full Screen in that program's PIF.

Execution	Checking the Background option tells Windows to enable full multitasking when this application is running. In other words, this application will continue to run in the background whenever you switch to another window. If a particular program causes problems whenever it is running in the background of a multitasking session, you may want to try setting the Execution option to Exclusive in that program's PIF.

Advanced 386 Enhanced Options

There are additional, advanced options that you can specify in the PIF of an application you expect to run under Windows in 386 Enhanced mode.

291

√ To See the Advanced PIF Options

▶ Choose Advanced in the 386 Enhanced PIF Editor dialog box.

Clicking on the Advanced button displays the Advanced Options dialog box shown in Figure 14.6. Options in this dialog box specify very precisely how Windows should set up and manage the virtual machines it creates during a 386 multitasking session. Several of these options are exactly what their name implies: advanced. Therefore, do not adjust them unless you know exactly what you are doing. Given the "beginners" nature of this book—and recognizing the wisdom of an old adage that proclaims a little knowledge to be a dangerous thing—I'll leave them unexplained. As you learn more about your system, and more about Windows, you'll begin to understand how these advanced options are used.

√ To Return to the Initial PIF Editor Options Box

▶ Choose Cancel.

Now that you have a basic idea of what the various PIF settings represent, let's outline the basic steps required to modify them.

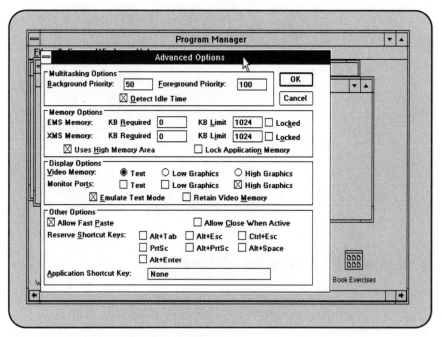

Figure 14.6. Advanced PIF options.

Modifying a PIF

To demonstrate the basic steps involved in modifying a program information file, I'm going to alter one setting in my WordStar PIF. Specifically, I'm going to tell Windows that I still use an earlier version of that venerable word processor, one that does not employ graphic screens.

> ▶ **Note:** Of course, unless you also own WordStar, you will not be able to perform the following exercise. Still, it will give you an idea of how to modify your PIFs, should the occasion arise.

✓ To Modify a PIF
▶ Choose File from the PIF Editor menu bar.
▶ Choose Open.
▶ Double-click on WS.PIF (the program information file for WordStar).

This calls in the information shown in Figure 14.7. This PIF contains the appropriate information for WordStar releases 5 or higher, which employ a graphic display for their Page Preview feature. I, however, use WordStar 4.0, an earlier version of WordStar that does not support Page Preview. In my case, therefore, changing the Video Mode setting to Text would free up additional memory on my system whenever WordStar is running.

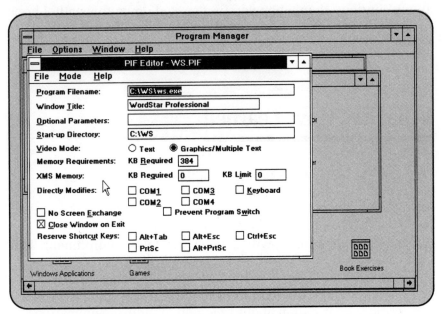

Figure 14.7. Windows default WordStar PIF.

293

√ To Change the Video Mode Setting to Text

▶ Position the mouse cursor in the circle to the left of the Text setting in the Video Mode field.

▶ Click the left mouse button.

That's really all there is to it. All that remains is for me to save the modified PIF back to disk, so its settings will be used the next time I load WordStar.

√ To Save the Modified PIF to Disk

▶ Choose File from the PIF Editor menu bar.

▶ Choose Save.

From now on, whenever I run WordStar within the Windows GUI, its windows will be configured for a character-based display.

We've covered much technical ground in this chapter. Still, knowing how Windows runs DOS programs and understanding the information a PIF contains is critical to getting the most out of your Windows environment. Luckily, it's also the last chapter in our tour of the Windows GUI. You can rest now, knowing that you know more about Windows than when you first started down this path. I hope the trip was fun. And I hope you have fun using Windows. It really does—both literally and figuratively—put a new face on your PC.

What You Have Learned

294

▶ The Windows DOS Prompt icon lets you temporarily suspend a Windows session and issue commands from the DOS system prompt.

▶ You can install standard DOS programs—that is, non-Windows applications—within your Windows environment. The easiest way to accomplish this is with the Setup Applications option in the Windows Setup accessory.

▶ Windows uses program information files, or PIFs, to record critical information about how non-Windows applications should be handled within the Windows GUI. Setup will automatically create a PIF for any programs it recognizes. Windows also includes a default PIF that should run most DOS applications successfully. If you encounter problems running a specific non-Windows application, you can create a new PIF—or, alternately, modify a currently existing PIF—to eliminate them.

Index

297

298

299

300

301

302

303

304

Reader Feedback Card

Thank you for purchasing this book from SAMS FIRST BOOK series. Our intent with this series is to bring you timely, authoritative information that you can reference quickly and easily. You can help us by taking a minute to complete and return this card. We appreciate your comments and will use the information to better serve your needs.

1. Where did you purchase this book?

☐ Chain bookstore (Walden, B. Dalton)   ☐ Direct mail
☐ Independent bookstore   ☐ Book club
☐ Computer/Software store   ☐ School bookstore
☐ Other _____

2. Why did you choose this book? (Check as many as apply.)

☐ Price   ☐ Appearance of book
☐ Author's reputation   ☐ SAMS' reputation
☐ Quick and easy treatment of subject ☐ Only book available on subject

3. How do you use this book? (Check as many as apply.)

☐ As a supplement to the product manual ☐ As a reference
☐ In place of the product manual   ☐ At home
☐ For self-instruction   ☐ At work

4. Please rate this book in the categories below. G = Good; N = Needs improvement; U = Category is unimportant.

☐ Price   ☐ Appearance
☐ Amount of information   ☐ Accuracy
☐ Examples   ☐ Quick Steps
☐ Inside cover reference   ☐ Second color
☐ Table of contents   ☐ Index
☐ Tips and cautions   ☐ Illustrations
☐ Length of book
☐ How can we improve this book?_____
☐ _____

5. How many computer books do you normally buy in a year?

☐ 1–5   ☐ 5–10   ☐ More than 10
☐ I rarely purchase more than one book on a subject.
☐ I may purchase a beginning and an advanced book on the same subject.
☐ I may purchase several books on particular subjects.
☐ (such as _____)

6. Have your purchased other SAMS or Hayden books in the past year? _____
If yes, how many _____

7. Would you purchase another book in the FIRST BOOK series? _____

8. What are your primary areas of interest in business software? _____

☐ Word processing (particularly _____)
☐ Spreadsheet (particularly _____)
☐ Database (particularly _____)
☐ Graphics (particularly _____)
☐ Personal finance/accounting (particularly _____)
☐ Other (please specify _____)

Other comments on this book or the SAMS' book line: _____
_____

Name _____
Company_____
Address _____
City _____ State _____ Zip_____
Daytime telephone number _____
Title of this book _____

Fold here
- -

BUSINESS REPLY MAIL
FIRST CLASS   PERMIT NO. 336   CARMEL, IN

POSTAGE WILL BE PAID BY ADDRESSEE

SAMS

11711 N. College Ave.
Suite 141
Carmel, IN 46032–9839